FEMALE TERROR

Other books in the Virgin True Crime series

FEMALE TERROR

Scary Women, Modern Crimes

Ann Magma

uFirst published in 2002 by

Virgin Books
Thames Wharf Studios
Rainville Rd
London W6 9HA

ISBN 0 7535 0718 8

Typesetting by TW Typesetting, Plymouth, Devon

Printed and bound by CPI Antony Rowe, Eastbourne

CONTENTS

INTRODUCTION

Cruella De Vil. Remember her? Fantastic woman. The car! The clothes! The hair! The attitude! The power. Wonderful in the original cartoon of *101 Dalmatians* and fabulous as reincarnated by Glenn Close. Cruella was a satisfying icon for any little girl uninterested in sappy princesses waiting for their hair to be climbed up by a man wearing tin cans. And those who liked Cruella would graduate to an affection for Beryl the Peril, Lady Macbeth, Kali and Tura Satana – any icon, in other words, who was shamelessly out to get what she wanted. The princesses wanted husbands; the bad girls wanted mayhem. And mayhem seemed so much more interesting.

Visual entertainment has dissolved the boundaries between what it presents as fiction and what it presents as fact, so that the thinking about the relationship between genuine non-fiction female criminality and constructive feminism has become unclear. It is difficult for those of us who (thanks to Faye Dunaway) have long revered Bonnie Parker as a glamorous villainess in stilettos to accept her reality as a cruel and silly woman who had, in the end, a loser boyfriend and a painful exit where, despite the fact that she had the courage to defect from convention, no purpose was really served.

It is difficult not to think of Aileen Wuornos (she who stalked the highways shooting men stone dead simply because she felt like it) as a B-movie heroine avenging herself on the dreadful male of the species on our behalf, like some big-breasted temptress from a Roger Corman movie.

It is inevitable that the real-life murderess should so often become the folklore goddess. Society likes a superbitch and women need women who can be angry on their behalf because, for the most part, that particular emotion has been denied them. If little girls were taught how to constructively actualise fury, it is more than likely that women would be less interested in those who implemented it *de*structively. As it is, we must enjoy ourselves vicariously and shamefully through the antics of the frenzied harridans who obey no rules and who dramatise our own dreadful desires.

It is no coincidence that, having suffered many long-haul flights under the fascist regime of rude air hostesses and bullying stewards, my favourite maniacs are the Mikula twins, who acted out my dream when they punched an air hostess in the face.

The sisters, Cynthia and Crystal, who had the added glamour of being beautiful, twenty-two years old and identical twins, were three hours into a United Airlines flight from San Francisco to Shanghai when, after a couple of drinks, they started punching each other. 'Open the door! I've got to get out of here,' Cynthia Mikula reportedly yelled. 'Let me off this airplane, I've gotta smoke, open this door!' When a flight attendant tried to intervene, Cynthia hit her on the nose. When one of the pilots escorted the twins back to their seats and sat beside them to prevent more trouble, Cynthia reached over her sister in the middle seat and hit him in the head. She later struck another flight attendant in the face and spat at one. Finally, the flight crew put her in plastic handcuffs, prompting her sister, Crystal, to put another flight attendant in a headlock. The four pilots opted to make an emergency landing in Anchorage, and the sisters were escorted off the plane, Cynthia Mikula still screaming. All of which is enough to make one want to go off and write a serenade for twelve wind instruments.

Are women becoming more violent? Has feminism unleashed a disgusting nightbreed of evil witches who disdain morality and shrug off society's pathetic attempts to clothe them in the guise of gentle mothers and creamy beauty queens? Is there a gathering horde of muscle-bound, gun-toting mutants who, having emasculated the male species, are set to take over the world by means of psychotic force?

No.

The truly psychopathic femme fatale is still a freak. The compulsive desire to commit motiveless murder, though less rare than it was, is still rare, as is evinced by the number of films that are made about this kind of woman when her actions come to light. She is interesting because she is unusual and very often defies explanation. She has the charisma of the dark mystery that is evil, and which is often augmented to fantastic proportions by screenwriters who boost her myth and provide her with a twisted iconisation that belies the truth, distorts her reality and encourages the mob to react to her in an emotional way rather than in a way that perceives her facts and sensibly assimilates the judicial implications. Fame is no friend to the person seeking parole.

The psycho-bitch is a statistical abnormality; the ordinary female criminal is not. The fact is that in England and America there are more women in prison than there have ever been. The numbers increase year by year and there is evidence to suggest that, in some places, they are showing an increased inclination to commit the kind of violent acts that have traditionally been committed by men – though in both countries these increases are explained by drug-related offences and the judicial systems to come down on them.

According to the Prison Reform Trust, in June 2002 there were 4,383 women in prison, ten per cent of whom were there for violent crime. The female sector represents only six per cent of the total UK prison population (which is around 71,000 and constantly rising) but the number has trebled in the last decade.

Exactly the same trend is reflected in America where women also represent six per cent of the prison population but the general levels of violent women are higher. There are 138,000 women in prison (of a total prison population of two million) and there was an increase of 108 per cent between the years 1990 and 2000 as opposed to the increase of 77 per cent of male inmates in the same period. It has been reliably estimated that 72 per cent of the women in American prisons are there for drug offences. I'll repeat that. Seventy-two per cent. That is a lot of mothers inside and a lot of children outside. About 150,000 at the last count.

The rise in the number of female offenders is not proof of some atrophy of feminism. To think of women felons in terms of political activism is a mistake; women who are in prison tend to be victims: of men, of their own inclinations, of their backgrounds, of their deprivation. Statistics show that they are abused, unemployed and/or homeless, and are far more likely to be incarcerated for offences connected to theft or to drugs than to violence. The female criminal is very rarely a privileged or educated person – she is more often a beaten person who sometimes reacts violently.

Sometimes she is clever, though rarely has she been advantaged by either education or beauty. She is more likely to be a woman driven mad by the stresses of motherhood or the violence of a partner. If she kills, she kills her intimates in a home environment, though the woman who orders a contract killing also reappears in the annals with great regularity and attracts little sympathy for so doing.

Domestic abuse as a defence is now a legal tic and is beginning to lose validity thanks to women who have lied about the extent that they have suffered, to the unfathomable contradictions that exist around provocation, and to the ever-growing voice of men who point out that they too are sometimes the victims.

The female delinquent is not a dissident who has read Jean Paul Sartre and is making a conscious statement, nor is she a sexy lesbian pulsating with the chained desire of a renegade heroine celebrated in the kind of camp prison movie that advertised 'corrupt floozies' and called itself things like *Barbed Wire Dolls* or *Ilsa, The Wicked Warden*.

Nevertheless, the facts about the female convict are very important and have only relatively recently being downloaded into relevant research and databases. Criminology and the social sciences have been slow to catch up with the facts of female criminality which means that, suddenly, the prisons are grotesquely overcrowded and human rights abuses proliferate, both because of this overcrowding and because, in America, the judicial system fluctuates to the ebb and flow of plea bargaining and is absurdly haphazard in its methods of punishment. Murdered your mother? One state will kiss you, another will kill you. It's a federal free for all.

Dr Alice Green, an executive director of a prisoners rights group in New York, encapsulated the current worries recently when she said, 'There has been little or no serious planning for the increasing number of women in the prison system.'

Post-feminist thinkers have warned and argued against the phenomenon of 'chivalric justice', where the female felon is able to operate covertly and escape blame thanks to a male judiciary that cannot believe in her reality. They want to think of women as sensitive and beautiful souls, because to accept the opposite is to accept a terrible threat. This denial negates the woman's right to be seen and judged as a person; that is, she must be viewed with the same objectivity as a male offender if she is to achieve the non-gender-specific individualism that promotes achievement. If she is to take her place as a visible member of society, able to fly a plane, fight on the frontline or paint a masterpiece, then she is as able to take responsibility for her criminal actions. Perceptions of these actions should not kow-tow to an old-fashioned hope that she is a gentle creature that can be manipulated.

The most recent cases, many of which are outlined in this book, show that chivalric justice is a thing of the past. For a start, many judges, lawyers and juries are female, and they can see an appalling woman for what she is. In England they put her away for life; in America they put her to death.

Pundit opinion is split between those who blame drugs and mandatory sentencing for the rise in the number of women in prison, those who think that women misunderstand (and need to learn) the difference between aggression and assertion, and those who think society is breeding a huge race of angry female killers.

Maggie Hall of the UK charity Women in Prison thinks that the number of women in prison reflects the system's inborn prejudices. She has said, 'There has been no massive crime explosion involving women, it's simply down to the fact that judges and magistrates seem to think it is not the norm for a woman or girl to commit a crime. As a result, they are harsher. Many women are jailed for a first offence of non-violent crime – something that does not happen to men.'

The rise in female violent crime in the United States is more tangible, documented in reports, boosted by guns, crack and widespread levels of serious urban desperation. Jane Warren, a university professor in Virginia, was asked to comment on female offender statistics collated from the state of Georgia, which showed higher levels of violence than the national US average. She saw an emerging group of homicidal women. 'I think we're clearly seeing that there is a growing number of women doing more cold-hearted murdering. We have some really violent women. It's a whole new phenomenon.'

1. GIRLS IN THE HOOD

Are rampaging crews of savage gang girls set to take over the lawless streets and cause mayhem in modern urban life?

West London – the areas of Notting Hill Gate, Ladbroke Grove and Shepherds Bush – is an urban terrain divided by gentrification. From the mid-1990s onwards huge houses and soaring property prices demarcated the territory invaded by the middle classes who, through the brute strength that is cash, successfully colonised a neighbourhood once dominated by London's West Indian population.

On one side of the street you have white men and women with all-terrain baby strollers and new Range Rovers, giving their properties makeovers and buying organic bread and scented candles. On the other side you have state-funded housing estates where the going is not so smooth: parents struggle and bored kids hang out on corners, penniless. Ladbroke Grove may be attracting the likes of Gwyneth Paltrow to its domain, but the local off-licence has not taken down its protective glass.

Ladbroke Grove has problems. It always has and it probably always will. Still, when a woman was attacked on the towpath by the canal near Sainsbury's supermarket on 25 July 2000, it was a shock. Petty pilfering, break-ins, drug dealing – these inconveniences are pretty normal in the area, but this was a gang rape; a woman had been set upon, teenage boys had gang-banged her – and they had been helped by their girlfriends. One had even held her arms down. The dark side of luxury life had been exposed. The neighbourhood made famous by Hugh Grant's film *Notting Hill* suddenly became as sinister as Central Park after dark.

The summer of 2000 was hot and a 'crew' began to collect around Drayford Close. The loose posse was young, fifteen to eighteen years of age, and the girls would egg the boys on, make them show off, get them to boast about their petty pilfering, build up their reps, and win the kudos that arrives with shop-lifting Kit-Kats.

The Grand Union Canal is a spooky place at night; by day it's OK, but at night, when it is dark, it is deserted and anything can happen. The locals know this, and most would not venture there after the pubs have shut. However, this victim had had a few drinks and her sixth sense for danger was slightly numbed by alcohol. She was tipsy and she risked it. The kids who approached her seemed OK, and she followed them when they offered her a joint. There were women in the group, after all, and their presence made her feel safer.

The attack had no motive. 'Unprovoked and savage' was how the police described it later. A pack of fourteen teenagers, having previously contented themselves with boasting and smoking dope, for no reason, and within a time frame of twenty minutes, suddenly turned into serious criminals.

First they pushed her into the canal, then, when she dragged herself out, they assaulted her. A girl named Claire Marsh punched her in the face and pulled her clothes off. Then four of the youths raped her while their girlfriends shouted encouragement. At one point the victim broke free and tried to run away, but they caught her, kicked and punched her and, at one stage, dragged her naked along a gravel path, lacerating her bare skin.

'They were just grabbing my limbs like an animal, sort of thing, just dragging me along the ground kicking me,' she would later tell the jury at the Old Bailey.

A fifteen-year-old boy tore off her trousers and raped her while the fourteen kids, one aged twelve, looked on. Then Marvin Edwards, eighteen years old and no rocket scientist, fell on her and raped her. Two other youths, aged fifteen and sixteen, were also later charged, but cleared.

When the assault was over and the boys were done, the gang girls threw the victim's clothes into the water, leaving her to run home naked, bruised and terrified.

The Drayford teenagers could not keep their mouths shut. They boasted to their friends about what had happened that night, and soon it was all over the estate what Claire had done, and who had run off because they were chicken. The strange thing was that everybody saw it as a dare. Nobody thought it was serious, least of all those who had been involved. It was just a lark, you know, and they went on to their mates about it.

Then it was in the newspapers – headline of the *Evening Standard* – and on the *Crimestoppers* television show. The phone calls started and it began to dawn on the dumb Drayford crew that they could be in trouble. Real trouble. The police started picking them up. It wasn't difficult, they knew who the troublemakers were anyway. It had been one thing after another on the estate that summer, and they had a lot of people willing to help them. People had had enough of it.

All fourteen members of the gang were detained. It soon emerged that several of them, including eighteen-year-old Claire Marsh, had been arrested just hours after the attack for a break-in at an off-licence.

Officers were struck by how unconcerned Marsh seemed to be about what had happened to the victim. She, and the others, seemed unnaturally uninterested. 'You could have been dealing with her for shoplifting. She certainly didn't seem sorry about what happened,' said one. 'I think that reflects the attitude of all those who were arrested. They just didn't see the severity of it. What was going on in their minds that night, goodness knows.' The officer went on to say it was unclear if the gang had had a 'ringleader'. It was more likely they simply developed what was described in court as a 'pack mentality'.

Describing Marsh as 'intelligent', one officer said: 'She had only been hanging around with the group for a couple of months. Perhaps she was showing off.'

Claire Marsh maintained that the gang's victim jumped into the canal herself and insisted she had struck the woman in the face only in self-defence. She went on to deny tearing her top off, or even being present when the rape occurred.

Judge Timothy Pontius described Marsh's involvement as 'a particularly vile and horrifying offence of sexual brutality'. She was sent to prison for seven years and was thought to be the youngest woman to receive such a conviction. But she is not the only one. Between 1997 and 2000, in London alone, a total of fourteen women were charged with rape.

Claire Marsh's face peered from various newspapers. She looked like an ordinary sullen teenager, but she was not, of course; she was a freak – a lone vixen in a country where bad girls are neither protected nor encouraged by a bad-girl culture.

In America, however, there are thousands of girls like Claire. Inured to hardship, fuelled by aggression, immersed in assault and battery and drugs and guns, the 'gangsta' girl has an identity of her own. From Los Angeles to Chicago, from Manhattan to Boston, she is a transcontinental bi-coastal phenomenon; a badass bitch with her own lyrics, her own icons, her own uniforms and an accessible MTV philosophy thanks to rap groups like Bytches with Problems and Hoes Wit Attitude. American street gangs such as the Sex Girls and the Turban Queens are a far cry from Miss Claire Marsh and the gormless renegades that hung out down the Harrow Road.

American 'gang consultant' Robert Walker warns that care should be taken by those who choose to 'handle' a female gang member. 'Use extreme caution,' he says. 'Never assume that just because she is a girl, she won't try to hurt or possibly kill you.'

The fact that female street gangs were proliferating from the mid-90s onwards remained unnoticed and/or unacknowledged by academics, cultural studies researchers and, to an extent, the police. At that time statistics were difficult to collate since there were no centralised databases of gang-related information. The authorities knew very little about gangs except for the fact that they were responsible for drive-by shootings, homicides and crack.

It is a sign of the racism inherent in the white American culture that so little was known about the Hispanic gangs on the West Coast, and ironic that racism should serve to temporarily protect their activities. Latinos were the first to establish themselves into street collectives. Wandering the barrios in the 1920s, they were joined together by language and family ties. While burglary and vandalism were the common crimes, the prime purpose was to protect the turf. Those who crossed the boundaries risked being knifed. A prison sentence was the ultimate prestige.

By the 1980s formal structures had evolved and the violence escalated as crack and cash entered the picture. The *veteranos* came out of prison and trained new recruits. By the 1990s trends had shifted again. African-American gangs controlled the South Central and

Compton districts of Los Angeles. They had originally been less organised and less violent, but this was to change and, gradually, they turned into lethal, well-armed, well-organised underground armies.

The notorious Crips formed in the 1960s and, after them, the Bloods, a group that collected to protect themselves against the Crips. Both sides held a truce during the LA riots of 1992, during which they joined together to engage in a guerrilla war with the Los Angeles Police Department.

'Operation Ceasefire', a concerted police effort to head off escalating gang crime, produced research that, for the first time, showed the presence of groups such as the Bad Mother Fuckers and the Champer Dames – violent all-female groups that were as ready as their male counterparts to commit any felony they felt like.

Now there are second- and third-generation family members in gangs; teenage mothers have given birth to gang babies; juveniles are used to carry weapons because they risk less. Loyalty means a fight to the death. And this is as true of the women as is it is of the men.

Robert Walker: 'Joining a gang, whether as a member of a predominantly male gang or an all-female gang, can be as dangerous and hazardous for the females as the males. Most must go through the ritual of gang initiation, which might consist of a beating with fists and/or clubs, an order to shoot someone, or participation in an act of violence, such as assaulting or beating a rival gang member or an innocent person.

'Many females are initiated by being "sexed in". The prospective member may voluntarily agree to have sex with some or all of the male members, and in some instances she may be raped. A recently reported trend to being sexed in is to have sex with someone who is known to be HIV positive.

'Female members frequently have one or more children and, as they grow older, feel the need to separate themselves from the gang life. This is sometimes as difficult and dangerous as joining the gang. Many gangs have a "jumping out" ritual that may include a severe beating. This could lead to permanent injury or death.'

As the Hispanic barrios were among the first to spawn male gangs, so too were they the first to breed all-female gangs. The Fresno Bulldog Babes came along; then there were Las Monas, the Latin Queens, the Diablas, the Playgirl Gangstas and many others.

One study entitled 'An Urban Ethnography of Latino Street Cultures' – initiated by Dr Francine Hallcom – details an environment where the teenager would fall out with the family and find themselves on the streets. Sometimes they were *tapada* (living with a man and doing as he told them) sometimes *tecata* (heroin addicts). All were *chola* (gang girl/rebel) – trapped between the values of the worlds of past Catholic Mexico and present urban America, sidewinding through both cultures, but never fitting in. It states:

'Girls' crimes appeared to be still largely "traditionally female": prostitution, shoplifting, running away, fighting with other girls and drug-related crimes. Actual scuffles among these young women involved knife assaults and/or scratching and kicking, which occurred frequently, sometimes against other women and often against males as well.'

The report observes the unbearable disparities that exist for Mexican girls growing up in America.

In many Mexican culture homes, it is normal for boys to be treated more leniently than girls, enjoying more privileges, being allowed to stay out later, and even dominating their sisters who must often iron their shirts to perfection and wait on them at the dinner table.

In the traditional Mexican family, the joys of motherhood and family security are highly prized. Typically, Mom always seems happy and both she and Dad are primarily concerned with providing for the children. The family is sacred. In the traditional Mexican family, Mom also stays at home and cooks and sews – even today with the economy virtually forbidding this practice any longer. In some Mexican homes, Mom has to work; nevertheless, she returns to the nest and puts in another shift cooking, washing, ironing, and nurturing.

Many young women are fed up with this double standard and express their exasperation vociferously. Given the further pressures provided by poverty-stricken environments, they become likely targets for gang recruitment.

In addition, in many of the homes Dads are not always present and, if they are, they are not necessarily able to provide much for their children.

Anne Campbell, writing the book *Out of Control* in 1993, interviewed various teenagers living in the gang cultures of New York and concluded that self-protection (rather than over-criminality) was an important purpose.

This is backed up by crime statistics that reflect the different profiles of male and female gang members. The women commit fewer violent crimes, although 78 per cent reported having been involved in gang fights and 65 per cent admitted to carrying a weapon. Drugs were the most common cause of arrest. In the 80s the women were dealing heroin; later crack and cocaine.

One survey, in San Francisco, found that male and female gang members had split over drug profits and the women had gone into business for themselves. This trend was also seen in Detroit, where unemployment was high, and figures showed a parallel rise in female dealers.

Campbell pointed out that many of the women attracted to gangs come from homes where they have seen their mothers beaten up.

'Less physically strong and more sexually vulnerable than the boys, they [the gang girls] find that the best line of defence is not attack but the threat of attack. The key to this is the development of a reputation for violence which will ward off opponents. There is nothing so effective as getting in a street gang to keep the message blaring out, "Don't mess with me, I'm a crazy woman." '

Weeza, who had founded the Sex Girls in New York, described a father who, when not in prison for dealing dope, would arrive home covered in lipstick and love bites and demand food and money from her mother. Later, when she was older, Weeza got into an argument with him and he tried to shoot her.

Connie, who founded the Sandman Ladies, saw her father die from heroin addiction.

'I remember being so lonely,' she told Campbell. 'Like an outsider, like I didn't really belong.' Then she, like Weeza, also learned to stick up for herself. 'I had to fight with a chick and I had my .25 automatic and I had my switchblade . . . if you leave her dead, leave her dead.'

Girls fated to survive in a brutal and brutalised urban landscape look for acceptance and safety. The female gang is a sisterhood, a sorority of like-minded toughies who will protect each other. And, like their whitebread counterparts in Ivy League schools, the street sorority will not accept just anyone. There are initiation ceremonies. It is particularly important that the new recruit knows how to fight, and win, so the initiations tend to involve a punch-up where the novice must show no fear and no pain.

By 1996 it was generally accepted that female gangs were not only extensive, but dangerous. A report in one social worker's journal noted a trend in Texas for carrying knives to school. This was explained by a fifteen-year-old girl. 'Hey,' she said, 'school's a dangerous place. You gotta do what ya gotta do – fist, blade, or pop (gun).' Another girl, aged fourteen, reported walking to the store with her nine-year-old brother and having to push him down onto the pavement to avoid the bullets from a car full of gangsters driving by. Baby-sitting had become just as dangerous as sitting in the back row of a biology class. No one was safe.

An individual crosses a female gang member at their peril. Rosanne Gervais told two twenty-year-old San Francisco homegirls to turn down the volume of their ghetto blaster. 'We can do what we like,' they said, at which point they pushed Gervais to the floor and kicked her, then punched her. She was punched in the face so hard that her jaw was broken.

Journalist Gini Sikes spent some years with the gang girls of Los Angeles, New York and Wisconsin in order to write *8 Ball Chicks: A Year in the Violent World of Girl Gangs* – a remarkable and horrifying book that illuminated not only the extraordinary levels of violence with which the gang girls had to live, but the misery of endless abuse, poverty, and levels of sexism that were almost psychotic, and which were, by and large, passively accepted by the women involved.

Sikes' pages highlighted the important fact that the last twenty years have bred large numbers of teenage girls who cannot feel pain, emotional or physical, and who were destined to be as cruel to others as life and their families had been to them.

Her chapters tell endless stories of stepfathers who rape pre-pubescent girls, of brothers who die of gunshot wounds, of mothers on coke and on the game, of scarred faces and knives and guns and photograph albums full of obituaries.

She came across girls with razor blades in their mouths and Glocks down their pants; schoolgirl mothers so focused on surviving the streets they did not even know which state they lived in; girls who risked their lives to guard their hoods, hoods that they did not own, and which, anyway, were urban hellholes of crumbling projects, crack dens and crossfires – ghettoes that did not seem to be worth affection, let alone the risk of a blade in the leg or a bullet in the back.

And, along the way, there were sixteen-year-old boyfriends called Shotgun and Psycho who punched them and fucked them and told them they were bitches and hos. Characters like TJ of the Playgirl Gangstas learned to break into houses by watching crime programmes on the television and could hot-wire a car in under a minute. As her self-confidence within the gang grew and she became more skilled in the crafts required by nefarious activity, so, at school, her grades became better and better. Then her boyfriend hit her until she lost the baby that she did not know she was carrying.

Shygirl looked like a boy and had Lennox (the name of her Latino hood) tattooed onto her forehead. She had a bullet lodged in her thigh and a .380 down her trousers.

Hear the Nasty Fly Ladies from New York talking to Sikes.

Tiny: 'Nowadays the fists don't work no more. You gotta have a knife or a hammer. Or a gun.'

Happy: 'First time I saw a girl put a razor in her mouth, she was flipping it around with her tongue, not getting cut. I thought, oooh, that's for me! So I got me a brand new razor, put it in the side of my mouth and cut myself. A lot of blood – after a while I got used to it.'

Carmen: 'A dealer shot my brother six times in the head. That's when I got really violent.'

In San Antonio, Texas, gang crime was characterised by sexual assault and highlighted when it came to the public's attention that a twelve-year-old girl had lured a thirteen-year-old into a trailer so that she could be raped by nine men.

The Lady Eights, the Queens and the LA Girlz were among the all-girl gangs. Sweetie, 300 lb, pulled a gun on a man who tried to rape her. Marie thought nothing of a fight when she was five months pregnant. Lynn's mother bought her a gun, and Alicia explained that she would rather deal with broken bones than reality. 'Pain makes me forget my anger,' she told Sikes. 'And I have a lot of anger.'

Sad Eyes, a Latin Queen, was drinking by the time she was eight, had had her first miscarriage at the age of ten and was seriously beaten up and raped at the age of twelve. At thirteen, and pregnant, Sad Eyes joined the Latin Queens. Aged sixteen she had a second child – its father went to prison for shooting a man who talked to her. At seventeen, carrying a third child, she started her own gang, jumping everyone in (beating them up) despite the fact that she was pregnant.

'I was always drunk and angry,' she told Gini Sikes. 'I know it had an effect on my son. To this day he is real mean.'

She stole a car and went to Chicago where her father enjoyed a career as a drug dealer. Squatting in an abandoned building, penniless, she started to sell the girls of her gang for sex. One, aged fifteen, called her Mom. 'I didn't care how she felt. I was drunk and wanted my money. I sold the others too.'

Sad Eyes achieved 'respect' in the hood especially after the time she disguised herself as a 'Spanish Cobra' (a rival gang) and infiltrated one of their parties. She and her friend Suzy Q lured two Cobras to an alley with the promise of sex, whereupon they were gunned down by their rivals in a car. Looking briefly at the corpses on the street, Suzy Q spat on one of them.

At the age of eighteen Sad Eyes attacked a fourteen-year-old and burned her with a cigarette. Charged with assault of a minor she went to prison.

'To me,' she explained, 'it's power to see someone get killed or having a gun in my hand, it's a natural high.'

In Milwaukee, Mama Sheik made a name for herself until she was shot down at the age of 25. A five-foot-eight drug dealer and gang leader, La Sheik was remembered for a *funk-elegance*; she and her girlfriends parading down the street, all in white fur coats.

She was rumoured to have thrown six policemen off a bridge when she was eleven, though this is thought to have been part of the Mama Sheik myth, bolstered by her accredited skills as a black-belt kick-boxer.

Hailing from the projects, one of four 'rough' sisters, she started the Lady Sheiks as a breakdancing group who attended competitions and then enjoyed a rumble in the car park afterwards. She was careful about whom she recruited; a Lady Sheik had to prove herself by fighting with a man 40 lb heavier and two inches taller than herself.

Mama Sheik was very violent; she carried a stiletto knife and her car was known to be full of pipes and chisels. One teenage girl was held down while she and four of her gang members beat the life out of her for failing to join with a gang chant. In 1985, at the age of eighteen, she walked into a Credit Union bank wearing a wig and armed with an automatic and robbed it. She was caught when the getaway car was followed by a member of the public who rang the police. Mama Sheik was sent to prison for six years, a term which successfully served to crystallise her criminal ambitions.

She came out and set herself up as a fully committed gang leader and drug dealer, commanding obedience from both men and women. Cocaine brought big money and she laundered it into businesses such as a limo service and a hair salon. She surrounded herself with young female lovers, whom she would claim by beating up the men who beat them; the irony being that the girls were no safer under the volatile 'protection' of the big mama, who was just as likely to punch them up.

Her sister Sharon, meanwhile, at the age of ten, founded the Baby Sheiks. Seven years later she was to tell Gini Sikes, 'I don't give a fuck about nobody. I'm a self-centred person, that's how I am. I mean I love me, I'd die for me.'

Then Mama Sheik's apartment was burgled – all her Christmas presents were stolen – and she took five hired gunmen out on a revenge ambush. La Sheik went down in the crossfire. Some said that she had been killed by one of her own men. Why? She had got too big, and she was sleeping with their women.

By 1997 the FBI was crediting gangs with half of the murders committed in Los Angeles and reporting that violent street gangs were operating in 94 per cent of America's cities, the trend being that they were appearing in the smaller towns thanks to relocation of families. A gang member would arrive in a new neighbourhood, his colours would earn him instant respect, and a new group would quickly grow around him.

So while overall crime rates were falling, gang membership was growing – a number of 600,000 was estimated at a Senate hearing on gang violence. Senator Dianne Feinstein, sponsoring a bill entitled the Gang Violence Act of 1997 (which was designed to provide more funds for federal prosecution), told senators that gang violence was a more serious threat than organised crime.

In 1999 the *Boston Phoenix* described the activities of the Doves, a female gang loosely affiliated with the Crips. One policeman said that the gangs of girls have become, 'much more volatile – participating in crimes such as robbery, assault and drugs.'

A year later Chicago's *New Expression* magazine reported that there were thirty female gangs in the Boston area, all with their own identities and titles such as the Corbitt Street Girls and the Green and Goldies. Their crimes? 'These girls fight with razors, knives and stomp other females with their heels on.'

Hear 'Pumpkins' on the matter. She used to get picked on. Four fights a week, at least. Not any more though. 'Whoever looked at us funny or tried to pull it, we just messed them up bad. I got this bleach spray bottle and when somebody do something dumb or something I don't like, I fuck them up. I sprayed this one girl's brand new pink Guess outfit, she had bleach stains everywhere, in her hair too.'

The Green and Goldies were founded by a pair of fifteen-year-old twins, one of whom was named 'Squeaky'. Squeaky claimed she got the name from 'Squeaky' Fromme – 'the coolest chick in the Manson family', but her twin sister told Boston reporter Sarah McNaught that, in fact, she was called 'squeaky' because, as a child, that was what she was.

'If you drive around Dorchester,' said Squeaky, 'the people with the phat cars, phat clothes and wads of cash are all gangbangers. It's the easiest way to get what you want.'

The Green and Goldies became notorious for challenging male gangs to fights. Having developed their own hand-signals and their own colours, the homegirls' pleasure was to slash tyres, mug commuters, snatch purses and beat up other girls, preferably after stealing their boyfriends.

'Make no mistake,' said Boston police officer Lieutenant Gary French, 'these girls are not girl scouts.'

As the thug culture of the streets was reflected in the gangsta chic of rap (whose stars tended to end up in jail or dead or, in the case of Tupac Shakur, both), so the girl gangs had their own breed of icons – bolshy female rap stars and R&B soul sistas who had lived the street life and who vocalised the endless pressures imposed on young black urban women. Certainly somebody had to stand up to the sexism purveyed by the swaggering roosters strutting all over the R&B charts.

The real girls living on the street were violent, but they were also strangely passive and defenceless when it came to accepting the atrocities meted out by their boyfriends. Female MCs were an important protest movement and lyrical activism was most effective when it came from the sisters who knew the hood.

So there is Eve, who once stripped to make money; DaBrat, singing about sex and weed, who once declared, 'Because of my profanity and my parental advisory stickers I'm never gonna be like a total household name. Some people try to make it negative that I cuss and talk and all that, but I think we should be able to talk about what we want to talk about.'

There is Missy Elliot, strong and fierce, and Foxy Brown, straight out of Brooklyn and onto Def Jam. An album (*Chyna Doll*) extolling the delights of Prada was complemented by headlines following an incident where

Miss Brown spat on two hotel clerks when they failed to provide her with an iron.

Gangsta Boo, meanwhile, ran with Three 6 Mafia and, at first, promoted herself as a tough hussy with hardcore credentials and songs like 'I Faked It Last Night'. Then, somewhat disappointingly, she found God and announced that she wished to be known as 'Lady Boo'.

Mostly, though, there is Lil' Kim – irrepressible, incorrigible, exhibitionist – a gangsta girl par excellence. Lil' Kim, Brooklyn born and bred, is patently not a criminal herself, and has pointed out that 'Lil' Kim is the character I use to make money. Kimberly Jones is me, the human being.' Nevertheless she has hard-woman pedigree. Her parents divorced when she was eight and her brother, Linwood, became her guardian. It was a volatile relationship which ended when Kim stabbed him in the shoulder. She ran away, lived with boyfriends, sold drugs. Then, when she was sixteen, she met Christopher Wallace, also known as The Notorious B.I.G., or 'Biggie' to his friends, and he did have friends, because he wasn't nearly as bad as he liked to make out. According to his mother, anyway.

Kim joined Big's crew, Junior M.A.F.I.A, released an album, *Hardcore*, and started to appear in neon wigs, porno hot-pants, sequins and feathers. Biggie, the most successful act from Puffy Combs' 'Bad Boy' stable, was a 400 lb six-foot-two ex-street hustler whose mobster look was credited with launching the gangsta rap phenomenon. He released two best-selling albums and fielded various police charges before going down in a hail of bullets outside the Soul Train music awards in Los Angeles in 1997. The incident, which had been preceded by the similar execution of Death Row's Tupac Shakur several months earlier, ignited a plethora of conspiracy theories and journalistic investigations which, though thriving years later, were not accompanied by any arrest.

The most feasible theory seems to be that the death of Shakur, at least, was a revenge assassination involving the Bloods (which Shakur superficially represented) and the Crips (who were implicated in his murder).

When Biggie Smalls died, Lil' Kim lost a friend. 'We (Biggie and I) were like partners,' she was to claim. 'Like Bonnie and Clyde for real.'

As Bad Boy released Biggie's posthumous album, bearing the eerily prescient track, 'You're Nobody Til Somebody Kills You', Kim found herself embroiled in record company legal problems that lasted four years until, finally sorted, she released *The Notorious K.I.M.*

'Rapping,' she said, 'is all about claiming your spot.'

She was eminently marketable, and she, more than anyone, understood this. According to Biggie's mother, Voletta Wallace (speaking to writer Cathy Scott in the book *The Notorious B.I.G. – The Murder of Biggie Smalls*), Lil' Kim played up her relationship with Biggie, adding to her gangsta cred.

She knew what the press wanted and she appreciated the showbiz glitz of burlesque. Fabulous in glittery corsets and jewellery, she easily grabbed magazine covers, pushing *Select* and *Vibe* off the newsstands as pop-eyed wannabe youth found a new gang-girl goddess to worship.

Reporters were pleased to note her affiliations to gangsta types such as Puff Daddy, Little Cease and Larceny. Her career suffered no setback after a shoot-out in New York in February 2001. Twenty shots were fired by five different guns at 3 p.m. on a Sunday afternoon when Lil' Kim's entourage came across that of Capone-N-Noreaga at Hot 9 – a hip-hop radio station that had been interviewing the rappers. No lessons, it seemed, had been learned from the similar shoot-outs that had claimed both Shakur and Biggie under similar circumstances of internecine rivalry between gang-affiliated entourages.

Lil' Kim, reported to be in her limo at the time, vehemently denied any involvement as, of course, did Capone-N-Noreaga. Police reported that words had been followed by bullets and a 31-year-old, Efrain Ocasio, had been shot in the back. Everyone limoed away and Ocasio had been left to make his own way to the nearest hospital, where he was described as being in a critical condition.

The speculation was that the gunfight had erupted as a result of a feud between Foxy Brown and Lil' Kim. Once childhood friends in Brooklyn, they had fallen out and insulted each other on their records, as is the rappers' wont. Brown had described Kim as 'lame' on a Capone-N-Noreaga record .

'Let the females cat fight,' Noreaga said at the time of this release, 'And whatever happens happens.' Whatever did happen, and a man nearly died.

'We're bigger than this,' Foxy Brown said on MTV news afterwards, and she expressed a desire to make up.

The homegirls saw Lil' Kim as a hardcore bitchin' chick to whom they could relate; a success story from the street who had had to dodge the gunfire and survive. Lately, though, there have been discontented rumblings from the fanbase. Hip-hop website BET.com's survey to find the 2001 Tackiest Diva of the Year placed Lil' Kim firmly on a short list where the only person to attract more venom was Mariah Carey. The voting forum turned into a ferment of bitchy postings about the MC where aspersions were made about everything from her 'horrible blonde weave job' to her 'fugly dresses' to her 'tacky ass Flower Bra barely covering those over-inflated boobs'.

The final word was supplied by a person posting under the tag, 'KHRPP': 'I USE TO LIKE LIL' KIM, BUT THAT WAS IN '96, WHEN SHE WAS TRULY HARD-CORE. KIM GO BACK TO YOUR ROOTS GIRL. GO BACK TO THAT REAL B****. YOU FAKE AS HELL RIGHT NOW, LOOKING LIKE A WHITE BARBIE DOLL. YOU USE TO GET MAD RESPECT FROM ME. NOW YOU GETS NOTHING.'

You won't catch Keke Wyatt in 'fugly' dresses, but then you might not see her at all since, at the time of writing, she has been indicted for stabbing her husband in the back.

Christmas morning in the Wyatt household took a violent turn as the R&B singer's understanding of the concept of goodwill to all men failed to extend to her husband. The 21-year-old was arrested at her Shelby-ville, Kentucky home and charged with second-degree assault after allegedly attacking him with a steak knife. At the time of writing she has been arraigned and has entered a not guilty plea.

Rahmat Morton, 28, who is also her manager, was stabbed five times in the chest, back and hand. Part of the blade broke off in his back and had to be retrieved by doctors. One could not possibly imagine that Keke Wyatt assaulted her husband in an effort to boost her record sales but, nevertheless, as Rahmat went down, so her units went up. As MTV news pointed out, her debut album, *Soul Sista*, released in November 2001, a month before the incident, 'First entered the Billboard album chart at number 60, dropped more than 40 places in its second week, and plummeted to 190 the week before the alleged knifing occurred. The week after her arrest the album bounced back by nearly 50 places and went on to peak at number 33 by the end of February with nearly 340,000 copies being sold.'

Death, as Biggie Smalls had so rightly pointed out, is the most effective career move for any singer and Lisa 'Left Eye' Lopes achieved it in when she died in a car crash in April 2002 at the age of thirty. One of the three sistas in the successful R&B group TLC, she was remembered for defending herself in a place where hip-hop women were too often the pawns of producers and managers. Lopes was always willing to fight for business interests and her creative control. She made a lot of friends and she had a lot of fans. Whitney Houston, DaBrat and Janet Jackson were among the ten thousand mourners who turned up to her funeral in Lithonia, Georgia. A legion of eulogies extolled her 'self expression and rebellion'. Treach of Naughty by Nature described her as 'a female Tupac' who once bought him an engraved axe. 'She was the thug out of the group,' he concluded.

She certainly was. In 1994 she set fire to her boyfriend Andre Rison's house. 'Andre and I were having a very traumatic domestic argument,' she explained later. 'There was drinking involved. There was hurt, anger and passion. He stormed off and I decided to barbecue his tennis shoes. I threw them in the bathtub because I thought the fire would contain itself that way, but it immediately blazed out of control and then the whole house burned down. It was awful.'

BET.com's Tonya Pendleton noted that 'Once arrested, Lopes was sporting pre-fire facial bruises, the marks of another of the couple's frequent fights. Hey, I ain't saying she was right, but I understand.'

Pendleton, who had interviewed the singer several times, put the incident down to Lisa's background in Philadelphia where she, her mother, sister and brother lived in a one-room converted garage with an abusive alcoholic father.

'He ran the household with military precision, waking Lisa and her brother and sister up in the middle of the night for transgressions as minor as a pen left in the middle of the floor. One night he beat Lisa's mother and threatened to kill the rest of the household, falling asleep with a knife clutched in his hand while Lisa and her brother and sister huddled wide awake in a corner. Lisa admitted that her relationship with Rison mirrored her parents' relationship, and her own battle with alcohol culminated in the torching of Rison's house.'

She concluded that Lopes was a 'feminist hero' who never got the headlines that double murderer Betty Broderick did, but, 'to some, she is the poster girl of female rage.'

Lil' Kim, meanwhile, told MTV news that Lopes and her group reminded her of herself. 'They were real street, but always had this girlie girl edge, just fun and not caring.'

The life patterns of gang girls are different to their male counterparts. Most gangstas end up in jail or in wheelchairs; the women have children and, unless they are unfortunate enough to be junkies, the kids tend to help them go straight, especially if they are keen to revoke the atrocities meted out by their own parents. It's a tough business, of course, but maternal protectiveness often kicks in. For many maturing gang girls the life of the mother precludes a life spent wielding an Uzi.

Gang girl Tiny told Gini Sikes, 'The violence, the robbing, all of this will stop when I find out I'm pregnant.' While Wanda's mother correctly predicted that her teenage daughter would 'grow out of it'.

The 28-year-old woman is a very different person to the 15-year-old girl and, in the event that she stays out of prison, she is less likely than a man to remain a violent recidivist eking out her jail sentences because she is trapped in a macho set of moral codes that simply serve to fuel the killing machine.

There is some evidence that the gang girl comes to regret her streetfightin' years. Sandra Davis was once a gang member, living on the streets, then her son was killed by a gang and she founded 'Mothers Against Gang Warfare'.

The website www.gangstyle.com has attracted many thousands of hits since its inception in 2000. It is designed to provide 'support, help and advice from gang and ex-gang members' and, to this end, is characterised by reflections on the dark side of street life. There is a long obituary 'remembrance' list devoted to all those who 'fell in the line of action': Thumper and Sad Eyez; Mad Killa and Solo Loco and many more.

Supplying information about tattoo removal, about making the transfer from prison to a new start, there are forums where religion is discussed and the rules are 'no hating'. There are many 'life stories' posted by kids who have lost friends, kids with regrets, kids who got lured in. But it is 'Shadow' whose words must provide the final conclusion. She posted this on the section of the site reserved as a forum for gang girls past and present.

'Girlz, I know you trynna be hard, and you wanna look like you da baddest bytch around. You wanna prove to yo man that you will do anything and everything. You wanna make that money, floss those thangz. You start slangin, that's the easiest way, then before you know it your man talkin bout he need more money, the whole time he aint doin nothin cept sittin on his ass drankin wit his boyz and smokin. You the one makin the money, payin yall billz, buyin his clothes, feedin his ass, and for what? To prove you love him. You wanna make sure he don't go nowhere

and mija you would sell your soul to keep him from leaving. Then yall start talkin bout movin out, yall wanna get an apartment of yall own. You know it's gonna take more money then you got rye now. Some nigga you know offers you money if you sleep with him. You know that's prostitution, but you want your man happy. You know if he finds out what you did he would whoop your ass and probably leave you anyway so you keep it quiet. Soon your sleeping with anyone for money, your nothin but a cheap whore.

Your still keepin your man in the tightest outfits, makin sure he has money in his pocket, buyin his weed, payin his bills. You begin to not give a fuck. You don't care what anyone says about you. You'll whoop there ass if they disrespect you, but don't you realize you are disrespecting yourself in the process?? You are hurting yourself more then he could ever hurt you. Then you talk to your homegirls and some of them are willing to help you do the same thing, so you begin to think that if your girls are doing it then it must be okay . . . babygirl, please sit down and remember as hard as you can all the hopes and dreams you had before you met this man. Is he worth the abuse your giving yourself? Is he worth the heartache? Even though you know he loves you, you are hurting yourself so much more then you know.

He will never love you as soon as he finds out your a hoe. He will leave you all alone. If you remember why you even started doing all of this, it was because you wanted him happy, sure you have nice cars, your bills are paid, your hair and nails are done, but look deep inside of yourself and you will see more emotional scars then you ever thought anyone could have. All this for a man? Girl, he ain't worth it.'

SOURCES

Campbell, Anne, *Out of Control, Men, Women and Aggression,* Basic Books, New York, 1993

Sikes, Gini, *8 Ball Chicks: A Year in the Violent World of Girl Gangs*, Doubleday, New York, 1997

Scott, Cathy, *The Notorious B.I.G – The Murder of Biggie Smalls*, Plexus Publishing, London, 2001

'An Urban Ethnography of Latino Street Cultures'

Boston Phoenix

New Expression

www.BET.com

www.usatoday.com

www.the411online.com

www.MTV.com

www.gangstyle.com

2. DEMENTED HOUSEWIVES

Sometimes cooking, cleaning and kids make you go mad. Most women commit their crimes at home.

In 1998 a 62-year-old Egyptian housewife named Fawakih Ibrahim Abdel-Latif discovered that the will of her husband Sayed Ahmed included arrangements that, to her mind, were both unsatisfactory and unfair. Ahmed had allotted less land to her than to other members of the family. Overcome with murderous resentment, she used the full weight of her thirty-stone body and sat on his face until he suffocated and died.

Replete though America is with endomorphs who could well use their fat butts in lethal ways, the weapon of choice is still a gun, though not always; sometimes the homicidal homemaker will grab a kitchen knife. In Colorado, Carolyn Gloria Banton used both. She shot her husband Peter and then chopped him up. No domestic goddess she – chunks of human flesh were found among her cooking utensils.

Michelle Antencio went for her disabled husband Ray with a butter knife at their cosy home near Denver. This turned out to be an unsatisfactory weapon as husbands do not slice up as easily as Utterly Butterly. She finished him off with a steak knife. In 1999 she sought clemency, somewhat optimistically claiming that Ray, despite being paraplegic, was a vicious man and the stabbing was in self-defence.

The domestic blade is easy, available and always at hand. It has been used in various ways, but no one used it with more effective finesse than Virginia housewife Mrs Lorena Bobbitt. She found herself promoted to the status of feminist superstar when, on the night of 23 June 1993, she rolled back the sheets of the marital bed and carefully sliced her sleeping husband's dick off. Then she walked out of the apartment with his appendage still in her hand, got into her car, and threw it out of the window as she drove down the road.

Police, having unsuccessfully searched for the severed penis in the Manassas apartment, retrieved it from the side of the road. They wrapped it in ice and took it to the hospital where it was successfully sewn back onto John Wayne Bobbitt who, despite his enormous loss was, according to a medic on duty, 'surprisingly upbeat'.

The testimony of a urological surgeon stated that Bobbitt had suffered a 'potentially life threatening injury'. If a wound of this sort is neglected over a period of time, a patient would be expected to lapse into haemorrhagic shock and could suffer 'morbid complications'.

Nevertheless the cut had been a clean slice. As one physician said, 'it was a very acceptable organ for replantation', and this enabled them to perform their task successfully. 'It is a very unusual operation,' the doctor admitted. 'There have been probably less than fifty in this century.' The prognosis was 'good for return of functions'.

Mrs Bobbitt had unintentionally enacted the suggestion propounded by the radical activist Valerie Solanas when she founded the Society for Cutting Up Men and issued her notorious SCUM manifesto. But Lorena Bobbitt was not a feminist; quite the opposite. She was tiny, and she projected an image that was shy and retiring. A good Catholic girl, born in Ecuador and raised in Venezuela, she came from a loving family where there was no violence. If her parents disagreed with each other, they talked it out.

At the age of eighteen Lorena came to America to work as a manicurist and hoped to be both a wife and mother. She thought her dream had come true when John Bobbitt walked into her life. She thought, as her defence lawyer put it, that he was her 'knight in shining armour'. In love, she married him in 1989 when she was nineteen.

Having successfully charmed her during their courtship with the performance of a gallant military type, he proceeded to embark on a saga of physical and emotional abuse that, by the end, left his wife battered and shaking at least twice a week.

'Rape, beatings, kickings, punching, shoving, slapping, dragging, choking and threats' is how her defence lawyer described their marriage. Unsurprisingly Mrs Bobbitt became depressed, but, having grown up in a culture where the woman was blamed for a divorce, she risked being condemned to genuine social shame. She stuck with her marriage for four years while her husband went on hitting her, sleeping with other women, taking her money, drinking and anally raping her. Then, when to her delight she became pregnant, John Bobbitt made her have an abortion – though he was to testify that it was a mutual decision.

Lorena's defence attorneys painted John Wayne Bobbitt as a cruel thug who drove his wife mad. Evidence against him was compelling, as various witnesses testified to the fact that his sexual thrill was to see women suffer, and others spoke of his wife's continuous bruising and misery. The prosecution, meanwhile, attempted to persuade the jury that the 25-year-old woman was a possessive, jealous, unstable thief who had often initiated the violence and whose bloody act was the malicious revenge of a wife who was about to be left by her husband. Furthermore she had once told a friend that castration was the correct punishment for an unfaithful man.

The facts became more and more elusive as the various attorneys attempted to unravel the Bobbitts' complex marital battleground, proving, if such a thing needs proving, that marriage is an unfathomable thing whose truths remain mysterious to the participants let alone any individuals attempting to observe them from the outside. It is possible that the most meaningful comment was delivered by witness Sandra Beltran: 'I heard an argument. I didn't see anyone hit anyone, they were yelling at each other, I separated them – this is like two children. I separated them, she said, "He hit me", he said, "She hit me . . .!" '

Dr Susan Feister, the psychiatrist speaking on Lorena's behalf at the trial, opined not only that Mrs Bobbitt was suffering from a major depressive illness, but that she showed symptoms of post-traumatic stress disorder and panic disorder. Untreated, under stress and alone, in Feister's opinion, the young woman had experienced a psychotic breakdown.

Feister's testimony, brilliant and convincing, was adamantly unaffected by confrontation; she was one of the few witnesses able to make the prosecuting lawyer look foolish and she certainly helped to push Lorena to victory.

The defendant avoided a possible twenty-year prison sentence when the jury hearing the case in Manassas, Virginia, in 1994, found her not guilty of malicious wounding by reason of temporary insanity. They had been forced to survey a range of bizarre evidence, not least photographs of Bobbitt's severed penis, and a pair of Mrs Bobbitt's 'panties'. They had heard people wonder how it was possible to drive a car while holding a penis, and they had heard how John Wayne Bobbitt had failed to give his wife any orgasms. In other words, he always came first.

Sympathy, in general, was not with John Bobbitt. Nevertheless, despite his painfully obvious defects, he became a media celebrity and embarked on a career as a porn star.

Crimes committed by women in the home are not necessarily of passion (motivated by jealousy) or self-defence (motivated by abuse) or even ennui (the endless monotony of cleaning and cooking). Some wives become murderers for reasons that are connected to a psycho-pathology that exists outside the tenets of explicable criminality. They are the ones looking for ant poison in the supermarket and they are the ones who are as likely to keep their husband in the freezer as they are gallon tubs of ice cream. And yes, they look like you and me.

In March 1998 one 54-year-old hausfrau was the first woman to be executed in Florida for 150 years. Judy Buenoano had poisoned her husband James and drowned her handicapped son Michael. She was caught when she attempted to blow up the car belonging to a boyfriend shortly after he took out a $500,000 life insurance in which she was the beneficiary. Buenoano spent thirteen years on death row knitting baby-wear.

Jackie Postma's crime bore some resemblance to that of many other homicidal women, bearing, as it did, the familiar noir themes where the bored married wife attempts to persuade her macho lover to kill the husband who is an impediment to her personal happiness and whose death would release a gratifying endow-ment of some sort.

Postma, a Florida housewife, tried for murder in 2002, briefly managed to persuade police that she had no part in the execution of her husband, Ed. Pregnant at the time of his death, she had joined her mother-in-law Karla Postma in handing out green ribbons as police searched for the supposed murderer. 'I wanted to see that bitch in jail,' was Karla's response when all the revelations came to light.

La Postma, 31, insisted that her relationship with her husband was volatile and unhappy. He had raped her repeatedly but she told the police that she still loved him. She had engaged in a passionate affair with ex-convict Michael Cordes and, she claimed, it was Cordes who had killed her husband when a planned 'discussion' about divorce went too far.

In August 2000 her husband, a 32-year-old mechanic, pulled into a car park in a convenience store in Duette, a town in west Florida. His wife had called him to say that she had run out of petrol and was stranded. When Postma arrived, his wife was not there. Michael Cordes was said to be there, armed with a handgun, as was his friend, Todd Martin, armed with a knife. The prosecution claimed that together they shot and stabbed him to death.

Todd Martin was sentenced to twelve years as an accessory; Cordes, a career criminal, was acquitted on the grounds of insufficient evidence. Cordes claimed that Martin had committed the murder alone and the jury believed him. Jackie Postma was charged with masterminding the killing in order to inherit her husband's $50,000 life insurance policy.

At first Postma lied. She lied about her relationship with Cordes and she denied that she knew anything about the ambush. Later she said she had lied because she was afraid that Cordes would beat her up. But Chrissy Rogers and Edward Turner testified that Jackie Postma and Michael Cordes had offered them $6,000 to kill Ed. And not only that, she had supplied them with a gun, Ed Postma's work schedule and the control unit to his garage door.

Jackie Postma: 'I wish the son of a bitch was dead.'

Chrissy Rogers: 'I thought it was like a joke . . .'

Various witnesses insisted that Jackie Postma, caring for three children, was a kind person, but the jury found her guilty of second-degree murder and sent her to prison for life.

Omaima Nelson might have been content in the traditional role of child-raising and homemaking, but she was not destined to enjoy the tasks that are characteristic to the life of a newlywed woman willing to please. Omaima Nelson's wifely duties were sadly remiss. She did not cook much. When the police looked in her fridge they did not find any delicious ingredients for the making of candlelit lovers' suppers. They found Mr Nelson. Or Mr Nelson's head, to be exact.

Omaima Nelson, an exotic-looking woman with high cheekbones and brown eyes, dressed and behaved like Tura Satana as Varla in *Faster Pussycat Kill! Kill! Kill!* – tight-fitting trousers, white shirt, black gloves. Omaima did not run from a catfight and she drove a red Corvette that added to the *femme fatale* image. But this was non-fiction. Omaima was a real devil-bitch from hell.

Omaima, an Egyptian, was born in 1968 and raised in Cairo where she was both sexually abused and circumcised, as was the primitive custom. These circumstances did little to aid healthy development.

She met up with Bill Nelson in a bar in California in 1991. He was 56 and an ex-convict but, as far as Omaima was concerned, he was kind and nice and she married him. Four weeks later she killed him.

She told a neighbour that Nelson had tied her to the bed, raped and cut her, and that she had knocked him out with a lamp. Then she had cut him up and decapitated him. She offered the neighbour, a man named Popovich, $75,000 to help her dispose of the body. Somewhat alarmed by these suggestions, he informed the police.

The police went to the apartment in Costa Mesa, a Los Angeles suburb. Here they found a mattress soaked in blood and the remains of Bill Nelson. Some of his organs and limbs had been dumped in a rubbish bin; other parts, such as legs, genitalia, fingers and hands, were in the fridge; some had been neatly wrapped in silver foil, some in newspaper.

Questioned by police, a neighbour said they had heard chopping noises and the garbage disposal unit had been whirring all night. Later Omaima Nelson told a psychiatrist that she had put on red lipstick, a red hat and red high-heeled shoes in order to mutilate her husband's body.

She was hypnotised by the red of his blood and dressed up to play a ritual. She described how she had hacked off his genitals and put them in his mouth. She explained that she had sliced off his finger because he would stick it up her when he came home, rather than kiss her. Later, when she was hungry, she cooked his ribs and ate them with barbecue sauce. Omaima Nelson received a sentence of 27 years to life in March 1992.

The fat housewife with wide staring eyes, plump maternal figure, and veneer of innocence has become an archetype among the roster of homicidal maniacs who characterise the dark side of domesticity. This woman was defined and encapsulated by Rhonda Belle Martin, but she has reincarnated many times since.

Rhonda Belle Martin murdered her mother, two of her five husbands, and three of her daughters. A bespectacled woman of twelve stone, she then married her thirty-year-old stepson and tried to poison him. It was at this point that she was arrested and sentenced to death in 1957. Rhonda Belle Martin enjoyed cooking and sewing and she professed to love her husbands and her children. She did not know why she killed them; murder was a compulsion that she could neither fight nor explain. When asked how she accounted for the love of the men who married her, she said she was a good wife – she cooked and cleaned – they did not have any complaints. 'Lord knows I didn't ever claim to be perfect,' she said to one journalist who visited her before she was due to be executed.

Mary Thompson, also plump and maternal, also middle-aged and bespectacled, was a Rhonda archetype. She was seen as a maternal figure by the community who lived around Eugene in Oregon. A consummate con woman, she had successfully set herself up as a high-profile anti-gang activist, giving lectures to parents and children about the dangers of street gangs and the damage caused by them. She drew on her experience with her son, Beau Flynn, who, at the age of thirteen, had helped to form the 74 Hoover Crips and had subsequently served time at a local juvenile prison.

Mrs Thompson received much publicity and veneration for her 'crusade' against criminality. She gained the trust and respect of local police and she was employed as a member of the Gang Prevention Task Force. Nobody realised that Mary Louise Thompson was damaged goods.

Born Mary Fockler in 1954, she was the youngest, unplanned child of an Ohio steelworker and a nurse. She was always a bully, prone to tantrums and violence, but she was by no means the only black sheep in the family. In 1968 her older brother, Bobby, had asked her other brother, Joel, to drive him to a local pizza restaurant where his wife worked. Bobby then strode in and shot his wife dead. This event was followed by the stress-related heart attack of their father and by the attempted suicide of Joel, who tried to shoot himself in the chest with a rifle, but failed. The bullet hit his spine and he was paralysed from the waist down.

Mary, meanwhile, contented herself with running up her mother's credit cards, writing bad cheques drawn against her account and stealing her furniture. She began to hang out with Ohio bikers and, at one point, attracted the fame that she sought by bringing a false charge of rape against five of them. She was a liar.

In 1978 Thompson pitched up in Wolf Creek, Oregon, where she earned money dealing speed. She gave birth to Beau and managed to convince her boyfriend that the baby was his, which it was not.

It took some perseverance to indict Thompson for the murder of Aaron Iturra, a 19-year-old gang member who had been shot in the head in the middle of the night in his bedroom. It was a Crip event. Joe Brown and Jim Elstad had committed it, while wearing their blue bandannas, in the hope of gaining 'respect'. They had been arrested and sentenced, but the police knew there was more to it than two hit men. They suspected that Mary Thompson had ordered the execution and, following a wire tap placed on her home telephone, she was charged and convicted.

Aaron Iturra had incurred Thompson's fatal hatred after a knife fight in which a youth was slashed in the stomach and after which Beau Flynn had been arrested. Iturra, who was not a gang member, but who had been a witness, planned to testify against Flynn.

At Thompson's trial a former member of the Crips testified that while Thompson's husband was at work, the housewife would invite gang members over to smoke crack, that she sold drugs and guns and organised burglaries. They called her 'Moms' and believed her claim that she had been a Crip for thirty years. She not only supervised the jumping-in ceremonies which launched the gang in their area, but she had incited the teenagers to turn against Iturra by insisting that Iturra was not only selling drugs to small children, but having sex with them also.

The jury found Thompson guilty of aggravated murder – that is, her actions had been the cause of the death of Aaron Iturra. She was sentenced to life in prison with no parole.

Dante Sutorius was also convicted of aggravated murder – the consummate crime of the manipulator. Sentencing her in June 1996 the Ohio judge Richard Neihaus opined that she was beyond rehabilitation. He compared the small 46-year-old woman to a lionfish. 'The outward appearance of the creature completely belies its deadly, poisonous, aggressive nature. The lionfish attracts its prey through its appearance and then consumes all that comes close to it. That creature is you,' he said. Dramatic words from a judge, but then the case was a drama, filmed for Court TV and played out in the press. Dante Sutorius was a good story; more interesting than your run-of-the-mill trailer-trash murderess, she had all the characteristics of a bona fide psychopath.

Mrs Sutorius went to prison for twenty years for shooting her sixth husband Darryl in the back of the head. She then attempted to make it look as if he had committed suicide, a gambit that nearly succeeded thanks, in part, to the fact that she had very nearly driven him to it. Dr Sutorius' friends and family had seen him turn into a very unhappy man. The burly doctor was terrified of his wife but tended to tell friends that he was frightened for his life, rather than that he intended to take it.

Forensic evidence came down against Dante Sutorius. Various experts in the field of 'suicidology' commented that those who shoot themselves in the head do not customarily shoot themselves in the back of it. Furthermore a couple of Dante's ex-husbands had emerged and their stories did her no favours. Indeed, their stories drew a picture of a deranged narcissist whose life of perpetual self-indulgence had oscillated from delusional grandiosity to arson.

Sutorius had spent her adult life destroying the lives of others by means of covert but vicious methods. Her close family, who knew her by her given name of Della, were unsurprised when she was charged with murder. Her mother, in particular, had always sensed that there was something wrong with her eldest daughter. The other six were all healthy and normal. But Della had always been a parasite, unwilling to work for her living, leeching, causing trouble wherever she went.

In the twenty years of Della/Dante's adult life, and in the years of childhood before that, there had always been lying and manipulation with episodic outbreaks of dangerous savagery. One sister recalled that when they were children, growing up in Cincinnati, Della, aged seven, claimed she had murdered a dog. 'Do you like what I did to it?' she said. 'I saved the best part for you. You get to do the eyeballs.' She then poked at the dead animal's eye sockets with a stick.

The same sister remembered that Della would stand over their mother when she was sleeping and hold a pair of scissors to her neck. Even then she was interested in how easy it would be to take a life. It hardly mattered whose. Her mother, Olga, could not explain it. There seemed to be no reasons. She simply knew it was true. Her eldest daughter had always been bad.

There were five husbands before Dante netted Darryl through a dating agency in Ohio. Five husbands whose bank accounts had been cleaned out, who had been stalked and followed and threatened. A stock trick, on rejection, was to inform the man that she was pregnant.

'If I marry her she will have an abortion,' her fifth husband David Bretteon told a friend. 'If not she says she will come after me for child support for eighteen years.' He capitulated and married her.

One of her many lovers woke up to find his bed on fire. Della denied it, of course. Later somebody broke into his apartment and smashed it up. Everything was broken. The fish died. Everything. Another, whose house burned to the ground, strongly suspected that Della had committed arson. She managed to wheedle her way back into his bed. He woke up the next morning to find the only possession that had not been burned in the fire had been stolen by her – his wallet and his cash. The very last things. She denied it, of course; told him she was pregnant and he would have to marry her.

Another man, in California, was threatened with a knife and was sure that Della was responsible for the fact that motor oil had been poured into his brake fluid, causing his car to lose control.

When things went wrong for Della she reverted to savage amorality. In one instance she did one of the worst things a woman can do – she screamed rape when nobody had touched her. In one case she actually slammed herself against the walls of a room and rang the police to claim that her boyfriend had beaten her up.

Jeff Freeman, a stockbroker, was made of sterner stuff. After a disastrous holiday where he grew tired of her cutesy voice, her snobbish airs and her endless grooming and whining, he tried to extricate himself from their relationship. She pretended she was pregnant and then pulled a gun on him. He brought a charge of 'terroristic threatening' for which she received a conviction.

Darryl Sutorius was a perfect target for this woman. A divorced doctor, he had advertised himself at the Great Expectations dating agency as somebody who was Protestant, white, very religious, with a $20,000 credit limit each on Master Card and Visa. He said he was looking for someone who 'needs me and appreciates my support'. Dante sent him her profile. She described herself as 'moral, loyal, cute and adorable.'

Darryl Sutorius' children saw none of these things. They saw a pretentious fake, stiff and cold and imbued with idiotic pretensions that were to prove a drain on their father's finances. Dante came over as a victim of an abused childhood She told anyone who would listen that her mother had tortured her. Certainly she had some symptoms. She was an obsessive compulsive who was phobic about germs. She was also needy, clingy, jealous and obsessed by appearance, particularly her own, which was a combination of cosmetics, cosmetic surgery, foil highlights and mink coats.

Destructive from the start, she was to become hysterical when her new husband agreed to pay for his daughter Deborah's wedding, an affair that would cost thousands of dollars.

Darryl Sutorius was unaware of his wife's past when he married her in March 1995. He gave her a white Lexus, fur coats, jewellery, a Mediterranean cruise, a new kitchen – everything she asked for, and she asked for a lot. She was the kind of woman who liked baby grand pianos, ornate mirrors, silver tea-sets and fake

Monets in gold frames. She often boasted about how good her taste was.

By January 1996 the doctor's wife had moved into her own room. The marriage was on the rocks and he became frightened for his life. She listened in to his telephone conversations and she rang him at his office to check up on him. He had already broken through the locks on her bedroom door and taken one gun from her – a .22 which was hidden under her bed. He told friends that his wife had threatened to destroy him by damaging his reputation – revealing his impotence, his financial muddles, even his lack of personal hygiene.

He was terrified that his standing as a doctor could be dismantled and his livelihood taken away. His state of mind was not helped by talking to his wife's mother and one of her ex-boyfriends, both of whom convinced him that she was genuinely dangerous.

On 7 February 1996 Dante Sutorius cleaned out her husband's cash accounts and used some of the money to buy a snub-nose Smith and Wesson revolver from Target World. On 16 February she shot him while he lay asleep on the sofa in his basement. He had planned to serve her with divorce papers the next day.

Dante Sutorius' personality accurately fits Anthony Storr's definition of an aggressive psychopath. In his book *On Human Aggression* the chapter on this condition notes that aggressive psychopaths are not mad in the clinical diagnostic sense. They do not suffer hallucinations or the debilitating distortions of reality that affect and fuel the behaviour of the criminally insane. Neither are they suffering from a mental illness in the way, for instance, that depressives are, or people who suffer from paranoid schizophrenia, conditions which can lead to the committing of violent crime. There is very little evidence of them suffering at all. Unlike many other psychic disorders (particularly those which affect women, who tend to internalise anger and take it out on themselves, rather than on others), aggressive pyscho-paths do not turn their hostility on themselves. They turn their anger outwards and this makes them very dangerous.

In clinical and legal terms they are easily identifiable as they all, men and women, tend to show similar characteristics. They all tend to be paranoid and they have an inability to control their immediate impulses.

'The aggressive psychopath tends to take what he wants at the time irrespective of the needs or the rights of other people,' says Storr. 'They carry a more than normal amount of hostility and they have genuine difficulty separating fantasy from reality; they also have an almost total disregard for the truth.'

Della Hall caused alarm, anguish and chaos before she was finally caught breaking the law in her latest and last incarnation, the expensively dressed, glossily groomed wife of a wealthy heart surgeon.

She used her femininity as her weapon; her cute womanly ways were wiles, often recognised by other women, rarely by men. She would flirt and pout and talk in a little girl's voice and make them pay. She wore thick foundation over her various face-lifts, she affected an upmarket accent and wore the kind of designer labels one finds in an American mall. Her nails were fake and so was she.

Other women saw her coming a mile off because Della Hall used an artillery with which all women are equipped and which they, at some point, choose to use. Those whose morals and outlook have aligned them-selves with the integrity of modern gender politics have abnegated the use of pouting to pull a pay cheque, but this does not mean to say that the behaviour does not resonate with a deep familiarity that serves to make it all the more irritating.

Men were Della's victims and they were her meal tickets. If she had been on some interesting post-feminist revenge kick then she might have gained some respect among the more militant of the feminist phal-anx. However, Della did not target bullies and bastards and take them to the cleaners; she homed in on kind men whose only real sin was to be imbued with an instinct to protect, who wanted to save and caretake, and who fell for her act of defencelessness. Her targets were the kind of men who liked to pay for women because it made them feel strong and manly. And they certainly ended up paying.

Deadly Della was subtle and clever, and very avar-icious. The twisted face of suburban America, she ate nachos and pizza rolls and wanted all the things suburban America is supposed to want.

Dante Sutorius' polished public appearance as the aspirant suburban housewife of the Symmes Township, Ohio was, outwardly, different to the performance enacted by Catherine Nevin of Arklow, County Wick-low, Ireland. But despite the distance between their environments and cultures, the two women had much in common.

Catherine Nevin's husband Tom, like Darryl Sutorius, was an inoffensive man who was terrified of his wife. He told friends that he was certain that she was capable of shooting him stone dead. Catherine Nevin, like Dante Sutorius, had a pattern of making death threats, and Catherine Nevin, like Dante Sutorius, very nearly got away with her crime.

Both women had completed modelling courses and both women were obsessed by their own appearance.

Both had had cosmetic surgery. Catherine Nevin's procedures had included an operation to enhance her sexual pleasure that had involved a metal stud being inserted into her clitoris. Both women needed to be the centre of attention. Both were pathological liars and both wielded information as if it was a weapon. Dante had a history of threatening her lovers with revelations that would destroy their professional lives; Catherine Nevin was the same, telling one cop's superiors that he was guilty of corruption. Making mud stick.

Both wives exerted terrible holds over their husbands but why did the men stay with them? Neither woman was beautiful or loving or clever or funny. The reasons for their power are unfathomable. Perhaps the answers lurk in the mysteries that lie at the midst of corrupt femininity. The siren as psychobitch.

Catherine Scully arrived in the life of poor Tom Nevin in 1976. At first she attempted to be a professional model, which was an unsuccessful career choice due to the fact that her face looked as if somebody had stepped on it while it was still hot.

Tom Nevin, born on a farm in Galway, had always wanted to own a pub and finally succeeded in this ambition when he bought Jack Whites in Brittas Bay, County Wicklow in 1986. His wife, still interested in beautification, opened a hair salon next door. Nobody wanted their hair done, apparently, so she was forced to work in the pub, overseeing the food served in the 'lounge' and the bed and breakfast business. Catherine Nevin was a slob who did not care whether her clients were satisfied or not. The sheets in the guest bedrooms went unwashed and the food served in the lounge was unaffected by any modish concepts of gourmet eating. Guests began to get food poisoning and clients began to transfer to the pub down the road where the atmosphere was friendlier and where one was not likely to be a victim of the idiotic prejudices of an uncontrolled bully.

If Catherine Nevin did not like the look of someone she would either bar them (this applied to Protestants and younger women wearing tight clothes) or drive up the price of their drinks until, correctly, they took the tariffs personally and started to complain. Then she would tell them to fuck off.

So of course she became a local joke.

The hostess did not add to the limited attractions of the pub. She tended to appear in a blue silk dressing gown and a pair of feathered mules. She was loud, rude, drunk, bullied the staff and often engaged in grotesque flirting with the clientele. Her husband, meanwhile, was popular because he was kind. Everyone liked Tom. And Tom, a very passive man, tried to please his wife. He bought her an expensive mink coat and gave her jewellery and did as he was told.

By 1989 Catherine Nevin, always a belligerent ego-maniac, was beginning to cause genuine trouble. Having banned all Protestants and given the pub a sectarian atmosphere, she attracted a number of local gardai (police) to the pub, and then spent years making their lives hell; one victim suffered seven statements and seventeen unfounded allegations over two years, ranging from corruption to sexual assault.

She also took to befriending criminals and planning a long-term conspiracy which would interweave with the extraordinary lies that she told, year after year, until they formed a concoction and turned her entire life into a fantastic formulation. Between 1989 and 1990 Nevin asked three men to help her in her quest to kill her husband.

One, a lover, was offered £20,000; the second, a member of Sinn Fein, was told 'I want you to get the IRA to kill my husband', and the third, a former member of the IRA, testified that she had wanted him shot dead. He had informed his 'connections' and they had warned her off. She came to one of these solicitations with her face bandaged and attempted to curry sympathy by claiming that her husband had beaten her up. The truth was that her face was bruised because she had undergone cosmetic surgery.

In 1995 Catherine Nevin invited various members of the IRA to hold a meeting in the pub. The presence of the IRA at Jack Whites could later be used as a means to cast doubt on her husband's death; if there were criminals around they could be blamed for the murder which was made to look like aggravated burglary.

Tom Nevin, described as a 'six-foot lamb', was shot dead on the night of 19 March 1996. The police arrived at the murder scene at 4.45 a.m. after the internal alarm was called. The two officers found Catherine Nevin with her arms tied behind her back and her mouth gagged with stockings. She told them that a hooded man had threatened her with a knife and demanded her jewellery. She told the police that her husband had been murdered and, later, she placed the word 'murdered' on his gravestone.

Catherine Nevin's trial – 42 days long – was the longest murder trial in Irish legal history. She was charged with her husband's murder a year after his death following gaping discrepancies in her evidence. She was an inveterate liar, and the stories that she created interwove with each other to compound a complicated fabrication, made more so by the fact that she had taken local criminals and local judges as her lovers. But, in the final analysis, her stories did not tally and she often contradicted herself. On 11 April 2000 the jury returned a guilty verdict of murder and three counts of soliciting murder. She was sentenced to life in prison. Making her announcement, the judge, Mella Carroll, said, 'You had your husband assassinated.' Mrs Nevin, in tailored navy suit and gold jewellery, was led away. She had joked, a couple of days previously, that Julia Roberts was not pretty enough to play her in a film.

Writing a book about this case, *The Black Widow*, author Niamh O'Connor comments that Catherine Nevin thought she was invincible. 'She believed she was literally going to get away with murder because, for a decade, she had managed to get away with so much. Throughout her marriage she was locked in a terrible bind with her husband. The more he put up with, the more she despised him. Tom Nevin was both unwilling to put his elderly mother through a second marriage break-down and afraid to leave his second wife. It was not enough for her to separate from her husband because she wouldn't settle for half the pub and property. She believed she was entitled to all of it.'

The passions of romantic disharmony have long spawned female killers. The woman in love is as combustible as the man in love – as prone to jealousy, obsession, rage and, in many cases, as prone to murderous violence. Most cases describe female cunning rather than spontaneous savagery. The annals of murderous spousal discord tend to reflect subterfuge: the enraged female will plan and plot and coerce an accomplice rather than simply let rip in uncontrolled frenzy. Some women, however, are swept away by the vagaries of the human heart. They just lose it. There is no plan and no premeditation.

Tracie Andrews was a woman who saw red and lost control in the throes of spurned love. She let rip. And not only did she let rip, she then displayed the cool head of a clever and shameless liar. England remains fascinated by Andrews and not only, presumably, because she was blonde – albeit a dyed one, and prone to blousiness. Andrews, in reality, is a little plain and dumb; certainly she is seriously disordered; she could have been an everyday Birmingham basket case, but her fame is forever swelling. When ITV aired her story on its *Real Crime* series in 2002, she attracted an audience of five million, double that for Jeremy Paxman's interview with Tony Blair which went out on the same night.

It all happened in the West Midlands in 1996. Ms Andrews managed to lure both the public's attention and sympathy when she appeared in a television appeal to find her boyfriend's murderer. Her story was that she and Lee Harvey, having been to a pub in Bromsgrove, were driving back when they were followed by a Ford Sierra which flashed its headlights at them for several miles. It then overtook them and forced them to stop at Coopers Hill near Alvechurch.

At this point two men leaped out of the Ford and one of them stabbed Lee to death, leaving Tracie, or Trace, as she is inevitably known to her decreasing coterie of friends, to weep hysterically by the side of the road, shrieking for help and covered in her boyfriend's blood.

It was a good story and it was believed by the police and by the first witness who came across her that night. The police launched an expensive and nationwide manhunt to find Lee Harvey's assailant. They found a spring and a pair of tweezers at the scene and these were judged to have fallen from a Swiss army knife which was thought to be the murder weapon but which was not found.

Then two witnesses came forward to tell the police that, yes, they had seen Lee Harvey's white Ford Escort in the area that night, but that the car was not being followed by a Ford Sierra, or, indeed, by any vehicle at all. At this point the spotlight fell upon Miss Andrews. Our Trace was no angel. She had a history of volatility and violent anger. And she was very jealous.

She had met Lee, a 25-year-old unemployed bus driver, through a dating advertisment and, by the accounts of friends and family, they had genuinely loved each other. At first it had been a delightful romance, of joy to both parties, who had much in common, in particular children of the same age by previous partners. They looked set to become one family when Lee asked Trace to marry him.

But the foundations were unstable, shaking on the jealousy and insecurity felt by both partners. There had been physical fighting. Lee was jealous of Trace's ex; Trace was jealous of everybody and, at one point, flew at him in a pub and bit his neck so hard that he looked as if he had been attacked by a shark.

Then Trace became pregnant. In August 1996 she had a miscarriage and was apparently devastated by it. It was only later, during one of their frequent rows, that Lee discovered she had, in fact, had the child aborted. And so the two continued their dance of death. Lee's friends knew that he was besotted by her, and that he stayed with her when he knew he should not. His family encouraged him to leave her but the two remained strangely trapped in the addiction of drama.

Lee's sister Michelle Harvey Gill never trusted Trace. She saw her as a troublemaker and a cause of misery and suspected that she was capable of worse. 'I knew she had done it,' she said in the *Real Crime* interview. But Lee's mum could not believe it. She wanted to believe the road-rage story; the opposite was too evil to address.

Lee's mum held Trace's hand when she appeared on the television appeal, teary and bleary and shocked, begging the public to find her fiancé's murderer. 'She deserved an Oscar for that,' Michelle commented.

As the police began to sift through the evidence that was gathering against Trace, they noted that her story about the cars did not tally with the reality of the road. Furthermore, forensic scientists, having examined Trace's clothes, noticed a bloodstain in the neck of one of her snakeskin boots which was the same shape as a Swiss army knife.

Events did not become any less bizarre as the net of suspicion closed in on Trace. She gave her own press conferences, declaring her innocence. She sent out a Photofit picture of the alleged killer which, to the investigators' amazement, bore an uncanny resemblance to one of their own team.

She took her lie all the way to Birmingham Crown Court, which begs the question as to whether she was so mad she believed herself, or whether she was imbued with the stupid optimisim so often present in the criminal personality. She told her story again for the benefit of press, public and jury. The Ford Sierra. Heavily built stranger. Knife. Blood on the road. And Lee down with forty injuries to the neck and back.

Ah, but, said the prosecution. Forensics show that Lee was stabbed while he was retreating. Furthermore the blood that had geysered onto Trace's face and clothes was consistent with the violent spray of arterial blood that would spurt forth in the event of a close-contact stabbing.

The conclusion was that Trace had murdered Lee after 'one dickens of a row' when he had finally tried to leave her. For good. She had lost it, attacked him, killed him, and then hidden the knife down her boot. On arrival at hospital to be examined for her own injuries, she had then got rid of the knife.

Mr Justice Buckley presided over the four-week trial. Trace stood by her story. The jury took five hours to deliver their guilty verdict. She went down for life.

In 1999, perhaps to encourage the affection of the parole board, Trace confessed. It was Lee's knife, she said. He had bought it in Spain and he kept it in the pocket in the side of the car. They had a row. She saw red. That was it.

SOURCES

James, Mike, *Women Who Kill Viciously*, True Crime Library, London, 1999

Jones, Aphrodite, *Della's Web*, Pocket Books, New York, 1998

Kane, Peter, *The Bobbitt Case – You Decide*, Pinnacle Books, New York, 1994

O'Connor, Niamh, *The Black Widow*, O'Brien Press Ltd, Ireland, 2000

Rosen, Fred, *Gang Mom*, St Martin's Paperbacks, New York, 1998

Storr, Anthony, *On Human Aggression*, Bantam Books, London, 1970

'Women Who Kill in Colorado' (www.dvmen.org)

www.CourtTV.com

3. LORD SAVE US

Death cults are usually founded and led by men, but, in a village in Uganda, followers made the mistake of believing the frantic rant of a homicidal 'nun'.

Descriptions of the village of Kunungu in Uganda differ. Some who have travelled to the isolated rural area describe an impoverished hell isolated by one dangerous road on which no one will travel unless necessity forces them to. There are no telephones, no televisions and the electricity supply is haphazard. Houses are huts and the nearest 'lodge' is 30 km away. Others point out that, by African standards, Kunungu enjoys relative wealth as there are banana and pineapple plantations as well as healthy livestock. The town is not a community of illiterate peasants – there are professional men and women, as likely to be teachers and business people as to be farmers or shopkeepers.

Nevertheless Kunungu would have remained anonymous if over three hundred people had not burned to death there on 17 March 2000. As the world press gathered in this unprepossessing East African village, and gruesome facts came to light, it became apparent that Kunungu had been home to a religious sect whose female leader, Credonia Mwerinde, was destined to join the premier league of murderers and maniacs that dominate the history of doomsday culture.

The congregation that had gathered in the tiny church were members of the Movement for the Restoration of the Ten Commandments of God, a collection of men, women and children who had succumbed to the apocalyptic dogma delivered by 'Sister' Credonia, a 48-year-old woman who, while often described as 'beautiful', with soft skin and a dulcet voice, was also clever, calculating, cruel, greedy and manipulative. The most powerful member of a triumvirate of 'apostles', she led the movement from simple beginnings based on Christian evangelism to a murder spree that was compared to Jonestown, where 914 people died in 1978.

Mwerinde's sect had gathered together in their tiny tin-roofed church on the morning that they believed the world was going to end. Witnesses heard the sound of singing and chanting and then a blast as a gasoline-fuelled explosion tore down the building. 'People said they heard some screaming but it was all over very quickly,' one policeman said after visiting the site.

Some saw the bodies of Credonia's male cohorts in the charred rubble of the church, but there was no sign of 'the Priestess of Death' herself. It was said that she had escaped through the hidden trails of the jungle over the border into the Republic of Congo, the country to the west of Uganda. The general conclusion was that she had taken her cousin Ursula, possibly her partner Joseph Kibwetere, and the money that she had spent some ten years slowly stealing from her followers.

The members of the Movement for the Restoration of the Ten Commandments had believed Sister Credonia when she told them that the Virgin Mary promised them an afterlife where Paradise was a land of luxury and where they would have no need of their material possessions. To surrender them was to buy redemption when the known world erupted into conflagration.

'The only thing that made Credonia really happy was making money,' her ex-husband Eric Mazima told one newspaper.

The immolation of Mwerinde's followers was followed by an investigation that turned up a series of mass graves. Four days after the burning of the congregation, six decomposing bodies were found underneath a latrine behind the church. They were all men. Five had been poisoned to death and one had been killed by a blow to the head. The flesh had been burned from their bodies with sulphuric acid. It was thought that this was Mwerinde's goon squad – the henchmen who had been responsible for helping her kill her cult.

On 24 March 155 bodies were found in a pit at Buhunga, a place near Rukungiri where the cult indoctrinated new members. Two days later 155 bodies were exhumed at the Rugazi property of Dominic Kataribabo, one of the leaders of the movement. A defrocked Roman Catholic priest who had earned a master's degree in Los Angeles, Kataribabo helped to compose the group's creed as the apocalyptic dogma that appeared in their handbook. He had taught courses in a primitive dormitory built behind his house.

Credonia's niece, Mary, was to later tell journalists that she had been locked up there for a week, only managing to escape from the room when somebody broke a window. She had fled to Kampala and hidden there, certain that her aunt would have her killed. Some of the dead had been buried in the priest's yard; some were found underneath a concrete floor in the house itself.

A further eighty bodies were buried in Rushojwa, on the farm of another cult leader, Joseph Nymurinda. Over half of these were children. Another 55 were disinterred at a site near Kampala.

Hundreds of corpses; mass graves; pits where the stench would linger for years. Women and children were stacked as neatly as sardines in a tin. Many of the victims had been poisoned; some had been garroted or stabbed or had their skulls crushed. Many were naked. They had been stripped of all their identifying features, and their bones melded together in an inseparable chaos of collarbone and hipbone.

Policemen who had initially addressed the case as a mass suicide realised that they were dealing with murder on a very large scale. Some people had been dead for a year and, without adequate forensic resources, it was impossible to separate one mangled remain from another, let alone officially identify the bodies and give them names, particularly in a far-flung rural area where people did not have either dental or medical records.

Dr Thaddeus Barungi, the pathologist who lead the forensic investigation, later delivered an official tally of 783. The question was, and still is, how these killings were perpetrated and by whom. No one was either charged or caught. An offical investigation set up to find out exactly what happened was quietly dropped due to lack of funds.

The truth remains obfuscated by confusing rumour and counter-rumour, easily cultivated in an isolated place where people believe in witchcraft and where the history of Amin's state terror has left a populace inured to the reality of individuals mysteriously disappearing overnight.

Nevertheless some facts rose to the surface as villagers, relations and former members of the cult were tracked down and interviewed by journalists.

Credonia Mwerinde's early life never came to light, but her immediate background was slowly revealed. She had started off as a simple businesswoman selling beer from a bar in the banana plantations around Kunungu, a tropical region 217 miles to the west of the Ugandan capital of Kampala.

'She was strong and clever but she was never a churchgoer,' Eric Mazima said. 'Men liked her because she was a prostitute, women liked her because she was friendly.'

In 1988 Mwerinde's business ran into financial difficulties. Credonia began to claim that she had seen a vision of the Virgin Mary in a cave in Nyakishenyi. This was a popular venue for mariological sightings. In the 80s a woman named Gauda Kamusha had enjoyed local fame after she claimed that one of the rock formations had transformed into the mother of Jesus before her very eyes.

'She took me to see the Virgin Mary,' Eric Mazima told a reporter. 'Between the caves there is a pillar of rock. She said she could see the Virgin standing with her back facing out to the world. She said that the Virgin was turning her back on people because of the terrible sins they had committed. I could not see it and I told her that. That was on 10 August 1988. On 24 August I told her I was finished with her. It was directly because of her so-called vision.

'I thought that because she was a prostitute she was wanting other men and this was a way to get rid of me. But others believed her. They said they could see the Virgin too. Men and women started following her and that's how it all started.'

Credonia claimed that visionary talents ran in the family. Her father, Paul Kashaku, had also seen apparitions. His deceased daughter Evangelista had appeared to him in 1960 and was followed 28 years later by Jesus, Mary and Joseph, a glittering council who informed him that he would donate his land to Christian believers.

Credonia met Joseph Kibwetere in 1989. A respected member of his community, and a relatively wealthy one, he had founded a Catholic school and had been a headmaster. A devout Catholic fascinated by the Virgin, Kibwetere also claimed to have had visions of the Holy

Mother. He had visited Rome in 1979 and returned from the pilgrimage determined to do good within his community. He had raised sixteen children with Therese, a retired domestic science teacher and his wife of forty years.

'We had a happy marriage,' she told one reporter.' My husband was very kind. The problems only began when we met Credonia Mwerinde.'

Credonia Mwerinde, her cousin Ursula Komuhangi and Angela Mugisha were already leaders of a Christian cult devoted to the Virgin Mary who, they said, had instructed Kibwetere to take them in. He agreed. They moved in to the Kibwetere home and lived there for two years.

Kibwetere formed an immediate bond with Mwerinde, to the dissatisfaction of his wife. Her anger escalated when Mwerinde was joined by an ever-increasing number of devotees ready to believe the orders channelled through her from the Virgin Mary and to do as she bade. Credonia was known as the 'Programmer' and her power was unchallenged.

'Credonia was humble at first,' Therese has said. 'She was silent and she stayed alone in a room. We would only see her when we went to mass and meetings. Her nephew used to pass us messages. She said she was receiving messages from the Virgin Mary and she spent the whole day writing them down.

'She began to mistreat me. She said I was bad, then she said she and her sister should sleep in the same room with my husband and I. He always supported them.'

As followers grew in number and began to gather into a community, Joseph Kibwetere was seen as the leader, although most agree that Mwerinde made the decisions that were to affect the sect.

Father Paul Ikazire, a priest who spent three years as one of the cult's leaders before defecting back to the Roman Catholic Church, recalled how Sister Credonia dominated. 'The meetings were chaired by Sister Credonia, who was the de facto head of the cult,' he said. 'Kibwetere was just a figurehead, intended to impose masculine authority over the followers and enhance the cult's public relations. I perceived her as a trickster, obsessed with the desire to grab other people's property. She told her followers to sell their property but she never sold hers.'

The Kibweteres' son Giles was appalled by the influence exerted by Credonia on his father who, until that point, had been a loving and community-minded man. 'They prepared nice food for higher ranks, but the rest could stay a day without eating. They would punish people. They would tell children not to go to school and they would say the world was ending. The leaders made them silent because they wanted to be obeyed without question.'

Joseph Kibwetere's family finally took action after an incident in which Therese's clothes were set alight and Credonia then attacked her. Kibwetere began to sell off his personal property in order to support his following. 'We called the elders,' Giles told a reporter.' They agreed to expel him. He told us he was going away and would never come back.'

In 1990 Joseph Kibwetere officially launched the Movement for the Restoration of the Ten Commandments of God and later registered it with the NGO – the Non-governmental Organisation Board – an authority set up to supposedly scrutinise the hundreds of sects that easily proliferate in a country where people are poor, scared, superstitious and desperate.

In 1993 he left his wife and family and moved to Kanungu where Mwerinde's family owned ten acres of land. Members of their sect observed a strict code of conduct that forbade private ownership of property. Converts surrendered all personal clothing and money to the cult. Followers took a vow of silence and communicated by sign language. Men and women were separated, except for Kibwetere and Mwerinde. Sexual intercourse between members, including married couples, was forbidden.

A rigid timetable was followed with Mondays, Wednesdays and Fridays as days of fasting, which started with prayers called 'The Way of the Cross' from 3 a.m. to 5 a.m. From 5 a.m. to 7 a.m., members would go back to sleep. Upon waking they would work till 1 p.m. followed by another prayer session until 2 p.m. Free time was from 3 p.m. to 4 p.m. and thereafter there would more work followed by supper at 8.00 p.m. and night prayers at 11 p.m.

On non-fasting days, the schedule was basically the same, but members had to clean the compound before breakfast. They also said a prayer, the Angelus, from 12 p.m. to 3 p.m. Lunch was a piece of sugarcane or a cup of porridge. Members were taught that light meals were a necessary part of sacrifice. But their leaders enjoyed lavish meals.

Members lived a life of prayer and meditation. Sunday was a 'Day of the Lord' when no work or activity was permitted. Ordinary dress was prohibited. People surrendered their clothes on entering the camp and were issued with uniforms – black for recruits, green for those 'who had seen the commandments' and green and white for 'those who were ready to die in the Ark'.

The movement aligned itself with the Roman Catholic Church and its members wore three rosaries – two worn around the neck, one facing the front and the other the back. The third was carried around in the hand. At times, a fourth would be hidden under the garments.

Baptism into the cult involved a ritual where the entire body and head were shaved and the nails were cut. Later the nails and hair would be burned and the ashes dissolved in tea or water, which the candidate would drink. Part of the ash was mixed with anointing oils and smeared over the candidate's body, after which he or she was considered clean.

In 1997 the cult started a primary school. A year later, education authorities closed it down due to poor sanitation, low academic standards and violation of children's rights. It was found that the young pupils were malnourished and sleeping on the floor.

Credonia was not a woman blessed with maternal kindliness, or any other kindliness for that matter. Juvenal Rugambwa, a son of Joseph Kibwetere, told a reporter that in the early 1990s she had forced sixty children to live in a 15-by-40-foot backyard shed in the village of Kabumba. The windows were nailed shut and the children were forced to sleep on the dirt floor, where many contracted scabies.

Mwerinde taught that children were as likely to be tempted by Satan as anyone else. She ensured that when families moved into the sect's compound, children were separated from their parents and then were forced to submit to the regime of relentless fasting. Having obeyed Mwerinde's nonsensical directives for months, Mary Kasambi finally left the cult in 1997 when she found her four starving children foraging for grasshoppers to eat.

There were no health facilities at the Kanungu camp, a policy that reflected the cult's fatalistic creed, the terms of which were 'channelled' by Mwerinde in the form of messages that she claimed to receive on a regular basis from the Virgin Mary and Jesus. These emphasised the restoration of the Ten Commandments as God's guide-lines to humanity and urged members to confess their sins in preparation for the end of the world on 31 December 1999.

The leaders wrote a sacred book – *A Timely Message from Heaven, The End of the Present Times* – which detailed their philosophy. The message was predictably conservative and evangelical. Satan and the Commandments were the dominant philosophical tenets. It said that 'hurricanes of fire' would rain down on those who had not repented. Evil lurked everywhere. Even cats and dogs were possessed by the Devil.

'Our Blessed Mother Mary says that we are like simpletons or fools because of having allowed Satan to dwell in us and make us do all sorts of shameful actions.'

Women were admonished for wearing 'see-through dresses without any underclothing', and these were seen as a 'symptom of an urge to violate the Sixth Commandment'.

AIDS (currently suffered by 8 per cent of the Ugandan population, and a possible explanation for the ease with which fatalist ideas disseminate, since the disease has lowered the average life expectancy to 43) was a punishment caused by beer-drinking and perverse sexual practices that 'increase the anger of the Almighty'. Members were told to read this book twenty times, after which they would receive anything they prayed for.

When the year 2000 arrived without any obvious sign of Armageddon, discontent arose among some members of the movement and, realising they had been duped, they began to demand the return of the property they had given to the church.

Obedience, previously aided by the rule of silence, was now forgotten as dissidents became more vociferous and more rebellious. Then the more aggressive rebels began to mysteriously disappear and, when questions were asked, it was explained that they had been transferred to other camps.

The 'apostles' told their followers that the Virgin Mary had extended the date for the end of the world to 17 March 2000. They started to sell everything in readiness. Cattle, goats, motorbikes, clothes, sugar – all went for a snip as the faithful sold them off in the belief that they did not need them any more because they were going to heaven.

On the evening of 16 March, Kaganga, who had once been a soldier, drove the cult's Toyota to the police station and deposited the title deeds there for 'safe keeping'. Using his designated sign language he attempted to indicate that the end was about to arrive but, perhaps understandably, little attention was paid to him.

Villagers knew little about the group of strangers in their midst. Many of them came from places and families that they did not know. They were isolated by their life-style and by their belief system and, even if they had wanted to communicate, there were few who would have had the patience to converse through sign language.

'I doubt they would have reacted even if I had slapped them,' said Henry Birungi, a taxi driver who had driven them from place to place and who, by saying this, perhaps reflects the observer's subconscious desire to slap those who have allowed themselves to sink into the blank-faced obedience of destructive indoctrination.

During the days preceding 17 March members of Mwerinde's group prepared for a celebration which involved the slaughtering of several cattle and the purchase of a large supply of Coca-Cola. Members based in other camps were exhorted to return to the base at Kunungu with the promise that the Virgin Mary herself was due to appear.

On the night of 15 March they held a party at which they consumed the beef and Coke. The following night was spent in prayer. On the morning of the 17th, shortly before dawn, Credonia Mwerinde flagged down a bus that was leaving to go to Kampala. Boarding the vehicle she walked up and down the aisle to make sure that no member of her cult was making their escape to the outside world.

Later that morning she led hundreds of men, women and children across the compound to the 'ark', a rude building which served as their church. It had been lined with jerrycans filled with gasoline. The doors and windows were nailed shut and, when the flames ignited, the fireball was so intense that skulls exploded.

But whither the Priestess of Death? Did she slip away as the screams echoed around the village and her devotees choked on toxic smoke?

The fire in the church was well planned, although confusion remained as to whether the windows had been boarded up from the inside or from the outside, and whether the door had been locked or nailed shut – key questions, of course, in any murder investigation.

Gervis Muteguya lost five relatives that day, including his mother, a sister and a brother. 'I tried to stop them but it was impossible,' he told a *Time* reporter who visited the charred church after the police had bulldozed the site. 'My sister came home to the village a few times. But they knew our home and they came and took her by force.'

Catarina Nansana escaped thanks to her daughter, who forced her to come home. She was 72. 'I had sores on my feet, my arms and my legs, but I didn't care. I believed what I was doing was right.'

A series of interviews conducted by *Newsweek*'s Lara Santoro leads to the fair supposition that Credonia

Mwerinde was a homicidal maniac as cold and as dangerous as the Reverend Jones himself. After speaking to dozens of survivors, cult members and officials, Santoro concluded that Mwerinde was a mass murderer who had always been obsessed by fire and that the symptoms of her psychoses were already evident when she was a young woman.

Twenty years before the fire in Kunungu she had torched the possessions of a man who had jilted her and she subsequently received treatment for mental disturbance. Later, when she owned a bar, locals became convinced that the blood she was seen washing from the floor was that of a passing motorist that she had murdered.

Others told Santoro that all three of Mwerinde's elder brothers died mysteriously and she was now the sole owner of the family land. It was suspected that she had poisoned them.

'She is crazy, and she is a murderer,' Dr Thaddeus Barungi, the chief pathologist, told Santoro.

Credonia Mwerinde was not the first prophetess in Uganda's recent history to lead a flock to their death and she may not be the last. The turbulence of East Africa's social history has created a climate where any woman with a mouth and a Bible can exert her will. Five months before Credonia's activities destroyed the life of Kunungu, nineteen-year-old Nabassa Gwajwa had been arrested by police after they raided her camp in Ntusi, west Uganda.

Gwajwa, who preached repentance, was said to eat only honey, and urged people to sell their property. She was arrested after local police decided that she was a 'security threat'. Her one hundred followers who were camping with her were forcibly transported back to their home towns.

Meanwhile Mary Snaida-Akatsa, known as Mommy, who preaches in the slums of Nairobi, is noted for the wealth drawn from tithes donated by the poor. When this unpleasant 'prophetess' accuses a member of her church of being a witch, a vision she says she has received from God, her disciples stomp their feet, throw rocks and chase the unlucky follower out of the church with yells of '*Ashindwe! Ashindwe!*' – Swahili for 'Be defeated!'

Snaida Akatsa once brought a 'special visitor' to her Sunday service. 'This is Jesus,' the preacher told her believers, patting the shoulder of a Sikh gentleman. 'You must repent.'

Mary Snaida-Akatsa started preaching when she was eight years old and developed her huge following by telling a story about how her mother died while giving birth to Mary, and how her father then threw her into the bushes, where she died for seven days before coming back to life, revived by God.

Like so many of those who hear the calling of the Lord, she has become rich from her church. She owns several cars. After the services she has been seen to sell fruits and vegetables grown on her many farms. She claims they are blessed.

Thousands of people have joined such cults across Africa. According to one source more than 5,000 indigenous churches have arisen over the last hundred years. Only four months after the tragedy at Kunungu local newspapers reported a re-emergence of an aligned cult in Nairobi. A group entitled Choma (meaning 'burn') was expounding Credonia Mwerinde's ideas and attracting hundreds of followers. Members were being told to sell their possessions in order to gain salvation. The identity of their leader, only known as 'The Patron', was a closely guarded secret.

Charles Onyango-Obbo, editor of *The Monitor*, Uganda's leading independent newspaper, has followed these phenomena closely and has said, 'These groups thrive because of poverty. People have no support, they live in a no-man's zone and they're susceptible to anyone who is able to tap into their insecurity.'

The annals of religious insanity are populated by megalomaniacs whose projects have done little to further any spritual cause but, to date, these unstable fantasists have usually been male. The tiny, mad domain of the rogue messiah tends to be built on a patriarchal structure. He, the ludicrous evangelist, leads a 'family' as Father, which explains the success of so many movements. Lone souls are attracted to the promise of the succour of friendship and loyalty often unavailable to them in the larger world. It is no coincidence that the Manson mob were actually called 'The Family'.

Jim Jones, like most ambitious charismatics, taught that women were subordinate and ensured that they took secondary positions in the social hierachy of his People's Temple. This administrative policy suited the needs of his rapacious sexuality. Most rogue messiahs fall in with similar patterns because most are both priapic and deviant. Both L. Ron Hubbard and David Koresh compulsively slept with pre-pubescent girls. The latter told his followers that God was forcing him to and he had to obey even though he was shocked by the nature of the Lord's request. Jeffrey Don Lundgren, the Mormon 'prophet' and murderer, took various 'wives' after God sent him visions of their vaginas. Women, then, tend to take a secondary position in the realm of criminal evangelism and have a pattern of easy supplication. Kathy Jones, the chosen partner of Lundgren, believed that he was God.

Historically, if women have been conflicted by the febrile fervour of divine calling, they have tended to resort to the self-flagellation and hysteria that are reflected in the lives of the saints and in the bizarre behaviour manifest in medieval convents. Always the handmaiden, the female apostate is sometimes a genuine visionary, often an independent thinker, but she is rarely the architect of secular Armageddon.

But in the poorest states of the sub-Saharan continent the dangerous *religieuse* has become a relatively common figure. She bucks a cultural climate where polygamous marriage is a part of life and where modern feminist thought has yet to hold sway. Women are taught to accede to the wishes of their fathers, brothers and husbands, and to demonstrate their subordination to men in most areas of public life. Even in the 1980s, women in some rural areas were expected to kneel when speaking to a man.

The nun on the make is aided by the predominance of Roman Catholicism, which allows for unquestioning reverence of a religious matriarchy, and where many lost and frightened souls are looking for 'Mother'.

In 1986 Alice Lakwena, a self-styled healer and prophet, was given command of an anti-government rebel battalion called the Holy Spirit Mobile Force. She claimed to be possessed by the *lakwena* from whom she took her name; *lakwena* means messenger and, according to Alice, the *lakwena* possessing her was an Italian who had died near the source of the Nile during the First World War. With his aid, Alice began to cure people of various diseases. As a healer, she attracted a great deal of support among the Acholi, the people of northern Uganda, who were engaged in a guerrilla struggle against the government forces of President Musveni.

In addition to leading soldiers into battle, Lakwena promised to cleanse the Acholi of evil spirits and witchcraft. This was considered to be most helpful and she quickly attracted a popular following.

Her soldiers had to undergo initiation rites in which they burned their old clothes and any magic charms, and swore by the Bible that they would no longer practise any form of sorcery. They would then be 'anointed with butter oil and made holy'. Alice told the men that this oil was so holy that it would protect them against bullets, which would bounce harmlessly off their chests.

In January 1987 the Holy Spirit Movement's army marched to Jinja, sixty miles from Kampala, whereupon they were easily massacred by the superior artillery of Musveni's army.

After hundreds of her soldiers died Lakwena fled to Kenya, where she is said to remain today. Her dedicated followers turned to the leadership of her cousin Joseph Kony, an eccentric transvestite who developed the Lord's Resistance Army, a group of uncontrolled thugs who proceeded to became notorious for atrocities committed both on local civilians but, more violently, on children, whom they abducted and recruited into their ranks.

In 1997 Human Rights Watch wrote a report entitled *The Scars of Death*, in which it accused the Lord's Resistance Army of turning the north of Uganda into 'permanent battle zones, filled with burned schools, ransacked homes, abandoned fields and a huge population of internally displaced people'. This, in other words, was the sum total of Alice Lakwena's legacy.

Two years after the grim disinterments at Kunungu, all that remained were bereaved relatives, unanswered questions and some interesting conspiracy theories. The authorities had simply bulldozed the church where the fire had been, but the stench of dead bodies remained, lingering over the site and identifying its history despite the fact that nature had taken its course – weeds had taken over the compound and cows belonging to local residents grazed in the overgrown paddocks.

Occasionally a local will attempt to sneak past the guard and steal a morbid memento; more often a child will steal the sugar cane. The banana plantation has been left to its own devices. There are graffiti on the walls. One message says, 'Kibwetere is in Israel.'

The place is supposed to be haunted. 'As dusk approaches we see figures of people moving up and down, as they used to before they were killed in the fire,' said one villager whose aunt and four cousins perished in the inferno. Strange voices have scared those living near the compound at Nyabugoto. It is said that they are the voices of the people who allowed Credonia Mwerinde to lead them to their deaths.

SOURCES
Newsweek, 6 August 2000
The Scars of Death, Human Rights Watch, 1997
Apologetics Index – news archives (www.gospel.com)
CESNUR – news archives (www.cesnur.com)
www.rickross.com
Dr Thaddeus Barungi

4. HELL'S GRANNIES

Age does not always bring wisdom; sometimes it brings homicidal tendencies

The evil crone is an archetype of the collective unconscious. In folklore the young are always the innocent while the old woman is inevitably a bad old witch fuelled by jealousy and driven to commit heinous crimes against those who are more pure and more beautiful than herself. In reality the geriatric sociopath is a rarity; it is the young who are delinquent and the old who are the victims of the young. They are the ones who are booted to the ground on wet urban streets, who are forced to give up their pensions at penknife point, who are endlessly scared out of their wits by the forces of teenagers who exert their wills on street life.

The mature lady does not often appear as a mask of female evil and there are various reasons for this invisibility. Most crimes are perpetrated by young(ish) women who are more than likely to face their mature years in jail, well out of the public eye. Further, the kind of crimes that women commit tend to be around children and around domestic scenarios; if they are going to commit them they commit them before they enter their twilight years. The same is true of sex-related crimes, which tend to be committed by pre-menopausal women who are relatively interested in sex and are likely to have lovers whom they kill or with whom they collude. Other crimes which require youthful energy to implement gratification – robbery, for instance, or arson or gang violence – are, again, more likely to be committed by the young woman who is angry, energetic and violent.

But there are exceptions. Occasionally a white-haired old dear will appear on the television screen or in the newspapers and she is not, for once, the victim of some grisly mugging or repellent rape – she is the mistress of felonies which are hard to believe in a person who looks as if she should be down the WI with her home-made boysenberry jam.

Dorothea Puente has competitors, but she remains one of the most hellish old women of all time. Cunning, greedy, murderous, duplicitous, amoral, Mrs Puente got away with it for years thanks to her successful enactment of a nice old lady who was just out to care for people who could not care for themselves. The granny that Mrs Puente put out to the world was the granny in which the world believed. But the true Dorothea was dangerous and deranged. And, at the age of 59, she was a serial killer.

In the mid-80s Puente bought a Victorian house in Sacramento, California, and took in tenants that were on welfare and in need of help. Once they were placed under her supervision, either by the church or by the social services, she would organise their lives – clean them up, feed them well and ensure that their benefit cheques were paid every month. Mrs Puente was clever when it came to bureaucracy; she knew how to work it.

Her tenants, living in clean bedsits, seemed to thrive. One, Bert Montoya, was seen to be well fed, wearing new shoes and clear of his psoriasis for the first time in years thanks to the kindly administrations of his landlady. No one thought anything of it when she started to collect his monthly $637 state benefit on the grounds that he was mentally unable to do so himself.

'She was,' his caseworker Elizabeth Valentine told writer Patricia Pearson, 'like the quintessential grand-mother'.

In the summer of 1988 Bert Montoya mysteriously disappeared for no reason and without a word. Montoya was an unwell 55-year-old man taking antipsychotics; it is unlikely that he would have made many decisions for himself. When his caseworkers asked Mrs Puente where he was they were told that he had gone to Mexico to stay with Puente's family. Their investigations led nowhere; they asked again. Mrs Puente told them that Montoya had suddenly decided to live with a long-lost cousin in Salt Lake City, which was even more unlikely than the first explanation.

Granny Puente became less pleasant in her demeanour and obviously resented the questioning. The mask of the kindly old lady began to slip as Montoya's allies began to become suspicious. Nobody suspected the worst because they could not. Often evil has to come to call before it can be imagined. And then it has to break the door down.

A conversation with another tenant, John Sharp, revealed some disturbing facts. He told them that Dorothea Puente was a secret drinker and that tenants often disappeared for no reason. He had heard bumping sounds in the middle of the night, and God knows what else. Furthermore there had been a smell around the house, a smell that he had recognised from his time working in a mortuary. It was the smell of dead bodies.

Even at this point the police were loath to investigate. Mrs Puente was a respected old woman. An old woman! She made pies for people. But, fired by some strange policeman's hunch, one detective working in the Sacramento homicide department started to do some research and discovered that there was a lot more to Mrs Puente than a tight perm and a pair of reading glasses.

For a start, she was on parole and had had convictions for fraud, theft and attempted murder. Her record showed that as a home-care nurse she had spent some years drugging her patients and then robbing them. This was a dangerous old woman.

Detective Cabrera led his men to the house on F Street and, after two days, they had dug up seven bodies from the garden, some of whom had been in Puente's care and who were still registered as alive by government agencies, their benefits going to Mrs Puente every month. One victim had had her legs removed. All showed forensic evidence of having been drugged with Dalmane, which, as Mrs Puente's bathroom cabinet revealed, was her drug of choice.

Granny Puente legged it. She simply walked out of the house and went on the lam. Chased as a wanted fugitive by the police and the FBI, she made off to downtown Los Angeles, the mecca for the city's down and outs, where vagrants, the handicapped, gang members and those who have simply slipped through the net crowd together to form one impoverished and unrecognised community subsisting on welfare cheques in welfare motels.

It was easy for the fugitive to slip into obscurity. She took a room at a hotel and stayed in it, having set a false trail by buying an air ticket to LA and not taking the flight. Then she made a mistake. She went to a bar, and not only did she go to a bar, but she succeeded in picking up a man, an achievement in itself, all things considered. Charles Willgues recognised her from a picture on the television. He told CBS news and a CBS camera crew arrived at Puente's room, accompanied by various members of the local constabulary. Asked for identification she handed over her driving licence and was arrested immediately.

The defence case rested on an argument that the bodies in the garden were of people who had died of natural causes. It emphasised the good that the kind old Mrs Puente had done and it went into her background.

She had been born in San Bernadino, California in 1929. Her parents were both alcoholics and the little girl had to scrounge around for herself. By the time she was six they were both dead. By 1946 she was married, but then her husband died and, desperate for money, she began to forge cheques. She was good at this, but not good enough. She was caught, sent to jail and paroled.

In 1952 she married again, a violent man who failed to support her. She took a job caring for the elderly in a residential home. In 1966 she divorced her second husband and married a third, Robert Puente, in Mexico City. He was nineteen years younger and unfaithful. Again, in order to support herself, Mrs Puente managed a boarding house for the homeless and destitute.

In 1976 Mrs Puente, having separated from yet another physically abusive partner, began to hang around in bars where men on benefit were easy pickings. She would steal their cheques, forge signatures and take the money for herself. Until she was caught. Again. And charged with 34 counts of fraud.

Unable to stop her compulsion to steal, Puente hit on Malcolm McKenzie, a 74-year-old pensioner who told police that he had invited her back to his apartment and she had incapacitated him with drugs. Conscious but unable to move he had watched as she stole his coin collection and removed a diamond ring from his finger. Mrs Puente received a five-year prison sentence.

During her time in the state penitentiary she made friends with Everson Gillmouth, 77, yet another kind old man who fell for her. He picked her up after she had served her term, gave her some money, and she began to implement her plans to run another boarding house. Soon she had rented a large establishment on F Street, the 16-bedroom Victorian house that was to become as famous in Sacramento as 10 Rillington Place had once been in London. She then murdered Everson Gillmouth and successfully persuaded a handyman to build him a coffin, saying that it was a box needed for storage.

The carpenter, Ismael Florez, had no idea he was building a coffin, even when his employer then rode with him in a car and told him to dump it by a river bank, with the explanation that it was full of rubbish.

On New Year's Day 1986 two fishermen found the casket half-submerged by the water. Local police opened it to find the remains of Mr Gillmouth. He was dressed in his underwear, wrapped in a white bed sheet and bound with black electrician's tape. The foul-smelling body showed no signs of wounding and was decomposed beyond the point of recognition. The only distinguishing feature was a wristwatch. Unable to identify the dead man, the crime went unsolved and the body's identity was unknown for three years.

Dorothea, meanwhile, collected Gillmouth's pension and wrote letters to his family explaining that he had not been in touch because he had been ill.

The boarding house was full of tenants whose perceptions were muddled by alcohol and drug problems. This enabled the dreadful landlady to do pretty much as she pleased. She would collect their post, spend their money, and then dole out small sums which they took to the nearest bar.

In the following months more mysterious disappearances were reported. Betty Palmer, a 77-year-old resident of Puente's boarding house, never returned from a doctor's appointment. Puente forged an ID card and collected Betty's state benefit. Leona Carpenter, 78, discharged from hospital and placed in Puente's care, also went missing. James Gallop, 62, disappeared soon after receiving hospital treatment to remove a brain tumour. Vera Martin, 62, moved into Mrs Puente's domain and was never seen again.

Dorothea's case opened in July 1993. She was to be tried for nine counts of murder. The jury heard the testimony of 153 witnesses and many of them were on the old lady's side. Confused, no doubt, by the ideological complexities, they took weeks to make their deliberations. On 2 August they announced that they were deadlocked. The judge told them to try again. Finally, on 26 August, Dorothea Puente was found guilty and sentenced to spend the rest of her life in prison.

Grannies who go on the run tend to be news. As Dorothea Puente had managed to give the police the slip, thanks to her convincing performance as a harmless old woman, so too did Margo Freshwater, who managed to live as an undiscovered fugitive from justice for 32 years. She was finally picked up, at the age of 53, in Columbus, Ohio, where she had been living under another identity and where she was known as a kind mother of three and an enthusiastic competitor in ballroom dancing competitions.

Margo Freshwater had been on the run, in effect, since the age of eighteen, but a low-profile lifestyle had aided her illusion. As a teenager living in Tennessee she was supposed to have murdered three men while on a 'spree' with her lover. They were arrested in Mississippi and her boyfriend spent several years in a mental hospital. Freshwater was sent to prison in Nashville for 99 years for one of the murders – a man working in an off-licence. Then she escaped.

In 1970, when she was 23 and pregnant, she and another prisoner scaled a fence, outran guards to a main road, and hitched a ride in a lorry. Ending up in

Baltimore, Freshwater slowly made her way towards Ohio and towards a new identity – that of Tonya McCartor, suburban mother and successful insurance saleswoman.

After she gave birth to a daughter, she started to live with a boyfriend and helped him to raise his child. Having received another social security number, she took various jobs, registered to vote, and received a licence to sell insurance.

In the late 80s she met another man and had another child. After his death, she sold insurance in Columbus, her hometown, where she never came across anyone who knew her and where she was never recognised.

In May 2002 investigators caught up with Ms Freshwater as she was spending the day with her son and grandchild shopping and going to Jolly Pirate Donuts. They finally approached her in the car park of a health club. Later they told reporters that Ms Freshwater had remained calm. She simply hugged her family and climbed into the police car.

Margo Freshwater was caught after some fastidious police work by the men at the Tennessee Bureau of Investigation. Suspecting that she was lurking under the assumed Christian name Tonya, they searched databases for Tonyas who would be the right age and came up with Mrs McCartor. The appearance of her driving licence confirmed their suspicions and Freshwater was arrested.

That same month America's public was embracing another lawless granny. Mrs Ann Trexler, a 54-year-old matriarch from Florida, organised a contract killing while she was having her hair done. Her hairdresser happened to have a boyfriend. He was working as the shampoo boy (answering the telephone, cleaning the tanning bed and so on), but he had underground connections. He could arrange for a hit. Mrs Trexler was a regular customer after all. A friend. The price was $50,000 but Granny Trexler beat them down to $10,000. Do not, my friends, try this in your own salon. It could have very serious consequences.

In May 2002 Mrs Trexler, grey hair by now coiffed into a neat short cut, stood trial for the murder of her former son-in-law Ron Stovall and was convicted of being a principal to first-degree murder. The jury believed the prosecution charge that she had hired Antonio Alberto Perez to execute Stovall in his home.

Ron Stovall was the father of Mrs Trexler's granddaughter Kierstyn. He had primary custody of the little girl following his divorce from Kierstyn's mother Tina who was Ann Trexler's daughter. Problems arose when Ron married again. His second wife Angeleka had a son of her own. They lived happily in Panama City, until Granny Trexler arrived. Keen to see more of her granddaughter, Trexler had moved from Virginia to be with her. She took up many of the motherly duties, often picking Kierstyn up from school and so on.

The Stovalls were unimpressed by Tina's achievements as a mother and, in 1998, filed a legal paper saying that she was 'neglectful'. Furthermore they wanted to move to Montana and take Kierstyn with them.

Ron Stovall worked for the post office. On the morning of 6 October 1998 he woke up at 3 a.m. and searched for his packed lunch. As he walked out of his front door a shot rang through the air. A bullet grazed his knee and he fell to the ground. At that point a man leaped out of the bush pointing a .357 Magnum.

The husband and wife backed into their house. Angeleka lay across the front door, using her body as a barricade. The hit man fired through the door, three shots. Then the killer put his hand through the door and fired another shot, making it six rounds.

Stovall, now seriously wounded and bleeding, dragged himself across the kitchen floor and then kneeled and looked up at Perez who fired two bullets straight into him, hitting him in the chest and thigh. Then he said, 'This is for her', and fired the final bullet into the back of Ron Stovall's head.

As investigation into Stovall's murder began, Antonio Perez robbed a 74-year-old man at a local motel. He stole money and took keys to a car that he parked, with evidence of enormous stupidity, right outside his house. It was as if he wanted to be arrested, and arrested he was. Police found a Smith and Wesson .357 whose ballistic evidence showed that it had been used in the Stovall murder.

At first Perez intimated that he was acting on his own, pursuing a personal vendetta against Ron Stovall because Stovall had been involved with his girlfriend, the aforementioned hairdresser, whose name was Kim Miller. It was not until he went on trial that he began to implicate Ann Trexler. Then Kim Miller confessed to having set up the contract but denied that there was any reason for a personal vendetta. The murder was motivated by money, she said, $10,000 to be exact, and when Ann Trexler had paid it she had apparently hugged Miller and said, 'I've never had a friend like you.'

Mrs Trexler's defence successfully cast doubt over Kim Miller, condemning her as a pathological liar and a coke addict who had long been in and out of trouble with the authorities. They further asserted that the large sums of money drawn from Trexler's account had been used to hire an attorney to negotiate custody for Kierstyn. A pastor took the stand and described Granny Trexler as a kind person who read the Bible a lot, which was not necessarily an aid, as many criminologists will tell you that reading the Bible compulsively is often a sign of advanced psychosis.

The jury believed the prosecution's portrayal of Trexler as a cold woman who had hired a contract hit on her son-in-law in order to gain access to her granddaughter. They took two hours to convict her of being a principal to first-degree murder and she was sentenced to spend the rest of her life in prison.

Talking to the press afterwards Ron Stovall's father Freddie said that seven-year-old Kierstyn was struggling to come to terms with the circumstances of her father's death. The judge, Dim T Sirmons, had echoed this sentiment in his conclusion to the trial. Addressing Ann Trexler he said, 'That child will bear the full consequences of your actions and others' actions for the rest of her life. That is truly a tragedy.'

In England, in 2002, the *Observer* newspaper described Evelyn Fleckney and Diane Morris as 'two glamorous grandmothers living dangerous double lives'. Fleckney was 'petite, blonde and highly flirtatious,' while Morris was 'tall, busty and prone to violent outbursts'.

The times they surely are a'changing.

These two, both in their late forties, had spent some years enjoying an enormous income from the successful sale of heroin, cocaine and Ecstasy. They were 'drug baronesses' apparently 'feared and respected throughout the underworld', and 'trusted by some of London's most notorious criminal families'.

London's notorious criminal families, so accurately portrayed by Britain's slew of 90s gangster movies, are noted for the thickness of their necks rather than the measure of their IQ. They are also noted for being an idiotic underground culture of macho-thugs where women rarely appear and, when they do, it is as stereotyped totty. This facilitates the purposes of the female gangster, as both culture and reality serve to camouflage her. British culture refuses to iconise her, so she can dip and dart and escape the attentions of authorities who are slow to believe in the power of the presence of the female species in these manly milieus.

It was easy, in these circumstances, for two mature ladies equipped with brains to engage in duplicity and to go a long way towards achieving their end. Both Fleckney and Morris, while shifting hundreds and thousands of pounds' worth of various Grade A substances, were also acting as police informants.

Fleckney, nicknamed the 'chairman of the board', helmed a drugs empire from a nice little house in Tunbridge Wells, Kent. She was once heard to brag, 'There are not many drug dealers like me. Go and find another bird that can get what I can get. I could have a million pills if I wanted.'

Morris, meanwhile, liaised with her husband Ray. Acting with violent extortionists around Tooting, Diane would have done well working for the Krays – intimidation was her thing and, on one occasion, she was said to have threatened a teenager with a baseball bat and a canister of CS gas. On another joyful day she dragged an off-duty police officer out of his car and beat him until he passed out. Ray went to prison in 1991 and his unpleasant wife, seeing a career opportunity, promoted herself and took over his racket.

In 1998 Fleckney and Morris met each other in Holloway prison. It did not take the two cunning women long to work out the advantages of their situation. Their target was Jeff May, a police officer to whom Morris had reported information.

Fleckney told the Criminal Investigation Bureau that she had bought heroin from Jeff May. Morris later repeated this claim, saying she also had bought narcotics from May. The two women were separated, but May was arrested and suspended.

Detectives working on the case began to see the patterns of a plot. The details did not match up and their suspicions were further confirmed when letters between Morris and Fleckney appeared to corroborate their collusion. May was reinstated but he had become clinically depressed and took early retirement on the grounds of ill health.

This sequence of events had serious implications in another case at which Fleckney had testified in 2000. Five police officers, known as the 'Groovy Gang', had been convicted of offences involving the sale of confiscated drugs back on to the street. The case had concluded a two-year-long inquiry and was described as 'one of the biggest anti-corruption investigations in recent years'.

The ringleader of this scheme was seen to have been Robert Clark, who was jailed for twelve years. It was Clark, working from the regional crime squad headquarters in east Dulwich, who had begun by supervising information fed to him by Evelyn Fleckney. He had then proceeded to have an affair with her, during which she twice became pregnant. The couple enjoyed themselves – staying in luxury hotels, holidaying in the Canary Islands and so on.

Fleckney told Clark about a drug drop outside a village in Sussex. She knew that a light plane was going to deliver packages of cannabis over a field. Clark's officers arrived to make the arrest, stole a couple of blocks and gave them to Fleckney who sold them and redistributed the profits among the participating policemen.

The activities of the crime squad were exposed when a drug dealer was arrested and, having been fleeced, complained about Clark and his gang to his arresting officers. They then reported the allegation to the Criminal Investigation Bureau, whose allegations achieved the necessary evidence when an east Dulwich officer had a Serpico moment and blew the whistle.

Neil Putnam's evidence sustained many of the accusations made against the 'Groovy Gang' and he, having received money for recycled drugs, was sent to prison for three years.

Evelyn Fleckney, meanwhile, having successfully got her sentence reduced from fifteen to eight years, looked forward to an early release.

SOURCES

Pearson, Patricia, *When She Was Bad*, Virago, London, 1998
the *Guardian* 5 February 2000
the *Observer* 19 May 2002
'Dorothea Puente: Killing for Profit' by Patrick Bellamy (www.crimelibrary.com)
www.CourtTV.com

5. MAMA, WE'RE ALL CRAZY NOW

When the Godfathers go to prison, the Godmothers come out to play. The Mafia is now run by women.

Erminia Giuliano, the definitive mafia mama, was arrested in December 2000 after ten months on the run from the Italian police. Keen to uphold her image as a folklore femme fatale, she endeared herself to her fans by refusing to leave her hideout until her beautician had arrived and lacquered her blonde hair into a suitable style. Usually opting for leopard skin and stilettos, Erminia's style has long been regarded with admiration. The most famous image of her is as a bejewelled guest at her sister Gemma's wedding where she was photographed standing next to the superstar footballer Diego Maradona.

Erminia Giuliano has been called 'the Queen of Naples'. She has also been described as 'big-breasted' and 'blue-eyed'. Her flat in Naples had been used, it was said, to run the gangland activities of her family, the Giulianos, a mafia clan who have long ruled over the Forcella neighbourhood, remunerating themselves with a business of protection and extortion that was founded by Erminia's brother Luigi.

Erminia Giuliano was one of the 'Giuliano Women' and the Giuliano women were famous. 'Everybody knows they are the real strength of that family,' Naples prosecutor Antonio Laudati has said.

Erminia's sister-in-law, 'Donna' Carmela Marzano, the wife of the *famoso* Luigi, had already received much public attention, not to mention admiration. Luigi managed to shrug off charges of murder and drug trafficking, but finally went down for mafia association, at which point his wife took over the territory and commandeered the army of youths willing to do her dirty work.

Erminia Giuliano was the most colourful of a long line of gangland matriarchs to be arrested in Italy in the last decade. The emergence of these shameless god-mothers has forced local authorities, and the world, to reassess not only the traditional macho mores of the Cosa Nostra, but to readdress beliefs about the ability of women to run organised crime. The new wave of mafia mamas have proved to be every bit as dangerous as their male counterparts and, in most cases, a great deal cleverer, which, in most cases, was not difficult.

Patrizia Ferriero, for instance, married to hit man Raffaele Stolder, organised for her husband to stay out of prison and in hospital by ensuring that doctors were supplied with (stolen) contaminated blood for tests. Later, when he had robbed a jewellery store, she prepared his defence. Dressed in mourning she went to the jeweller, produced a photograph of Stolder, and commissioned a medallion on which his image would be engraved. Then, during the case, when the jeweller identified Stolder as the man who had robbed him, Patrizia Ferriero produced the medallion with Mediter-ranean flourish and drew the jury's attention to the fact that the jeweller had not recognised her husband during the long process of engraving his face onto a medallion.

She is, said her lawyer, 'a very clever woman. Cleverer than he is, actually.'

Stolder eventually went into hiding and his wife took over his business and directed the activities of his men, who obeyed her orders. She imported cocaine from South America, ensuring that connections with other traffickers were maintained, and took charge of the network of distribution. Ferriero set up an executive meeting with other families, to ensure old and necessary alliances were stabilised and she divided the merchandise with various representatives, which called for a talent for diplomacy – in this environment any lapse in the farcical comedy of manners known as mafia protocol is to slip haphazardly into a gang war.

Along the way, Ferriero bought friends in the judiciary and in the police force and made the bribes needed to block investigations into her husband's activities. She handled these arrangements with the finesse of a cool-headed female boss who knew exactly what she was doing and, if she had been set down in another place, would doubtless have been running rings round suits in an office tower-block in New York.

In 1990 she built an underground bunker underneath her flat in Naples. This had reinforced steel doors and was entered via a garage with a door opened by a remote control. Secret passageways led into the flat and down into the sewers. Cars would arrive from the Netherlands, bags of cocaine hidden in the door panels, and then be taken apart in the garage. The drugs would be weighed, wrapped in cellophane and stashed in a safe under the floor of the flat.

Ferriero was eventually betrayed by one of her men – an ex-policeman who had become addicted to cocaine – and she was arrested. The prosecution described her as 'the brains of the organisation'.

Some people have argued that statistics showing the global rise of crime committed by women represents the dark face of feminism, the liberation of an urban animus traditionally suppressed by the expectation of cultural mores; if this is true then nowhere is it better represented than by the recent emergence of the *mafiosetta* into a territory once inhabited solely by men.

Rosetta Cutolo, who ran her brother Raffaele's 'business' while he was in prison, was actually described as 'the first feminist criminal' by one Italian anti-Mafia prosecutor. Raffaele, serving a life sentence for murder in the 60s, set up the Nuova Camorra Organizzata from the comfort of his cell. A criminal body, the NCO was the kind of structured committee that gave 'organised' crime its name. Its purpose was to unify the strength of the mafia and, by so doing, promote it to a position where it would entirely control Naples.

Rosetta was 'director' of this board and the power behind her brother for fifteen years. Powerful though Raffaele was, and adored with the inexplicable reverence that arises among those who are threatened by bullies, he was said to be in awe of his older sister.

The NCO subsisted on protection and extortion – the families of the men in prison would be supported by the NCO under the proviso that the ex-con then served the NCO when he left prison. The other local mafia families (known collectively as the Camorra) united against the NCO in order to protect their own territories. They launched the syndicate known as Nuova Famiglia and the result was a war for the control of Naples.

Raffaele Cutolo, always unstable thanks to the paranoia that so often arrives with megalomania, began to have his closer allies murdered. His sister went into hiding for ten years, a time during which she was said to see much of her priest, and to spend her hours in the quiet pursuits of gardening and embroidery, pursuits which do no harm when a Godmother needs to plead her case for the defence.

She gave herself up in 1993 and was sentenced to five years for mafia association. She was charged with, but cleared of, three murders, including that of her brother's right-hand man Vincenzo Casillo, who had been suspected of embezzling money from the organisation and died as the result of a car bomb. His girlfriend followed soon after this, buried alive in a cement pillar.

The press were disappointed to note that the 55-year-old Rosetta looked more like a dowdy housewife than the most evil woman in the western world, but Cutolo's understated image was intentional; a dull front and a place in the background had always worked in her favour. Female cunning knows that infamy is no friend to freedom.

In an environment that bred this savage new species, it comes as no surprise to learn that one of Rosetta Cutolo's most dangerous enemies was also a woman – Anna Mazza, matriarch of the Moccia clan, a Camorra family dedicated to bringing down the Cutolos' NCO.

Anna Mazza's husband, Gennaro Moccia, had set himself up as the successful ruler of Afragola, a small town near Naples. Moccia was murdered in 1976, and his family, lead by Anna, set about ensuring that their status as criminal overlords remained intact. One Neopolitan magistrate described her as not only a *capo* in her own right, but 'one of the most dangerous, certainly one of the most bloody'.

The Moccia family wiped out the other mafioso clans in their territory by sheer force of violence. They were simply able and willing to murder more people. The Moccia brothers were savage sociopaths but they did not make a move without asking Mama first. She was known as the Black Widow of the Camorra.

Neopolitan magistrate Giacamo Travaglino told Clare Longrigg, author of the ground-breaking book *Mafia Women*, 'They are serious killers but none of them would have moved a muscle without the word from la Signora Mazza.'

Longrigg met Anna Mazza in the late 90s and describes her as an angry woman with dyed red hair, a Gucci handbag, black shades with diamante clasps, black jacket with shoulder pads, black trousers, shiny pumps, mulberry lipstick and plump fingers knuckle-dustered with gold rings. You get the picture. The Black Widow of Camorra looked like any bourgeois matron going window-shopping in Milan.

Mazza told Longrigg about her relationship with Rosetta Cutolo. Whereas some women make friends with other mothers in the back row of the school play, or at the school gates, these two bonded when Mama Mazza's psychopathic sons were arrested and sent to Poggioreale prison, which was ruled by Rosetta's brother Raffaele. Mama Mazza, knowing a dangerous murderer when she saw one, was aware that her sons' lives could be in danger if they did not address the humble politesse that was required by, and served to sustain, Raffaele Cutolo's majesty. She sent cigarettes into the prison as currency to protect her boys, and she asked Rosetta Cutolo to deliver them, thus initiating an important friendship.

But the Moccia brothers failed to do as their mother told them and were unwilling to show deference. The families fell out, and the Moccias joined the Nuova Famiglia. Mazza's son Angelo took a leading part as director of this crime syndicate, a position that caused his mother as much pride as if he had been made a secretary of state. Angelo turned his family into what Clare Longrigg describes as an 'efficient and imaginative killing machine controlling an extortion racket that brought in millions'.

As women working on the straight side of the law struggle up the corporate ladders of the western world, so the women working in the underworld syndicates of Sicily ascended to the top. Promoted by their intelligence, careerism and connections, they became the executives. All Versace skirts, shoulder pads, vermilion hair and gold jewellery, they hid guns in their underwear drawers and drove around in bulletproof cars.

They command gangs of hatchet-jawed Italian youth, dressed in cliché wide-boy suits, armed and dangerous and modelling themselves on gangster movies. If there is one thing the police are guaranteed to find during a raid on a mafioso house it is the full complement of Coppola's *Godfather* films.

The rites of the traditional mafioso subculture, infused as they are by twisted morals and ludicrous machismo, had specifically excluded women for reasons that oscillated between sexism and common sense. The wife who was told nothing, who knew nothing, was protected by this secrecy. The woman who knew nothing about the criminal activities of her husband could cause no trouble if questioned by the police, nor could she be implicated as an accessory. This tradition was underpinned by a belief, held until the 90s, that women did not have the intellectual facility to conduct business or the amorality to commit crimes.

In Italy she was the blessed Madonna, an untouchable virgin or mother, protected by the invisible magic that was the Catholic idea of femininity. The prominent anti-Mafia hero judge Giovanni Falcone told an interviewer in 1989 that the Mafia was a totally male organisation. 'Either there are no women or they have a subaltern support role.'

This was of much use to the purposes of the Cosa Nostra and responsible for the fact that women operating in the Mafia crimeworld got away with murder, extortion and drug trafficking for years on end. The credulous idealism that lurks behind chauvinism had allowed women not just to complicitly encourage the actions of their husbands but to commit atrocities themselves – for far longer and with more impunity than their murdering brothers, cousins and fathers.

Sicily is the largest island in the Mediterranean, but it is still tiny in relation to neighbouring landmasses and illuminates the odd rule that the notoriety of a country in the scheme of global history bears no relation to its size; the smallest places have the largest reputations in world affairs – Ireland, the Falkland Islands and Rwanda to name only three examples. Sicily, then, might be small but, for the last century or more, it has been notorious thanks to its main export: criminals. Why should this unprepossessing island of olives and oranges breed such a large number of drug-trafficking psychos?

The island's cultural history provides some answers for it was always conducive to breeding a lawless society where internecine violence grew naturally from a tradition of blood feud. Furthermore Italy's poor have always been very poor; not an excuse, but a fact. The peasants had little and what little they had was taken away from them by people willing and able to resort to brutality. Usury, the historical mainstay of Mafia 'business', is a tradition that dates well back into the nineteenth century. Loan sharks have long thrived in the warmth of a Naples slum and the business of lending was often run by women.

Sicily has a long history of being conquered and consequently a long history of distrusting those who had set themselves up as rulers. This made it easier for indigenous paralegal groups to win the trust of those who had learned not to relate to the state. The Mafia arrived around 1860 in the absence of any strong official law. They were *campieri* – men with guns and horses, employed by landowners to protect their estates. The *campieri*, aggressive and dishonest, became richer and more powerful and eventually collected into self-protective secret cells, or 'families'.

They etched positions in the top strata of local society, which they further strengthened by marrying each other and by developing a subculture, designed to exist outside the state, protected by codes of 'omerta' (silence) which allowed crimes to be committed without the law being either alerted or aided. Add the perceived charisma of the anti-hero to the Sicilian distrust of authority and you have a picnic ground for mobsters, though the reality rarely reflected the glamour of the myth.

One prosecutor, Antonino Caponnetto, having spent months interrogating various mafiosi, noted that the human raw materials from which they were made were 'depressingly squalid'. These peculiar criminals were 'coarse characters who left you wondering how they were able to run a criminal organisation on that scale'. Nevertheless, they were, and still are, an immovable part of the infrastructure of southern Italy.

Between 1973 and 1983, after Marseilles fell as a port through which heroin was distributed, Palermo, the port on the north coast of Sicily, replaced it and became the host for a huge portion of the world's narcotics trade. The result was that the Mafia – which had already bought itself alliances in local politics and in the legal system – not only became very rich, but continued to forge the powerful underworld connections that had sustained its international strength from the days when the first Italian immigrants made their way first to New Orleans, then to Chicago and other US cities.

Giovanni Falcone once said that the Cosa Nostra was 'not invincible', but the current global picture says otherwise. The Sicilian Mafia have long outgrown Italy. By the end of the 90s they had made operational business connections with global fraternities that ranged from the Russian Mafia and the Colombian cocaine cartels to the Triads and Yakuza.

The destruction of national boundaries as a result of European integration and the emergence of the Internet presented the Mafia and their ilk with new business opportunities which transformed them into 'trans-national' crime syndicates. They have become major players in global economic activity and they have genuine political power.

While the dissolution of national boundaries opened the door to Europe for East European and Asian gangs, it also allowed Southern European gangs to go east. The Italian gangs were quick to take advantage of these new territories while, at the same time, increasing their connections with the new criminal groups from Russia, Estonia and Poland. They were laundering millions of dollars through the Internet. They were still successfully buying legitimate businesses and politicans. They had increased their interests to include the trafficking of radioactive materials – moving mercury and uranium through Eastern Europe to laboratories designed to make nuclear weapons.

At the end of 2000, as Palermo readied itself to host a UN Conference on fighting organised crime, the *Guardian* noted that a CD-ROM guarded in the local prosecutor's office recorded the existence of 190 families with a total of 5,192 members. Their combined assets were estimated to be enough to pay Italy's national debt.

For years, of course, the law has fought the Mafia, which is now global and increasingly corporate. In Sicily, investigators and prosecutors were impeded not only by a folk culture that supported the godfathers, but by their violence. Judges and policemen and anti-Mafia politicans all risked assassination.

Slowly the curtain started to rise on the reality of the mafioso lifestyle. This was aided, in particular, by the La Torre law which allowed the state not only to confiscate mafioso assets but, as importantly, to prosecute for 'mafia association', which meant that for the first time the women involved in the families could be imprisoned for allowing their names to be used for such things as fake money-laundering companies and for aiding the illegal activities of their family businesses. This was followed later by a law which allowed for the state protection of witnesses. The result was that many gangsters, having been arrested and wishing to save themselves, defected from their clan and exposed the workings within it.

One of the first mafiosettas to come to the country's attention, in 1982, was the 74-year-old Angela Russo, known as 'Granny Heroin'. Described, on her arrest, as 'tough and bossy', Angela Russo was seen to be the brains behind the family's drug-running operation, which she ran with the aplomb of an experienced and cool-headed businesswoman. As a Sicilian newspaper put it: 'From the quiet apartment on Via Abela where she lived with her son, daughter-in-law, grandchildren and paralysed husband, she issued telephoned instructions for consignments of "shit", "keys", "snow", "junk". Her business earned a comfortable livelihood for seven people, including her sons and daughters-in-law.'

Her father, Don Peppino, was an old-fashioned mafioso 'man of respect' at a time when the Mafia in Palermo did not, according to Russo, 'kill anyone unless it was absolutely sure it had to'.

Gangsterism was in her blood and she behaved like the son that her father had always wanted but had never had. She was pleased to be 'macho', to go out hunting with him, to take up gang business and to run it like a *capo di capi*.

'I was never afraid of anything,' Granny Heroin told one interviewer. 'Even as a child, as a little girl, I never took fright at anything . . . I was strong.'

When her son Salvino defected and turned state's evidence, his mother claimed he had gone mad as the result of the meningitis he had suffered as a child. Salvino's testimony initiated many vendetta murders – including the assassination of his brother – and resulted in his mother spending five years in prison. Granny Heroin made it clear that she felt he should die for his betrayal. 'Salvino knows he's a condemned man,' she said. 'He knows he'll get out and they'll kill him. They don't forgive . . .'

Over the next five years it became apparent that not only did the women of the mafia families know about everything that their husbands were doing, but they were also running the businesses when the men were murdered or when they went to jail. 'The state has no idea how much a mafia woman knows,' said Giacominio Filippello, who later turned state's evidence in order to avenge herself on the men that killed her lover, Mafia boss Natale L'Ala.

Ann Drahmann Coppola, the wife of Trigger Mike Coppola, was proud to be married to a 'boss' and, indeed, had purposively set her sights on one as an English Sloane Ranger sets her sights on a Lord. In order to find out the things he would not tell her, she would open his mail then sift through the various stashes of money and documents that he had hidden around the house. And she would eavesdrop, hide behind the door and listen as the fat mobsters gathered in her house and discussed the business of murder.

Others, though, were not content with such petty roles and stretched themselves well beyond secret eavesdropping, or the petty secretarial tasks of answering their husbands' telephones and helping to manage their dodgy books.

'Nitto's sister is even more mafiosa than his wife,' state witness Antonino Calderone said of the sister of gang boss Nitto Santapaolo, a man most famous for strangling four children because they stole his mother's handbag. 'Nitto would even take her along on heists.'

It soon became apparent that hussies and harridans from Palermo to Catania and from Catania to Calabria were running arms and drugs around southern Italy. They were collecting protection money, they were organising hits, and they were ensuring that their family's power remained intact. As one Neopolitan prosecutor said, 'In some families women are at the very top. There are women who take decisions to commit murder in exactly the same way as men do.'

Thus Giuseppa Condello, married to Antonino Imerti (known as 'the vicious dwarf'), took over the business in Calabria when a mafia war forced her husband to live in hiding in the foothills there. She oversaw the payments made by extortion, a complicated business which required some accounting skills, and she made the necessary visits to the tradespeople of Villa San Giovanni to collect the monthly payments.

Thus Maria Filippa Messina took over from her husband Antonino Cintorino when he was arrested in 1993. She was 24. She bought guns in from Yugoslavia, armed her men and controlled the extortion network. She was tough and she was bright and that was all that was needed. When other families attempted to break into her territory – areas around Calatabiano and Giardini Naxos – Messina planned her offensive with the cool skill and nerveless amorality of some sociopathic army general. She employed hit men and arranged for them to come in from Catania, then she organised a bomb to blow up her enemies. Nobody was going to survive. La Messina was arrested in 1995 and charged with everything from trafficking to extortion and murder. She is currently serving a thirteen-year sentence.

Maria Rasaria Buccarella managed to hide from the authorities until her arrest in December 1997. She was believed to have been the 'godmother' of the Sacra Corona Unita, an organised crime syndicate which rose in the Apulia region of Italy in the 70s.

Maria and Teresa Zappia were arrested in 1999 on suspicion of heading the Calabrian crime syndicate known as the Ndranghetta while Concetta Scalisi, arrested in the same year, controlled drugs and extortion in the area around Mount Etna.

Scalisi's father, a godfather named Antonio, was murdered in 1982. His son Salvatore took over until his own assassination five years later. Scalisi was accused of ordering the murder of three opponents and managed to avoid police for some months, alternating her hide-outs, and evading surveillance.

When the police bore down and Scalisi saw that there was no escape, she slashed her stomach with broken glass in an effort to be sent to hospital rather than prison – a ward, of course, is always more comfortable and always less secure. The recalcitrant outlaw was described, on her arrest, as 'a robust woman wearing dark glasses and a distinctly displeased expression'.

As more and more godmothers were arrested, the Italian judiciary began to appreciate the depth and gravity of their naivete with regard to the reality of the role that women were playing as leaders in the Cosa

Nostra. And the Italian people began to understand the dangers that lay within the confines of their culture.

The mobster was being created at home. He was a product of his environment, bred to the gun by a loving mama who, married to a mob boss, hit man or simple aspirational foot soldier, was perpetrating a moral climate that allowed her children to be indoctrinated with a twisted code of honour that instilled the idea that revenge was honour and extortion was for the good of the people.

The mamas, so sacrosanct and untouchable, were sending out conveyer belts of killers who had no need of conscience because their consciences had been moulded from childhood to uphold and believe in gangster ideals. They grew up with relations who believed in the same thing. So the mamas made sons who could kill and maim and know that they would be loved for it. And the daughters? The daughters married sons of mafiosi and waited until the inevitable happened – the assassination or the jail sentence that would promote them to the forefront of the family business.

'It's not as if you get up and join Cosa Nostra,' said the Mafia defector Leonard Messina. 'They keep an eye on you as a child, they bring you up, they teach you to shoot, to kill, to plant bombs.'

'I brought my sons up well and taught them religion,' Antonina Brusca announced to the press when her two lovely boys were arrested for detonating the 1992 bomb that killed Giovanni Falcone.

In June 2001 police finally caught up with Maria Licciardi, one of the most powerful godmothers. At the age of fifty, she helmed the Secondigliano Alliance, a collection of the most vicious clans around Naples. Licciardi's elusiveness had been legendary. One raid had led helicopters and several hundred heavily armed police to a ramshackle building in Secondigliano – here there was an attic guarded by a surveillance camera, complete with marble floors and jacuzzi, but empty of the woman known as 'The Princess'.

The daughter of a mob boss, Licciardi took control after her brothers were imprisoned and her husband and nephew were murdered. After a warrant for her arrest was issued she went on the run for two years, hiding out in Eastern Europe, but returned to run the family business – a network involved in the sale of guns and drugs which she ran with indomitable efficiency.

Reporter Rory Carroll described her as 'diminutive, powerful and calculating', and went on to note that she had 'exceptional intelligence, charisma, supernatural calm, and the brains of a ruthless tactician. She is not psychotic but practical and therefore merciless. She is a leader.'

Licciardi was at the centre of a mafia war responsible for hundreds of deaths. People were stabbed, beaten and gunned down in the streets around Naples; no cafe was safe. The Princess found herself in the limelight, a position that she did not crave, for like the other clever women of this milieu, she knew the shadows of the background were her only protection. She wanted power, not fame, and she understood the difference.

The war started in April 2000 after a consignment of heroin arrived from Istanbul. Unrefined and potent, it was therefore very dangerous to a junkie clientele unaccustomed to banging up pure smack. Licciardi decreed that the drug should not be sold, as such, but the Lo Russo family chopped it up anyway, poured it into the envelopes and sold it, initiating a spate of fatal overdoses that littered the place with junkie corpses as the Princess had predicted.

This not only damaged the marketplace – killing the client is not good business – but it initiated a police crackdown. Various gangsters were hauled off and the friable infrastructure created by the Princess began to dissolve as the hit men began to shoot each other. Four of her men were gunned down on her home turf, the suburb of Secondigliano. She retaliated with a vicious counter-assault and ended up on the list of Italy's most wanted criminals.

In May 2002, trouble broke out again on the streets of southern Italy and again the godmothers were at the centre. An old-fashioned shoot-out in Lauro, south of Naples, left three dead and five critically injured. It was, as one policeman said, 'like something out of a Hollywood movie'.

The corpses of Las Madrinas lay bullet-ridden and dead on the scene. The three fatalities, including a sixteen-year-old, were members of the Cava crime family. The Cavas were found to be armed with knives and scissors and a machine gun had been involved. Five injured women – three Grazianos and two Cavas – were taken to hospital and placed under armed guard.

The two clans had been feuding since 1972 when a Graziano was murdered by a Cava. The Grazianos had controlled the village of Quindici and wanted to expand into the Lauro valley with their network of extortion rackets. It propelled its sons into the bureaucracy by getting them elected to the local authority.

The Cavas, meanwhile, had also built up a portfolio of companies but wanted more, and so forged alliances with local families that built their power and disgruntled the Grazianos.

The arrest of Biagio Cava for various alleged offences triggered a series of disruptions in Quindici as the rival godmothers began to fly at each other. The bloodbath resulted after a chance meeting when both their cars came across each other late at night.

'We are still trying to establish who fired the first shot,' said a spokesman at the time of the massacre. 'We are interviewing several witnesses who have told us that they dived for cover because of the amount of bullets that were flying around the place.'

'The noise was terrific,' said one witness. 'People were hiding in shops and doorways or behind benches. I heard gunfire and looked around to see two groups of women shooting at each other.'

There was speculation that Italy was ready to enter a state of Amazonian warfare; handbags at dawn, as it were, as middle-aged mamas clattered onto the turf armed with machine guns. But *Guardian* writer Rory Carroll, who has long reported on the Mafia sagas, pointed out that the families of the Camorra, around Naples, have always been wilder than their Cosa Nostra brethren in Sicily.

Visiting Lauro after the shoot-out he described the washing of the blood from Via Canalone. 'The mountain village of Lauro is too high and far from the sea breeze of the Bay of Naples to entice tourists. It is not especially pretty, there are no renaissance steeples and much of the nearby oak forests have been stripped, leaving a grim, bare landscape. Sunday night gave another reason not to visit.'

SOURCES

Longrigg, Clare, *Mafia Women*, Chatto and Windus, London and Glasgow, 1997

Siebert, Renate, *Secrets of Life and Death, Women and the Mafia*, Verso, New York, 1996

Daily Mail, 28 May 2002

Evening Standard, 27 May 2002
the *Guardian*, 14 April 1999, 11 January 2001, 29 May
    2002
www.ABCNews.com

6. MOTHER DOES NOT ALWAYS KNOW BEST

Infanticide is a crime that has been committed by many women, for many different reasons, for many years.

The annals of infanticide are full of stories about the sick, the mad, the sad and the confused; while some mothers are driven to desperation by abuse and poverty, others calmly kill and then cover themselves with stories of cot death or mystery attackers. While some of these murderesses are repulsive harridans for whom there is no excuse, others are easier to sympathise with. Andrea Yates falls into the latter category.

The 36-year-old Houston mother had long suffered from a series of depressive disorders, ranging from endogenous episodes to schizophrenia. When she started reading the Bible more and more her husband, Russell, did not complain. He is a religious man and he did not see how he could complain about somebody reading the Bible. But Andrea Yates heard voices and she felt Satan's presence and, on 20 June 2001, she drowned her five children in the bath, one by one. Noah, seven, saw what had happened to the baby, Mary, and tried to run away. His mother caught him and held him face down in nine inches of water until his struggles stopped. The other children's bodies were lying on a sheet in the bedroom, but she left Noah floating there in the bath. Then she telephoned the police and her husband.

Officers arrived at the Yateses' clean suburban home to find Andrea soaked in water and five dead children. There was a poster of Jesus Christ 'the saviour' in the bathroom. The case received all the exposure that it is possible to receive in America. Aired on Court TV and the subject of an extensive *Time* investigation, it was called one of 'the most sensational murder cases in years'. Yates' mental health records, photographs of her children, details of her life, all were posted on the Net and into newspapers, which was ironic in the light of testimony that said one of Yates' overriding characteristics was her guardedness. She never revealed her true feelings to her friends or even to her husband. This was one of her problems. Her immutable defence system. The more details emerged, the more possible it was to understand how such a tragic event had come about.

The case of Andrea Yates – unlike crimes perpetrated by other frenzied and desensitised women – was not about savage abuse or deprivation or brutish criminalisation or sleazy amorality. It was the story of a modern woman driven to the worst-case scenario by the pressure to be a perfect wife and a perfect mother, while all the time presenting a perfect face to the world. In her drive to be good, Andrea Yates became fixated by evil, in the old-fashioned sense of the idea. She thought she was Satan, as so many schizophrenics do, and she wanted to die.

No matter how many perfect cookies she baked or how well she taught the children painting or how much she drove herself to achieve, she could reach neither stability nor equanimity nor any basic sense of fulfilment. If Andrea Yates had resentments she kept them to herself. She tried her hardest but, in the end, she blew. Russell 'Rusty' Yates, a computer engineer working for NASA, had not been aware that Andrea's family had a history of mental illness. Andrea's mother Jutta had had recourse to anti-depressants, a brother and sister were being treated for depression and another brother was bipolar.

After Andrea was arrested Rusty Yates told *Time* magazine's Tim Roche of his belief that Andrea was innocent and that her insanity lead her to kill. This was her defence: not guilty by reason of insanity. The prosecution, meanwhile, pushed for the death sentence. It was a capital crime and this was Texas. Texas executes more people than any other state in America.

Rusty Yates met Andrea in 1989 when they were both 25.They spent some time living together, reading the Bible and praying, then they got married in 1993. Noah was born in 1994. The morning after he arrived, Andrea had a vision of a knife and somebody being stabbed, but she did not tell her husband. She became pregnant again in 1995 and began to become more isolated, an emotional condition to which she was prone anyway.

In 1996 the couple leased out their house and moved to Florida to live in a trailer while Rusty worked on a temporary NASA project. Andrea conceived again. By 1999 she had three children – Noah aged four, John aged two, and baby Luke – three little boys all under the age of five. And she was pregnant again.

On 16 June 1999 Rusty found his wife suffering the onset of a serious nervous breakdown. She was crying hysterically and her body was shaking. That night she took an overdose of pills in an attempt to kill herself. Rusty told a social worker at the hospital that his wife had 'guilt about showing anger'. Some friends and members of the family said later that they thought Andrea had quite a lot to be angry about as Rusty was both undermining and controlling.

Testifying at the trial two years later, her friend Debbie Holmes told the court that she had been so worried about Andrea that she had kept a diary. 'A couple of times I called her husband and I was crying and sobbing.

' "She needs help now! Not next week!" ' Holmes went on to say that Russell Yates could not understand why his wife could not keep up with her responsibilities. He admired another woman in the neighbourhood who had nine children. Rusty Yates, meanwhile, told the prosecutor, 'Man is the breadwinner and woman is the homemaker. It's the way it's been for years.'

In 1999 the homemaker left the hospital with a prescription for the antidepressant Zoloft, but she got worse. Showing classic symptoms of chronic depressive illness, she stayed in bed, scratched herself until she was bald and scored her arms and legs compulsively until they were red. This was an angry woman taking it out on herself.

The voices and visions, meanwhile, were getting worse. On one occasion her husband found her with a knife pressed against her neck threatening to kill herself. She was readmitted to hospital and she was catatonic. The antipsychotic drug Haldol was prescribed. She told the psychologist there that she was terrified of acting out on the violent commands resounding in her head. Better to kill herself before anything happened.

Rusty Yates moved his family out of the bus in which they had been living and bought a three-bedroom house in Houston. Andrea, on Haldol, improved and concentrated on becoming the Perfect Mother. She taught the children at home, she baked cakes, she sewed costumes and she studied the Bible three nights a week. She also attended to her invalid father who, suffering from Alzheimer's, was slowly dying in front of her.

In March 2000 she became pregnant again. It would be her fifth child. A doctor warned that this could make her very ill indeed. At the beginning of 2001, when the new baby Mary was three months old, her beloved father died. She read the Bible. A lot. The scratching began again. She was rehospitalised and went back on

Haldol. There were regular suicide checks. But she never said anything during the group therapy sessions. Despite the fact that she was withdrawn, despite the fact that nobody really knew what was going on in her head, she was allowed to go home. She came off the Haldol and this, a doctor was to testify at her trial, was responsible for the onset of her psychosis. Dr George Reinholz, a neuropsychologist, saw Yates as an undiagnosed schizophrenic.

'She stopped taking medication two weeks before the killings,' he said. 'This would have dramatically increased her symptoms.'

On the morning of 20 June Rusty Yates left for work. He told the court that though he knew his wife was sad, he thought she would be able to cope for a couple of hours until his mother arrived to help out. But his wife did not cope. She filled the bathtub.

She told the homicide sergeant Eric Mehl, who interviewed her after the deaths, that she had considered murdering the children for two years. 'Since I realised I have not been a good mother to them,' she said. She told him that she wanted to be punished for not being a good mother and that this was a way of getting the criminal justice system to do it. In other words, she saw herself as receiving the death sentence which, in her view, was the necessary retribution for her failure to come up to her own standards.

Andrea Yates felt that the death of her children was a way of saving them from the torment of hell; they could only be saved when the state executed her. She told a doctor who interviewed her when she was in Harris County Jail that she wanted her hair shaved so she could see the number 666 on her scalp.

Minister Byron Fike of the Clear Lake Church of Christ in Houston officiated at the funeral of the five children killed by Andrea Yates and gave an interview to CNN. Describing the service that he had planned he said that the theme would be 'From Tragedy to Triumph because of the death and resurrection of Jesus. We believe these children will rise again as well . . .'

And what, asked the CNN reporter, did the minister plan to say about the children's mother? 'I won't be saying anything about her at this particular service,' he replied, but added that, in his opinion, 'we live in a fallen world.'

Rusty, meanwhile, told the television programme *60 Minutes*, 'I don't blame her a bit. If she had received the medical treatment that she deserved, then the kids would be alive and well. And Andrea would be well on her way to recovery.'

He set up a website devoted to his five dead children. It was designed to resemble a family photograph album: the visitor to yateskids.org could see photographs of their smiling faces and read of Noah, seven, who had enjoyed drawing rainbows, of John, five, who liked trucks, of Luke, three, who was well behaved, of Paul, two, who was a 'determined' toddler and of baby Mary who appeared in her crib.

In Houston the National Organisation for Women (and various other civil liberties organisations) announced that they planned to raise money to defend Andrea Yates, whose legal costs were, of course, very high and whose very life was at risk.

'Harris County is infamous for its indiscriminate seeking of the death penalty,' Texan law professor Jordan Steiker said during the time of the Yates case.

Deborah Bell, the president of Texas NOW, told Court TV, 'It gives us a platform for something that obviously needs education. One of our feminist beliefs is to be there for other women. Some good may come out of this tragedy.'

In January 2002 a jury was selected to try Andrea Yates. It consisted of four men and eight women, two of whom had psychology degrees and seven of whom had children.

Harris County had hosted the trial of Yolanda Salivar in 1995. Salivar had shot the singer Selena and her trial was inundated by fans lining up at 4 a.m. In May 2000 the courtroom had been packed for the trial of Angel Maturino Resendiz who had confessed to killing nineteen people.

Andrea Yates' trial started on 18 February 2002. On 19 February the *Houston Chronicle* noted that of the 50 seats allotted for the public, only half were filled, and those were occupied mainly by members of the Yates family. Representatives from women's organisations and anti-death penalty groups were 'nowhere in sight'. Outside one eccentric protester sang songs of prayer in support of the defendant. Two days later, after Yates' face had appeared in papers and on the Net, the same newspaper reported that interest had ignited and 'spectators outside the courtroom began pushing and shoving one another in an effort to get prime seats'. On the fourth day a court official attributed the increase in public interest to the grimness of the testimony to be presented. This was to include police photographs of the dead children and Yates' audiotaped confession.

At the end of March 2002 the Houston jury rejected Yates' insanity defence and found her guilty of murder. They also decided that she was not a future danger and would therefore not be eligible for death by injection. After the so-called 'penalty phase' of the trial, a panel decided that she would serve a life sentence. Forty years.

The court had felt that, although Yates was mentally ill, at the time of the infanticide she knew right from wrong, and this was the criterion for determining the legal definition of insanity and, consequently, the degree of her culpability.

As she began to serve her term, the district attorney announced that his office would be studying the culpability of her husband, Rusty, in the light of the questions asked, in particular as to why he had left his unstable wife alone with her children on the morning of her death.

'It is a tragedy that Rusty now has to defend himself after standing by his wife,' said his lawyer.

But Andrea Yates' family had been critical and, after her trial, was more vociferously so. Her brother, Brian, in a television interview, described Rusty Yates as 'unemotional' and said he simply had not done enough to help a woman with five children. In his defence, Yates said that some people 'don't understand the nature of biochemical illness'.

Andrea Yates' case reignited discussions about the relationship between postpartum illness and infanticide and it reintroduced the idea that postpartum psychosis could be used as a defence in cases where insanity was being argued. While Texas prosecutors argued that Mrs Yates deserved to be executed because she knew the difference between right and wrong, various legislators debated the issue with more sympathy.

Postpartum depression is recognised as a legal defence in 29 countries, including Great Britain. The infanticide laws tend to state that if a woman kills a child below the age of one and she can prove that the balance of her mind was disturbed, the charge will be manslaughter, and the sentence more likely to involve probation and counselling. That is, the law does not see the woman as a murderer, so much as someone who has killed and who is in need of help. The law in England limits this defence to the first year. A woman who kills her one-year-old can be charged with manslaughter but the woman who kills her older toddler is a murderer although, as any woman knows, the circumstances that could lead to murderous impulses may well be the same in both instances.

Medical knowledge says that although 80 per cent of women may suffer from 'baby blues' up to 22 per cent suffer actual depression, although postpartum psychosis is very rare – a statistic of one in 2,000 is suggested by the Reproductive Mental Health website. It is regarded as a definite clinical condition that is more likely to affect women who have had a history of bad depressive or psychotic illnesses such as schizophrenia or bipolar disorders.

A classic psychotic episode is a terrifying thing but it is recognisable thanks to its common characteristics. These include auditory hallucination (voices), delusions and chronically chaotic or illogical thought processes. This, in the view of some clinicians, represents a psychiatric emergency tempered by the fact that the mother may not know how ill she is – that is, she should be hospitalised for the sake of her own welfare and, in extreme cases, for the sake of her baby.

Law professor Michelle Oberman, author of the book *Mothers Who Kill Their Children: Inside the Minds of Moms from Susan Smith to the Prom Mom*, warned that psychosis as a legal defence is difficult to prove because of the fluctuating nature of hormonal imbalance.

A woman driven mad by natural chemicals may appear sane and rational when she is in court, making it difficult for a jury, particularly the male members of it, to empathise with the reality of a seriously disordered mind.

Houston defence attorney George McCall Secrest successfully defended Evonne Rodriguez in 1997 when she killed her four-month-old child in the belief that it was possessed by demons. 'The jury is going to have to focus not only on the facts of the actual offence on trial but they are going to have to understand the mental state of the accused,' he said at the time of Yates' trial. 'This is not an easy thing to deal with.'

Both society and the law are schizoid when it comes to attitudes to women who kill their children. Society may scream, but it still enjoys the movie. Diane Downs, in particular, has been immortalised. She shot her three children at point-blank range with a .22 Ruger on a road in Oregon in 1983, and then pretended they were the victims of a violent assailant. One child died and two were seriously maimed but survived after hospitalisation. The eldest, Christie, was called as a witness to her mother's trial. 'Who shot you?' prosecuting attorney Fred Hugi asked the eight-year-old. 'My mom,' she said.

A bitch of the first order, Diane Downs was supremely marketable. She appeared on Oprah Winfrey's chat show and, in 1989, was played by Farrah Fawcett in the film *Small Sacrifices*. Such celebration may have been personally gratifying to her, but it did not help when she attempted to get her life sentence revoked. She lost the appeal in 1999.

The mother who kills her children touches many nerves and high-profile cases inevitably promote appraisal about the pressures of motherhood and the difference between genuine criminality and stress-related causes. The law reflects little uniformity in the meting out of punishment. The outcome of a case is by no means predictable and the mother is by no means protected by an argument of mental illness.

In Texas, Darlie Routier went to death row but still protests the truth of her claim that an intruder stabbed her two children to death in 1996. There are some people who argue that Darlie Routier is innocent of the murder of her two young sons, Devon, six, and Damon, five. Campaigners fight on her behalf in the media and on the Net where several websites are devoted to arguing that she is a victim of a miscarriage of justice.

Routier, aged 26, was arrested after her two little boys were violently stabbed to death at their Georgian-style house in a plush suburb near Rowlett in Texas. The mother herself had suffered a knife wound to the throat. Another child, baby Drake, was asleep upstairs. Her husband Darin, 28, had been awoken in their bedroom upstairs by her screams at 2.30 a.m. The police arrived to find two maimed children, one dead, one dying, and the smell of blood. A search for an intruder revealed nobody. There was a bloody butcher's knife in the kitchen.

Routier stuck to her story that they had been attacked by an unknown assailant who broke into the house as they all lay asleep on the sofa having spent the evening watching television. The police could find little convincing evidence of an intruder. Routier had pointed to a screen, slashed with a knife, which showed no sign of a body climbing through it. A lot of witnesses spoke of their amazement at the woman's calm in the face of this tragedy. Trauma nurses dealing with the incident described her as 'cold as ice.' The media saw her, variously, as a trailer-trash mama gone psycho or a materialistic bitch for whom the kids had become an unnecessary expense. But if this was the case, why did baby Drake survive?

She was reported to have been raised in Lubbock, Texas – the child of a broken home who sometimes exhibited herself in order to attract attention. Darin Routier was her high school sweetheart and they were married in 1988. Darin's computer business was, at first, successful. He made money and it was quickly spent on the trappings that boast American prestige – a two-storey house with a fountain in the garden; a new Jaguar car; an entertainment centre with a huge television. All that.

Darlie, very concerned about her appearance, spent a fortune on clothes and paid to have her breasts enlarged to an EE cup, which was a surprising decision for somebody who was not a porn star. Some of her neighbours were critical, saying the children were not supervised enough, that Darlie Routier only thought about shopping and it was that shopping that eventually brought the family finances into disrepair, causing stress to her husband and, in the end, nearly bankrupting them. Darin's business hit a lean period and the family spending was not tempered to cater for it.

Things got worse. The marriage started to suffer. Darlie grew fat and the diet pills did not work and an entry in her diary, written a month before the murder, revealed that she was contemplating suicide.

The police were dissatisfied with her story, wondering, for a start, why the dog did not bark, why there was so little evidence of two adults struggling, why a bloody knife with her fingerprints on it was left behind, why there was no trail of blood marking his exit and why the children were killed first when an adult posed more threat – although this could be explained if the intruder was psychotic. The mother's wounds, furthermore, were said to have the traits of 'hesitation', the blade having been cut slowly into the skin, while the children's wounds were clearly delivered in a frenzy.

Then she held an extraordinary posthumous birthday party for Devon's 'seventh' birthday – a 'celebration' held at his graveside. As the pastor attempted to introduce solemnity to the proceedings, Mrs Routier sprayed a can of Silly String in the air and, laughing and singing, screamed, 'I love you Devon and Damon!'

These proceedings, recorded by investigators on a secret camera, were very odd, but a critic might say that they could easily be explained as the behaviour of a mother whose mental state was unbalanced by severe shock and grief. Very few women behave rationally when their children die.

Four days after this, on 18 January, Routier was arrested for murder and, as a young, blonde, normal-looking suburban mom, found herself promoted to the fame reserved for the media-made criminal. As the prosecution went for the death sentence, Darlie's parents remortgaged their home to pay for the legal fees. The bank, meanwhile, repossessed the Georgian house that Darlie and Darin had lived in. In February 1997 the jury delivered the death sentence. The defendant did not cry, but then she never cried in public.

Various supporters claimed that there was evidence that should have been seen by the jury – the bruises on Routier's arms, for instance, which could have showed evidence of a struggle. Since then some jurors have admitted that (in an environment that was baying for blood) they had succumbed to peer pressure when, in fact, they were not entirely convinced of the mother's guilt.

Her attorneys filed an appeal citing fourteen points of error. In March 2002 they were still fighting, citing in particular a faulty court transcript that, they claimed, prevented the correct raising of important legal questions.

As Mrs Routier awaits execution by lethal injection, the detached observer can only see a case of great complexity where there seem to be equal amounts of truth both for and against her, particularly if madness is part of the equation, either on the part of the mystery assailant, or on the part of the woman. Darlie Routier, however, never claimed that she was insane; she claimed that she was attacked. And, like Dr Sam Sheppard of *Fugitive* fame, she is sticking to her story.

Juana Leija received probation in 1986 after she threw six of her seven children into a bayou and killed two of them. Her lawyer argued that she had been driven insane by her husband. Diane Lumbrera was given a life sentence in 1990 when she was convicted of suffocating her four-month-old son. Her other six children had died in her care over a fourteen-year period and she told authorities that they had died young because her mother-in-law had placed a curse on the family. In 1995 23-year-old Christine Kibble confessed to drowning two of her children, suffocating one and attempting to suffocate another. She pleaded guilty in exchange for a life sentence.

There are some who think that Sheryl Hardy's crime was unforgivable. 'She's an evil person, a murderess,' detective Paul Schaill told reporters in November 2001, eleven years after Hardy had watched while her husband Thomas Coe rammed her two-year-old son Bradley's head down the loo as if it was a 'plunger'.

Schaill had led the investigation in Florida in 1990. The child was the product of a rape and, at the age of four months, had been placed in foster care. When the foster parents said they wanted to adopt him, Hardy reclaimed her son and, 66 days later, watched while her husband Thomas Coe murdered him. This was after the child had been tortured by both his stepfather and his mother. The case prompted Florida to overhaul its child protection laws and spend $79 million hiring more social workers to work in the field of child abuse. One social worker involved in the case was convicted of failure to report child abuse and placed on three months' probation.

After serving nine years of a ten-year prison sentence Sheryl Hardy relocated to Illinois, where she had been born, and successfully applied for the custody of her nine-month-old son by her new husband Randy Hardy. 'This baby is going to end up dead too,' Schaill warned. But the judge believed that Hardy, having received parenting classes in prison, was capable of becoming a 'sensitive and nurturing' mother.

It is difficult to sympathise with Hardy, as it is difficult, too, to care about the fate of Melissa Drexler, the so-called 'prom mom'. She arrived at her senior prom, gave birth to a six-pound son, strangled him, threw his body in the dustbin, and returned to the party where she ate dinner. It was widely reported at the time (though retracted later) that she requested the Metallica song 'Unforgiven' to be played for her boyfriend.

Drexler pleaded guilty to aggravated manslaughter and received a sentence of fifteen years. She was released from prison in 2001 and, at the age of 23, went home to live with her parents. Her lawyer, Steven Secare, said that his client was hoping to work in the fashion industry.

In Philadelphia in 1999 Marie Noe, at the age of seventy, finally confessed to eight counts of second-degree murder. She had smothered her babies over a nineteen-year period and, having suffered a long series of mental illnesses, was sentenced to twenty years of probation.

In Maine in 1954 Constance Fisher was committed to hospital after drowning three of her children in the bath. After five years she was declared cured and returned home. In 1967 she drowned three more. She was found innocent by reason of insanity and, in 1973, succeeded in drowning herself in a river near her hospital.

New York, inevitably, has seen its fair share of infanticide, as that city has seen more than its fair share of all kinds of crime. Waneta Hoyt is serving a 75-year prison sentence for the murder of her five children. In 1995 she confessed that she had smothered them between 1965 and 1971 in order to stop the crying.

Gail Trait, aged 26, stabbed her four children to death and told the police she was trying to save her soul. Sent to prison in 1978, she served ten years before an appeal court overturned the conviction and declared her insane. She spent the next ten years in psychiatric hospitals.

Mary Beth Tinning received a twenty-year sentence for suffocating her daughter in 1985. She confessed to killing two sons, and is suspected of killing all eight of her children.

In 1990 Maria Amaya stabbed four children to death then attempted to commit suicide. Her plea of insanity was accepted and she was hospitalised.

The story of Christina Riggs was particularly sad. The Arkansas mother smothered her two children, Justin, five, and Shelby, two. A few months before the deaths, the impoverished single mother pawned her television and VCR so Justin could have his birthday party at Chuck E. Cheese, as she had promised him the year before. She did not hate her children. She was overcome by the struggle to support them and she lost the will to go on.

Her defence was 'not guilty by reason of mental disease or defect'. The jury was instructed on all levels of homicide: capital murder (premeditated and deliberated intent), murder in the first degree (purposeful intent), murder in the second degree (knowing intent) and manslaughter (under extreme emotional disturbance). It was expected that Riggs would be convicted of something less than capital murder, considering the uncontradicted testimony about her longstanding bouts of severe depression and its effects on her. The jury, however, convicted her of capital murder. She collapsed to the floor crying and asked to be sentenced to death saying: 'I want to be with my babies. I started this out seven months ago. And I want you to give me the death penalty . . .'

The testimony was that Christina Riggs' depression had two sources. She had been sexually abused as a child, and she was genetically predisposed to severe depression because it ran through several generations of her family. Expert witnesses testified that child sexual abuse can easily lead to severe depression in the victim's adult life, as well as extreme feelings of low self-esteem. Her problem was exacerbated by a pattern of internalisation of feelings of contempt, depression, and guilt. She felt that suicide was the only option left to her and, in this, she followed a family predisposition. Her mother, a sister and a cousin all attempted suicide. Her grandmother had been twice committed to an Oklahoma mental institution, her great-grandfather had committed suicide in a mental institution, and a cousin had committed suicide.This was a family that killed themselves.

Christina Riggs worked twelve-hour shifts plus overtime as a nurse at Arkansas Heart Hospital, but she could not manage financially. Day care and babysitting were huge expenses. She was cashing cheques as an advance on her pay at a cashing company. She was, in effect, borrowing at 15 per cent interest per week. She had been told by Jacksonville Municipal Judge Bob

Batton that another 'hot' cheque' would land her in jail
for a year. She had written some, and she was afraid of
going to jail. Her car licence and insurance had not been
renewed, and she had been fined. She had to struggle to
keep the electricity on. She was working as hard as she
could, even asking for and being granted overtime shifts,
in an effort to help make ends meet. It still was not
enough.

The fathers of both children did not live with her or
provide regular support. She had divorced Shelby's
father Jon Riggs because he hit Justin in the stomach so
hard that he had to be taken to the doctor. Her mother
spent a lot of time with, and caring for, the children, but
Justin suffered from Attention Deficit and Hyperactivity
Disorder (ADHD). He was hard to handle.

Planning her suicide, Christina Riggs was afraid that her
death would separate them and, though their lives had just
begun, the children truly were inseparable. She feared that
Shelby would go to Jon Riggs and Justin to his father, and
she did not want the children separated in their childhood.
She had been separated from her sisters in childhood and
she did not want that to happen to her children.

Defence experts argued that the decision of taking her
children with her, in her mind, was an act of love, of
euthanasia, and it was an extension of her own suicide.
In her mind she was actually protecting them. As Dr
Bradley Diner testified, it was an expression of love and
desperation to prevent the children from being separated from each other as she had been after the family
was disowned by her father. She was terrified of leaving
them to a life where they would be unwanted and
unloved and uncared for.

Riggs did not talk about her depression, fears or plans
for suicide with anyone. Considering her history of child
sexual abuse, this was normal. It had been instilled in

her not to tell what she was thinking and feeling or suffer reprisal. She thought about her suicide for three weeks. On 4 November 1997 she obtained Elavil from her pharmacist. She also had morphine that had come home in her nurse's uniform pockets from the Arkansas Heart Hospital and had obtained some potassium chloride from the hospital. Potassium chloride is highly toxic. It is also, ironically, used in lethal execution injections and has been the subject of controversy because of the pain it causes.

On the evening of the suicide attempt, Riggs gave her children a half Elavil each to make them drowsy through the night. She then put them in their own beds. After they were asleep, she planned to inject them with potassium chloride so they would die painlessly. But it did not work as she expected.

At 10 p.m. she injected Justin with undiluted potassium chloride while he slept. He woke up, crying out in pain. His mother held and rocked him, crying herself, to try to ease his pain. It did not work. She then injected him with morphine to ease the pain. But he did not die quickly as she expected; he was crying and in agony. She smothered him with a pillow to end his misery.

Realising she could not kill Shelby by the same method of injection, she smothered the little girl, also with a pillow. Then she carried the children to her own bed, laid them together, side-by-side, and covered them with a blanket. She wrote a suicide note to her mother, which she left on the nightstand. She also wrote a letter to Jon Riggs, Shelby's father, which she left in her mailbox that night which explained her suicide and the death of the children. She took 28 Elavil tablets, an amount that could have easily killed her on its own. Then, she injected herself with 10 cc of undiluted potassium chloride, fully expecting to die.

The poison did not make it to her heart and kill her as she expected. Instead it ate a hole in her arm and caused the vein to collapse. She passed out but she did not die. She did not show up for work the next day, 5 November. Her mother, Carol Thomas, went to the triplex to see if anything was wrong. She found the children in bed and her daughter on the floor. She called 911 on her cellular telephone, crying, 'My daughter and her babies are dead!'

The first officer on the scene also thought Christina Riggs was dead because she was cold to the touch. They rushed her to the Emergency Room at Baptist Memorial Hospital in North Little Rock. Meanwhile the police, conducting a crime scene search, found the suicide note, the bottle of Elavil, the morphine and the used syringes.

Riggs was moved to the Intensive Care Unit and kept under constant police guard. She was charged with two counts of capital murder; one count for each of her children. She pleaded not guilty by reason of mental disease and called Dr Bradley Diner, a psychiatrist, and Dr James Moneypenney, a forensic psychologist. Both testified that she was suffering from mental disease and could not appreciate the criminality of her actions in the killing of her children. To her, their deaths were an act of love and an extension of her own suicide. In rebuttal, the State called Dr Wendall Hall, a psychiatrist, and Dr John Anderson, a forensic psychologist, both with the Arkansas State Hospital. They testified that she was not sufficiently depressed at the time to not appreciate the criminality of her conduct.

The jury rejected her defence and convicted her of capital murder. In the penalty phase, she asked to be sentenced to death, and the jury obliged.

She was executed by lethal injection on 2 May 2000. It took the execution team fifteen minutes to find her vein and Riggs ten minutes to die. Her final statement? 'Now I can be with my babies as I always intended.' It was the 31st execution in the United States that year.

Susan Smith, a far less sympathetic character, could have received the death sentence for murdering her two children in 1995, but a South Carolina jury spared her, despite the wrath she had incurred in the community of Union, a small textile town.

Smith had enjoyed an affair with the son of a rich businessman until he informed her that their romance was doomed. He did not want to take on the responsibility of another man's children. A week later she drove to the shores of a local lake, unlocked the handbrake of her burgundy Mazda Protege, and allowed the car to sink into the water with Michael, three, and Alex, fourteen months, in the back seat. She then told the police that the children had been abducted by a 'carjacker'. A black man had jumped into her car, forced her to drive along the road at gunpoint, and driven away with her children.

The sheriff's department launched a massive hunt to locate the car, while the local community, sympathetic to her supposed trauma, spent a week forming private search parties and organising 'prayer chains'.

Susan and her husband David appeared on national television appealing for the safe return of their children, their father David being unaware of the lie in which he had been unwittingly involved. The search went nationwide and tips poured in from all over America.

Nine days later Susan Smith, the woman once voted 'Friendliest Female' by her high school, confessed to the murder of her children. Their father David told the jury that she should be put to death for her crime. The defence, however, successfully painted a picture of a woman who had tried to commit suicide twice, who had been molested by her stepfather and whose father had committed suicide. She was sentenced to thirty years in prison.

New Jersey teenager Amy Grossberg pleaded guilty to manslaughter in 1996 following the death of her newborn son. She had killed him in a Delaware motel. Her boyfriend Brian Paterson threw the body into a dumpster. They claimed that the child was stillborn, but a state medical examiner said it was killed by a trauma to the head. Petersen was sentenced to two years; Grossberg received a thirty-month jail sentence.

There is a difference between neonaticide, which is the disposal of a baby who has just been born, and the murder of an older child. In the United States, every year, hundreds of women commit neonaticide. Prosecutors sometimes don't prosecute; juries rarely convict; those found guilty almost never go to jail. Barbara Kirwin, a forensic psychologist, reports that in nearly 300 cases of women charged with neonaticide in the United States and Britain, 'no woman spent more than a night in jail'.

Steven Pinker, writing in the *New York Times* at the time of the 'Prom Mom' case, commented that much of 'the leniency shown to neonaticidal mothers' reflects the fact that they are standardly 'young, poor, unmarried and socially isolated', although it is notable that similar leniency is rarely extended to young, poor and socially isolated male murderers.

'It's hard to maintain,' he continued, 'that neonaticide is an illness when we learn that it has been practiced and accepted in most cultures throughout history. Neonaticidal women do not commonly show signs of psychopathology. In a classic 1970 study of statistics of child killing, a psychiatrist, Phillip Resnick, found that mothers who kill their older children are frequently psychotic, depressed or suicidal, but mothers who kill their newborns are usually not. It was this difference that led Resnick to argue that the category infanticide be split into neonaticide, the killing of a baby on the day of its birth, and filicide, the killing of a child older than one day.'

In England, where Home Office statistics show that a floating average of three people a year are convicted of infanticide (it is around 250 in America), one of the highest-profile cases is that of Sally Clark, a solicitor who, in 1999, received a life sentence for murdering her two baby sons. Clark claimed that Christopher, eleven weeks, and Harry, eight weeks, had both died of natural causes in their cots. She had been advised to plead guilty to infanticide to avoid imprisonment, but she has always claimed her innocence.

In July 2002 she achieved an important step forward in her battle to clear herself when she was granted the right to appeal following the emergence of new evidence that Harry had died of natural causes. Her husband, Steve Clark, extracted medical notes from Macclesfield Hospital among which were details of a test showing evidence of a bacterial disease known to kill babies.

'I've always known that my wife was innocent,' he said, 'and have been determined to find justice for her. After more than four years of struggle, I hope the system will now move quickly to give it to us.'

Cot death is a complex issue in this area. Unfortunately for women such as Sally Clark, police are well aware that cot death has often been the excuse given by mothers who have purposely smothered their babies. Paediatrician Professor Sir Roy Meadow has unofficially given his name to the so-called (and controversial) 'Meadow Law' where, in the case of these deaths, two is said to be suspicious and three is said to be murder.

Sally Clark was sent to prison after a jury was told that there was a '73 million to one' chance of her two baby boys dying of cot deaths. It has since emerged that both children died at the height of lung epidemics, which was not known at the time of the trial.

The London *Observer* newspaper pointed out that 'The Crown presented no evidence that Clark was a bad mother with a history of violence against her children. Instead the jury heard a welter of contradictory medical evidence that she had shaken or smothered her babies to death – charges virtually impossible to disprove.'

Clark's campaign to clear herself has long received creditable exposure. In May 2002 it was announced that she would not be struck off the roll of solicitors.

The possible reversal of her conviction was seen to have a bearing on the implications around the case of another British mother, Angela Cannings, who was sentenced to life imprisonment for murdering her two baby sons, despite her claims that they were cot deaths.

In April 2002, Winchester Crown Court convicted her of smothering seven-week-old Jason in June 1991 and eighteen-week-old Matthew in November 1999. Charges over the death of Gemma, twelve weeks, who died in 1989, were dropped. Judge Dame Heather Hallett, the mother of two sons, offered an expression of sympathy as she sentenced Cannings, a 38-year-old shop assistant from Salisbury.

'There is no medical evidence before the court to suggest there was anything wrong with you at the time of the deaths of your children. But I have no doubt that for a woman like you to have committed these terrible acts of suffocation of your own babies there must have been something seriously wrong with you. All the evidence indicates that you wanted these babies and you cherished both of them.'

The judge, apparently sensing that postpartum depression was the background to this case, went on to say, 'It's no concidence that these events took place within weeks of you giving birth. There could be no other explanation as to why someone like you committed these acts when you had such a loving and supportive family around you. This in my judgement is a classic kind of injustice that can be caused by mandatory sentencing. In my opinion you will be no threat to anyone else in the future.'

Cannings consistently denied harming her children, and her husband Terry had stood by her. The defence portrayed her as a devoted mother, causing no concern to the health visitors.

The evidence against her was a hospital test that showed somebody had tried to suffocate Jason, but it was not until Matthew died ten years later that suspicion began to fall. A pathologist testified that investigation into both children's deaths reflected suffocation by intentional smothering with a hand or pillow. This was accompanied by the fact that both children had suffered near-death incidents before the final 'cot death'.

As Professor Roy Meadow's opinions about cot-death statistics had done much to condemn Sally Clark, so the professor turned up at the Winchester trial, as an expert paediatrician, telling the court that it would have taken Cannings two minutes to smother her children.

Angela Cannings herself said that she regretted having herself sterilised because otherwise she certainly would have tried for another baby. 'I don't know how or why or what I have done to deserve all this sadness,' she said.

These issues are further complicated by the mothers whose children have genuinely died for no reason but feel responsible, as if they *are* murderers. Bristol mother Michelle Uncles, for instance, developed 'false memory syndrome' through feelings of guilt over the death of her five-month-old baby.

Jade was a victim of cot death in 1989. Ms Uncles was charged with murder after walking into a police station and confessing to the 'crime' six years later.

Dr Christopher Cordess, a forensic psychiatrist, said, 'A lot of mothers whose babies have died in cot death at sometime or other want to take on responsibility of having done it. My view from talking to the accused is that this was the situation in this case.'

Uncles, a single mother, was cleared of murder at a Bristol court. Mark Evans QC, prosecuting, said the post-mortem examination had given rise to 'no suspicion of a direct act' by the defendant.

Infanticide is sometimes addressed in the light of modern feminist thought where proponents emphasise the complexity of the crime and the variants within it. The continual prevalence of female infanticide in overpopulated countries is seen to reflect the most brutal and destructive manifestation of the anti-female bias in 'patriarchal' societies. This is arguably linked to the phenomenon of sex-selective abortion, which targets female fetuses almost exclusively, and/or the neglect of girl children, so that at best they are not fed or educated, at worst they do not make it to adulthood.

Infanticide is also viewed in terms of evolutionary psychology. It is a crime against nature, but it is also a crime of nature, existing in the animal world where birds are thrown out of the nest or pecked to death and where some mammal mothers must protect their babies against older males of their own species.

In the human race infanticide tends to be committed by women, both in the Third and First Worlds, whereas, according to anthropologist Glenn Hausfater, infanticide in non-human primates 'is carried out primarily by migrant males who are unrelated to the infant or its parents and is a manifestation of reproductive competition'.

Scholarly studies conclusively show that infanticide has been practised on every continent and by people on every level of cultural sophistication, from hunters and gatherers to advanced civilisations. In the ancient Arab world, for instance, females were seen as an undesirable burden to a family struggling to survive. A common proverb held that it was 'a generous deed to bury a female child'. Nevertheless, the Koran, which collected the writings of Mohammed, introduced reforms that included the prohibition of female infanticide.

Infanticide is related, in general, to poverty and population control. Since prehistoric times, the supply of food has been a constant check on human population growth. One way to control the lethal effects of starvation was to restrict the number of children allowed to survive to adulthood. Darwin believed that infanticide, 'especially of female infants', was the most important restraint on the proliferation of early man.

The phenomenon of female infanticide remains a concern in a number of Third World countries today and, notably, the two most overpopulated – China and India. Estimates have indicated that 30.5 million females are 'missing' in China, 22.8 million in India, 3.1 million in Pakistan, 1.6 million in Bangladesh, 1.7 million in West Asia, 600,000 in Egypt, and 200,000 in Nepal.

The costs involved with the raising of a girl, and eventually providing her with an appropriate marriage dowry, were the most important factor in allowing social acceptance of the murder at birth in India.

Writing in the *Los Angeles Times* John-Thor Dahlburg pointed out that 'in rural India, the centuries-old practice of female infanticide can still be considered a wise course of action.' He described the case of Lakshmi, a mother living in an impoverished village in the state of Tamil Nadu.

> Lakshmi already had one daughter, so when she gave birth to a second girl, she killed her. For the three days of her second child's short life, Lakshmi admits, she refused to nurse her. To silence the infant's famished cries, the impoverished village woman squeezed the milky sap from an oleander shrub, mixed it with castor oil, and forced the poisonous potion down the newborn's throat. The baby bled from the nose, then died soon afterward.
>
> Female neighbors buried her in a small hole near Lakshmi's square thatched hut of sunbaked mud. They sympathized with Lakshmi and in the same circumstances, some would probably have done what she did. For despite the risk of execution by hanging and about 16 months of a much-ballyhooed government scheme to assist families with daughters, in some hamlets murdering girls is still sometimes believed to be a wiser course than raising them. 'A daughter is always a liability. How can I bring up a second?' Lakshmi, 28, answered firmly when asked by a visitor how she could have taken her own child's life. 'Instead of her suffering the way I do, I thought it was better to get rid of her.'

Her words bear similar resonance to the explanations of impoverished western mothers who, despite their environment, suffer third world deprivation that leads to exactly the same action for exactly the same reason.

One is reminded of Khoua Her. Khoua Her was a Hmong immigrant living in Minnesota. She had suffered abuse in a Thai refugee camp and then in her marriage. She strangled her six children so that they would not have to suffer in the way that she had and she claimed that her act was a loving one. Her attempt to hang herself was unsuccessful and she was sentenced to fifty years in prison.

In China, economics also played a significant role since it is a poor country with one of the lowest rates of agricultural output per acre of arable land in the world. With an extremely high infant and child mortality rate, because of sparse food supply and medical care, a married couple needed to raise three sons in order to ensure the survival of one into adulthood. Females were only consumers and a serious financial burden to a poor family. They were therefore often killed at birth.

The colonists brought infanticide to America from England while at the same time finding that the Indians practised it as well. In 1646 the General Court of Massachusetts Bay had enacted a law where 'a stubborn or rebellious son, of sufficient years and understanding', would be brought before the magistrates in court and 'such a son shall be put to death'. 'Stubborn child laws' were also enacted in Connecticut in 1650, Rhode Island in 1668 and New Hampshire in 1679.

The attitude of rigid parental control over the discipline of children is seen in a comparison to concern over animal welfare. Henry Bergh founded the Society for the Prevention of Cruelty to Animals (SPCA) in 1866. After first completing his campaign to improve the plight of cats and dogs, Bergh brought the case of Mary Ellen to the Supreme Court of New York. He claimed that the child's custodians had beaten her cruelly and that she should be brought under the protection of the court. The resulting publicity led to the founding of the Society for the Prevention of Cruelty to Children.

History, then, has long documented the propensity of parents to murder their children in an assortment of stressful situations. In nineteenth-century England infanticide was so common that a debate over how to correct the problem was carried out in both the lay and medical press. An editorial in the medical journal *The Lancet* noted that 'to the shame of civilization it must be avowed that not a State has yet advanced to the degree of progress under which child-murder may be said to be a very uncommon crime.'

The same could be said today.

Matricide is an altogether less common crime. No matter how tense some mother/daughter relationships become, most women manage to prevent themselves from killing their mothers.

Not so Sabrina Van Schoor. Miss Van Schoor, 22, was the daughter of the South African racist-killer Sybrand Jacobus Lodewikus van Schoor – known as Louis to his friends (and he did have friends, friends who covered up for him for years before his propensity to murder any unarmed black man he felt like murdering came to light), he was finally charged as apartheid collapsed and the South African political climate hauled itself into a more enlightened era.

A former policeman turned security officer, Van Schoor was reported to have shot at 101 people and killed 39. In 1992 he was charged with nineteen murders but convicted for killing seven people (including two teenage boys) and sent to prison for twenty years. His daughter was twelve at the time. In June 2002 she was hailed as a 'heroine' among the black residents of East London for hiring a hit man to slit her racist mother's throat.

Beverly Van Schoor was a successful businesswoman in Queenstown. Her daughter helped her to run her florist business and a bridal boutique. But her friends and her boyfriends were 'coloured', an inclination that caused violent rows between mother and daughter. Beverly beat her daughter and attempted to confine her to only associating with people of whom she approved, white people in other words.

At the age of eighteen Sabrina became pregnant by a 'coloured' boyfriend and her mother made her have an abortion. A year later she became pregnant again. She gave birth to a daughter, Tatum. The child was black and Beverly went berserk.

At the beginning of 2002 Sabrina Van Schoor hired Feza Mdutshane to kill her mother. He walked into Beverly's bedroom and slit her throat with a bread knife. 'Are you sure she is dead?' Sabrina asked him before paying him with her VW Golf and her mother's mobile telephone – items which led police easily to the assassin, who was arrested.

'I did ask him to kill my mother,' Miss Van Schoor told the judge. 'I did it out of anger and to liberate myself.'

SOURCES

the *Guardian*, 25 May 2001, 13 June 2002
the *Observer*, 15 July 2001, 6 January 2002
The Times, 17 April 2002
'Darlie Routier – Doting Mother/Deadly Mother' by
    Joseph Geringer (www.crimelibrary.com)
'Diane Downs – Her Children Got in the Way of Love'
    by Joseph Geringer (www.crimelibrary.com)
'Susan Smith – Child Murderer or Victim?' by Rachel
    Pergament (www.crimelibrary.com)
'A Brief History of Infanticide' (www.infanticide.org)
'True Crimes – The Ultimate Crime Resource'
    (www.karisable.com)

www.CourtTV.com
www.fathers.ca/
www.gendercide.org
www.Time.com

7. YOU CAN RUN BUT YOU CAN'T HIDE

The female terrorist is a woman with ideals in her head and grenades down her bra.

Wafa Idris made world headlines in January 2002 when she calmly left her home in a refugee camp on the West Bank, travelled to a busy shopping centre in the middle of Jaffa Street in west Jerusalem, and blew herself up.

Suicide bombers are common in that part of the world, and thirty had been recorded in the sixteen months leading up to Idris' protest; in the months after they were an almost daily occurrence as the violence in the Middle East escalated throughout the year. But Wafa Idris was a woman, and her cool walk to her own end was seen to symbolise a new radicalisation in the desperation of the Palestinian struggle. It was a radical act – a 10 kg bomb packed into her rucksack.

Wafa Idris was angry, but she was not unstable. She had no history of extremism or fundamentalism; she was not twisted with religious bigotry though various male journalists were quick to point out that she was childless and divorced, the subtext being that if a woman does not have a man or a child her empty life will turn her into a suicide bomber. Most reports described a woman who, though moving in an environment where politicisation starts at birth, was relatively equanimous. She was Muslim but modern in her approach to Islam, willing to wear make-up and unwilling to cover her head. She was not particularly devout and she was not officially affiliated with the militia groups of the Palestine Liberation Organisation.

Yet she blew her body to pieces outside a shoe shop. Her body was so mangled it took two days to identify. An Israeli man was killed and a hundred people were injured.

'Wafa has honoured the family,' said her brother Khalil, who had been imprisoned for eight years for his part as a member of Fatah, Yasser Arafat's nationalist faction of the Palestinian Liberation Organisation that constantly pits itself against the Israeli army. 'Anger turned her into a bomber. She felt that this was a war against Israel in which men and women were equal.'

Idris was intelligent and caring and, judging from her photographs, very attractive. Unfortunately for her, she was also sensitive. She had worked for two and a half years as a volunteer for the Red Crescent emergency service, arriving regularly to help with the victims of the Intifada, the name given to the Palestinian insurrection against Israeli control on the West Bank. She, like most Palestinians, had suffered as a result of a war characterised by fighting in the streets of her neighbourhood. She lived, penniless, in a grim refugee camp; she had been hit by rubber bullets three times and she had been beaten up by Israeli soldiers.

Idris had been particularly appalled by seeing children shot and killed during confrontations. A few weeks before she hit Jaffa Street she had been despatched to help clear up the remains of a man hit by a tank shell, a task which involved collecting his flesh and putting it into a sack. Her friend Mouna Abd Rabo told the *Washington Post*, 'Wafa's work destroyed her psychologically . . . she told me she wanted to do something to the Jews.'

Idris' mother, Wafiyeh, sixty, with whom she had lived in the Amari refugee camp near Ramallah, told various members of the world press that she was proud that her daughter was a martyr. 'She saw Palestinian youths killed and Palestinian people under seige. I hope this is just the beginning.'

Idris' fame was instant, although its aspects were different in different parts of the world, some seeing her as a lethal terrorist, some seeing her as the ultimate heroine. *The Washington Post* described the atmosphere in her native Ramallah:

'They called Wafa Idris' name from the minarets this morning, the loudspeaker's message echoing through the teeming side streets and trash-choked alleys of this squalid Palestinian refugee camp. "All hail Wafa Idris!" boomed the announcer as shoeless children stopped and looked up in wonder. "All hail the first woman to carry out a suicide bombing operation!"'

The Al Aqsa militant faction, part of Palestinian leader Yasser Arafat's movement, published a leaflet saying Wafa Idris had carried out the bombing in response to Israeli military actions. Posters said that she was a heroine of the Aqsa Martyrs Brigade, and she was described by Fatah as 'one of our female fighters'.

Her friends and family commented that Idris had no official connection with these groups; they were cashing in on her reflected 'glory'. Iraqi president Saddam Hussein, an enemy of Israel, called for a statue of Idris to be erected in a square in the middle of Baghdad.

A couple of days after her death thousands of women mourners held a mock funeral in her honour as some Palestinians called for more women to join the battle against Israel. A procession of three thousand marched through Ramallah with an empty wooden casket, led by Rabeeha Thiab, head of the Fatah women's movement. Idris may have scored her place as the first female Palestinian suicide bomber but women have long been involved in the struggle against Israel.

The nature of the struggle on the West Bank means they could hardly fail to be – as an urban struggle it is felt on all levels, whether it is the closure of the schools, the unemployment, the lack of health care, the imposed curfew, or the sight of children – the so-called 'Shebab' street brigades – throwing stones at Israeli soldiers and running away.

The Fatah is well organised, well funded and well equipped to recruit. The various branches, divided into sectors and cells, are found in every village, camp and high school, with strong branches at the universities. Disseminating its ideas of self-sufficient nationalism, the Fatah proactively encourages young people to take up arms and provides them with military training so that it is easy for the 'graduate of Intifada' to step from stones to anti-tank missiles.

Wafa Idris was one of many who had grown up with the culture of struggle where every Palestinian must decide how far they are going to involve themselves in the fight for their nation's independence against a force that is loathed.

Eileen Macdonald, who wrote the 1991 book *Shoot the Women First*, about female terrorists, visited the West Bank in 1989 during the time of the first Intifada. 'Everyone appeared to be involved,' she wrote, 'from stone throwing toddlers to eighty years old, but none more so than the women.'

The Shebab street fighters were an accepted and respected form of resistance and young girls were as much a part of it as boys. They were as quick to attack and as likely to be beaten by soldiers. This was a climate where a fourteen-year-old girl could be put under house arrest and sent to prison for throwing a stone, and where a twelve-year-old girl was breaking the law if she carried a text book to a school that was only open because teachers chose to work there illegally.

As Eileen MacDonald wrote, 'On General Strike days the girls joined the boys in stoning anyone driving a car or attempting to work. The Shebab was a powerful force, the girls possessing as deadly an aim with the stone or Molotov as their brothers.'

The older women, meanwhile, formed an organised resistance movement, providing safe houses, acting as lookouts, hiding weapons underneath their robes, smuggling money, distributing food, organising 'charitable' collectives which were political in their intent to support the Palestinian fight.

MacDonald: 'As the insurrection developed and tens of thousands of men were detained by the military, women took over the fight. With their men gone there was no-one else to do it, but it was more than that. The women became aware of their own importance and they were no longer prepared to be bystanders or widows. Participation was all.'

One woman told her, 'We have made children into fighters at three years old. I wonder what it will be like when they have grown up. I know that they will be full of hatred and bitterness if we do not win.'

It is somewhat surprising, considering these circumstances, that the PLO has not bred a greater number of violently radical women and that terrorism remains an unusual rather than commonplace political choice.

The most famous Palestinian female terrorist is still Leila Khaled, whose popularity rested on her youth, on her beauty, and on the fact that she had not actually murdered anybody. She was the perfect pin-up with her gun and revolutionary credibility; explosives in the handbag, a gun down her pants. She was an icon of the early 70s, a poster girl, up there with Che and the Grateful Dead.

She was young, she was brave, she was bright. She was the perfect frontwoman for the PLO, who wanted to be seen as freedom fighters and not as terrorists. Khaled, born in 1944, was four when her mother evacuated her eight children from their village of Haifa, which was being bombed by the Israelis. Her father joined the resistance and her mother took the family to Lebanon in the hope of providing them with safety. Their departure was delayed when their car was blown up by a shell.

At the age of fourteen she carried food through battle zones to Palestinian fighters. In her twenties she became a member of the illegal Popular Front for the Liberation of Palestine. In 1969, at the age of 25, she decided to join the organisation's military training camp in Jordan. Her mission, the one that made her famous, was accomplished on 29 August 1969 when she and a young male accomplice hijacked an aeroplane flying from Tel Aviv to Los Angeles.

Holding a hand grenade over the pilot's head, Khaled forced him to reroute and land at Damascus airport. 'I felt very calm,' she told Eileen MacDonald. 'But I always feel calm inside myself especially when something violent needs to be done.'

At Damascus airport the passengers were evacuated and Khaled blew the plane up. Held, briefly, by the Syrian authorities, she was then released to return to the PFLP base in Jordan. Accompanied by a cohort of bodyguards, Khaled then became a celebrity 'states-woman' touring the Middle East on behalf of the Palestinian cause.

In 1970, having had extensive plastic surgery to alter her features in an effort to make them unrecognisable, she and an accomplice named 'Patrick' boarded an El Al plane in Amsterdam. 'I had hand grenades down my front and flight plans in my underwear,' she told MacDonald.

The mission to hijack the plane went wrong. She was recognised by a sky marshal and overcome as, carrying grenades in both hands, she tried to kick down the door of the cockpit.

'Patrick' was killed in the struggle and Khaled was beaten within an inch of her life. The plane landed at Heathrow and she was incarcerated at Ealing police station where various men wrote her letters asking her to marry them, and where, angry rather than afraid, she skilfully navigated interrogation and refused to reveal anything that could compromise the PFLP.

Then the PFLP hijacked a British plane, forced it to land at Dawson's Field and held the passengers hostage until Khaled was released from prison. They succeeded in their demands. She was flown to Cairo and the safety of Egypt. From there she returned to her unit in Lebanon and, between combat duties, would tour refugee camps and urge women to join the armed struggle.

In 1982 she married a physician and had two children. In 1999, at the age of 57, she appeared in London where she was interviewed by the *Guardian* newspaper. Asked if she would still die for the Palestinian cause she sucked on a Rothman cigarette and said, 'Of course'.

Khaled's story is different, and happier, than many of those who fought for their causes. Kim Hyon Hui was condemned to a life of house arrest after blowing up a Korean Air Flight in 1987. The 350-gramme bomb killed 115 people, which must make Miss Kim one of the highest scoring murderesses of our time.

She escaped from the aircraft as she had left the device behind in the plane when it stopped to refuel.

She had thought she was on a holy mission. She was said to have been brainwashed. After she was caught she failed in her attempt to commit suicide (she did not bite down on the cyanide capsule properly) and she was subsequently shaken with remorse. This makes her different from other female terrorists, most of whom plant devices with cool aplomb and explain that death is necessary for the progress of the cause.

Miss Kim was a North Korean agent so beautiful she had once been a movie star. Recruited to become a spy while she was at university, she trained for seven years before receiving her mission. She was known as the 'Virgin Terrorist' and enjoyed a status as an Asian sex symbol, made safe by her self-renouncement.

'Our personal lives were to be sacrificed on the altar of reunification of the fatherland,' she said, subsequently. 'I was prepared to die. I saw myself as a bomber pilot who was on a combat mission in the enemy's zone.' Kim was sentenced to death in 1989 by the Seoul government, which later granted her a special pardon. She lives in protective custody, always in danger of being assassinated.

The forces that propel civilians to move between urban mayhem and political struggle on the West Bank and Gaza Strip are similar to those in Belfast. In both places the areas involved are relatively small, combatants live side by side, street by street, while history tells of oppressive authorities and religious schism. Violence leads to violence in localities where everyone knows everyone and it is impossible to forget. All families suffer losses and hatred and deprivation. No one is unaffected.

As street armies gestate on the streets of Ramallah, so too do they on the streets of Belfast, where the IRA recruits in the same way and for similar reasons that the

YOU CAN RUN BUT YOU CAN'T HIDE

Fatah recruits and where British soldiers are attacked in the same way and for similar reasons that Israeli soldiers are attacked – as imperialist invaders who have no right to be there.

There are many parallels between Belfast and Gaza and it is no coincidence that the history of women's roles in both revolutionary processes has reflected similar aspects. In 1916, at the time of the Easter Rising, women were members of Cumann na mBan (the women's army). Involved in intelligence work they would act as couriers on bicycles, concealing weapons underneath their long skirts, secure in the knowledge that they were unlikely to be searched by police.

Women such as Maud Gonne were (and still are) viewed as courageous revolutionaries, poetic figures, dignified, articulate, beauteous and fiery, fighting for women's rights and political rights alike. It was a woman, Mary Ellen Butler, who came up with Sinn Fein (Ourselves Alone) as a name for the burgeoning party.

Today, militant Republican women are seen (by both the British and most of the Irish) as terrorists, the enemies of the English and the Irish alike, fighting for minority beliefs with bombs that kill people in public places. And most recently they have been seen as a serious obstacle to the peace process.

In the 70s, when the British soldiers began to be hated by the Catholics, whom they were supposed to protect, and to be seen as forces of Protestant domination rather than as political allies, the IRA re-emerged as a paramilitary rebel force. It began to successfully recruit new soldiers, often young, often women. They were as driven and as dangerous as any male member of any other underground resistance, but they were never to achieve the glamour bestowed upon other 'freedom fighters'.

During this time, as the struggles escalated, women would lure soldiers to places where they would be shot. Others carried 'baby bombs' in prams into shopping centres. The so-called 'Duck Patrols', night units of British soldiers whose purpose was to conduct arrests and, in the eyes of many Catholics, to invade their homes, were met by a solidarity in which doors were left open to allow for the free movement of hunted men. Women began patrolling the streets to warn the neighbourhoods of army patrols, like a politicised neighbourhood watch scheme. They would blow whistles and bang dustbins lids on the pavement and became known as the 'Hen Patrol'.

Relatives of activists who had been imprisoned set up underground committees to exchange information. Women organised protests against the curfew and what they saw as acts of abuse implemented under the terms of the Special Powers Act.

Women, initially part of a special and separate sector of the IRA, became more active. The unit restructuring was expanded to admit them on an equal base and thus the 'progress' of rights within the underground militia was seen, by those involved, as reflecting the progress of women's emancipation in a more general sphere.

By December 1972, three hundred Republican women had been imprisoned. Nevertheless, when a truce was called in 1975, the females in the Army were not consulted. The website Irelands Own notes, 'For these women who had risked their lives and been arrested just as the men had been, this snub rang clear the politics of gender.'

Subsequently women who had organised themselves, particularly those interned in Armagh prison, made demands on the infrastructure of the IRA and were granted the right to a voice, which was seen as a success against the 'double standardisation of female roles previously held within the IRA'.

'Irish women,' notes Eileen MacDonald, 'wanted to fight, and they wanted to be treated as equals.'

Ireland's legacy had been coloured by the likes of Rose Dugdale, who hijacked a helicopter; Anna Moore who bombed a pub in Derry and killed seventeen people; Marion Coyle who kidnapped an industrialist; Ella O'Dwyer, who was sentenced to life for a plot to bomb sixteen British seaside resorts, and Jennifer McCann who was sentenced to 22 years for the attempted murder of a policeman.

Josephine Hayden was sentenced to six years for being in possession of a shotgun in Dublin in 1995. She was incarcerated in the C wing of Limerick prison, where conditions have been condemned by various civil rights groups and where women, who were in the minority, were supervised by male staff. If trouble broke out in C wing, the 'kickers', ten or twelve of them, would arrive to teach the 'bitches' a lesson.

Hayden suffered two heart attacks that she attributed to these conditions. Released in July 2000 she continues her work as an activist, giving speeches about the conditions in prison and hailed, by some Republicans, as one of their heroines.

Marion Price, born in west Belfast, grew up with activism. Her aunt had had her hands blown off while moving hand grenades. Marion and her sister Dolours, known as the Sisters of Death, were believed to have commanded an IRA cell in London. In 1973 she was jailed for her part in planting four car bombs in London; two of them exploded and two hundred people were injured.

Price, then, was nineteen. 'I have dedicated my life to a cause,' she wrote. 'And because of that I am prepared to die.' In 1980 she received the Royal Prerogative of

Mercy – that is, she was released for humanitarian reasons on the grounds that she was suffering from anorexia nervosa. Her sister Dolours, also released, married the actor Stephen Rea.

Marion Price recently re-emerged as a spokeswoman for the 32 County Sovereignty Committee (see below) and makes public speeches opposing the terms of the peace strategy.

Mairead Farrell, born in Belfast in 1957, joined the IRA when she was eighteen. A middle-class ex-convent schoolgirl, she was unusual in that she did not come from a family blighted by the tragedies of the 'Troubles' despite growing up in the Catholic Falls Road of Belfast. In 1972 she was fifteen and, after Bloody Sunday, developed a political fervour.

In 1976 the IRA launched an offensive in Ulster to protest the removal of political status for its jailed members. Farrell, an 'operative', had already been called in on an assassination. She took part in this wave of bombings and legend has it that when two of her colleagues objected to the shooting of a target on the grounds that he was unarmed, she threatened to have them shot.

On 5 April 1976, with two male terrorists, or 'active servicemen' as they are known in Republican parlance, Mairead Farrell carried a Colt 45 and a suitcase bomb into the Conway Hotel in Dublin. She was caught as she ran away. Two hours later the bomb exploded. Three days later she was in Armagh prison. She was given a sentence of fourteen years.

As the first Republican woman to be refused political status, Farrell devoted her term to leading organised protests and teaching classes in Irish and politics. In 1980 she engineered the 'dirty protest'. Locked in their cells for 23 hours a day, two to a cell, the women refused to slop out. They smeared faeces on the walls and did not wash. The windows were boarded up to stop them emptying pots into the yard below so they sat in dark bare rooms surrounded by their own filth.

Released in 1986, she took part in the IRA operation to attack Gibraltar and, to this end, landed on the Rock with Sean Savage and Danny McCann in March of that year. All three were shot in an SAS ambush. An eye-witness testified that Mairead and McCann, seeing guns pointed at them, raised their hands in surrender. As a consequence, in 1995, the European Court of Human Rights decided that the three terrorists were unlawfully killed in breach of Article 2 of the European Convention of Human Rights. 'I hope I am still alive when the British are driven out,' she once said.

Evelyn Glenholmes, an Irish terrorist, was suspected of being involved in several IRA bombings, but she dodged the Special Branch officials chasing her through the streets of Dublin in 1986. She went on the run to Cuba where she was suspected of having engaged in various clandestine activities on behalf of the Republican cause before Tony Blair, as part of the peace negotiations, allowed her to go home to Belfast in 2000.

The new face of Republican zeal has metamorphosed. She is no longer the 1916 revolutionary, wearing combat coat and Colt, she is a woman in cardie and pearls with a cup of tea. She is articulate, intelligent and knows how to make friends with students – a middle-aged activist with children and grandchildren. She is a woman like Rita O'Hare, once imprisoned for the attempted murder of two British soldiers, who went on to edit a Republican newspaper.

Bernadette Sands-McKevitt has a safe 'mumsy' appearance and she would be wise to cultivate such an image, for she and her husband Michael McKevitt have been linked to the Real IRA, a savage (and very unpopular) militia, who were responsible for a bomb in Omagh in 1998 which killed 29 people.

The Real IRA was formed in October 1997 as a splinter group who objected to the cease-fire and to the Provisional IRA alliance with the peace settlement. They announced their intention to continue with the armed struggle in the name of British withdrawal and Irish sovereignty.

Bernadette Sands-McKevitt founded the 32 County Sovereignty Committee in December the same year. The intention was to strive for British withdrawal and full independence, a political aim that she believed her brother Bobby Sands had sacrificed himself for when he starved to death in the hunger strike at the Maze prison in 1981. In 1998 Bernadette was described by the *Boston Globe* as gracious and modest, wearing an understated suit and looking like 'one of the yuppies who have done well in Ireland's booming economy'.

'I have three small children and I run a business,' she told the reporter. 'Explain to me in God's name where would I find the time to be in the IRA and why would I even want to?'

After the Omagh bomb the McKevitts moved their three children out of their home in Dundalk following protests from local townspeople and, a week or so later, Ms McKevitt was escorted from the premises of her shop The Print Junction, in a nearby shopping centre, following pressure from other traders which threatened to escalate into a 'breach of the peace'. Her solicitor, meanwhile, announced that he was advising her to issue proceedings for defamation against various members of the press.

Three years later, in March 2001, Michael McKevitt was arrested in Dundalk and charged with being a member of the Real IRA and with directing paramilitary activity. At the time of writing he is in prison awaiting trial in Dublin.

Japanese terrorist Fusako Shigenobu evaded the authorities for twenty years before she was finally arrested in Osaka in November 2000. She had checked into a hotel disguised as a man, but was recognised by officials thanks to her distinctive style of smoking a cigarette – she held it like a pipe and blew smoke rings.

The leader of the Japanese Red Army was particularly wanted in regard to her suspected involvement with the 1974 siege of the French embassy in The Hague. Shigenobu, nicknamed the 'Empress', was once a beauty who propounded free love and anti-imperialism. These philosophies, which earned her the status of icon among left-wing radicals, formed part of a field of human ideas which was a great deal more popular in the 60s and 70s then it is now.

As one Japanese news agency commented, 'To many Japanese who experienced the student protest movements in the 60s, Shigenobu was an extraordinary figure.' Her beautiful long black hair had become indelibly imprinted in the minds of her generation. Photographed on the bullet train to Tokyo, the middle-aged woman raised her shackled hands to give the thumbs up sign. The impression was of a 'highly spirited grandmother'.

Shigenobu, having dropped out of Meiji University, founded the Japanese Red Army in 1971. Her goal? Worldwide communist revolution. This was to be achieved by an armed uprising intended to overthrow the Japanese government and monarchy. In order to orchestrate this optimistic plan, Shigenobu entered Lebanon and made friends with the Popular Front for the Liberation of Palestine. Here she fell in love with a guerrilla and, in 1973, bore a daughter, Mei.

In 1972 the JRA attacked Tel Aviv airport and killed 26 people. In 1973 they blew up an empty plane in Libya. The following year they blew up an oil refinery in Singapore and in 1975 they raided various embassies in Kuala Lumpur and held 53 hostages in exchange for jailed JRA members. In 1977 they hijacked a plane and received six million dollars ransom. In 1986 they implemented a mortar attack on three embassies in Jakarta and in 1987 they launched rockets on two embassies in Rome. The following year they bombed an army club in Naples and killed five people.

By the end of the 80s the JRA's funds had dried up, there were fewer safe havens and its members had aged. Preceding the arrest of Ms Shigenobu, three JRA members had already been taken into custody after they were expelled from Lebanon. Mei Shigenobu was interviewed at the time of her mother's arrest. Having broken her cover, she was working as a teacher in Tokyo. It could not have been easy knowing that Mossad was after your mum, but Mei remained loyal. The 24-year-old described her childhood as a 'very nice experience', despite the fact that it was lived in war-torn Lebanon under a false identity, despite the fact that there was not always quite enough to eat, and despite the fact that she rarely saw her mother who was busy elsewhere, blowing things up.

Just as the authorities were slow to find Fusako Shigenobu, so too did they take twenty years to find Sara Jane Olson, who had spent her life living as a suburban 'mom' in Minnesota before she was arrested in 1999 and charged with activities connected to terrorist acts committed by the Symbionese Liberation Army in the 70s.

The SLA were most famous for kidnapping Patty Hearst and demanding that her rich family give $6 million to the poor. Hearst then took up a gun and joined them in the robbery of a San Francisco bank in 1974. Captured, she claimed that she had been raped and brainwashed. She was sent to prison for seven years, served two and received a pardon from President Clinton.

Olson, originally known as Kathleen Soliah, was sent to prison for twenty years in January 2002 for her part in a plot to blow up a pair of police cars in Los Angeles, charges for which she had been indicted in 1976.

Voices of Guns, a 1977 history of the Symbionese Liberation Army by Paul Avery and Vin McLellan, noted that the Soliah family were middle-class and conservative.

'Kathy's vita was resplendent with teenage honors: Girl Scout counselor, junior high yearbook editor, churchgoer, "pep chairman" for Palmdale High, from which she would graduate with honors.'

She studied theatre at the University of California and dated James Kilgore, who has been charged with murder and who is still a fugitive. At that time he was an economics major and, like many of their contemporaries, the couple became engaged in demonstrations against the Vietnam war. Ever more radical, Soliah joined the Food Conspiracy, a commune who pooled their money to buy organic produce from local farmers.

Acting in the local theatre she met and made friends with Angela Atwood, who was to become a founding member of the SLA. Atwood then died in a police shoot-out and her death was said to have crystallised Soliah's militancy.

As the police had launched a search for the SLA after their various acts, she fled to Zimbabwe where she taught English and met her husband Dr Fred Peterson. They returned to America to live in the St Paul suburb of Minnesota. Here she led a normal life, raising three daughters, and even engaged in an unsuccessful campaign to make her husband mayor.

In May 1999 the television programme *America's Most Wanted* featured a story about the SLA and a reward was offered for capture of the members. A month later police picked the 52-year-old mother up while she was driving her minivan near her house in St Paul.

At the time of writing she is also due to answer a murder charge pertaining to the death of Myrna Opsahl, who was shot dead when the SLA robbed a bank in California in 1975 and made off with $15,000. Mrs Opsahl's son, Jon, who was fifteen at the time of her murder, told reporters that he never gave up on the idea of bringing his mother's killers to justice. He was particularly haunted by a comment made by one of the robbers, quoted in Patty Hearst's autobiography, that his mother's death did not matter since she was a 'bourgeois pig'. Olson has said that she is innocent of this charge and that she was not involved in this robbery.

Basque terrorists have long conducted a campaign in Spain. The underground organisation's unremitting and regular acts of lethal violence have created as many problems for the Spanish as the IRA have for the English and Irish. Women have long been an intrinsic part of Eta. One shot a politican in the face (but did not kill him) in San Sebastian in September 2000. Another was seen to be the getaway driver for the two assassins who shot a town councillor in Barcelona. A woman named Josefina Mercedes Ernaga was sentenced to 1,588 years in prison for her part in the bombing of a supermarket, which killed 21 people.

Euskadi Ta Askatasuma (Basque Homeland and Freedom) was formed in 1958 to fight for a separate socialist Basque state. The participants believe that the Basque people are the oldest nation in Europe; they have their own language, Euskara. The separatist campaigns fared badly under the oppressive Franco dictatorship, but when the Fascist leader died in 1975, Eta rejuvenated itself.

Since then, against the opprobrium of both Basque moderates and of the Spanish population, the group is thought to have killed between eight hundred and a thousand people.

In the year 2000 Spanish authorities told reporters that Eta had been taken over by a woman. Maria Soledad Iparaguirre Genetxea named herself 'Anboto' after a mountain in the Basque country. As leader of its executive committee she is considered to be the principal strategist of this violent underground organisation.

Thought to be 39 and known to be a beauty, Anboto's appointment followed the capture of Ignacio Gracia Arregui, who was arrested at gunpoint by a French antiterrorist squad. She was seen to represent a re-hardening of the Eta stance after a fourteen-month cease-fire (begun in 1998) and negotiations with the Spanish government.

The Spanish Prime Minister, Jose Maria Aznar, had pressured moderate Basque nationalists to cut links with the radicals that sympathised with the terror campaigns of Eta.

Anboto has been a member of Eta since she was a teenager and her commitment hardened in 1981 when her boyfriend was killed by security forces. Since then she has been very active, on one occasion spraying a police patrol and Spanish television crew with machine-gun fire before she escaped to Basque safe houses in

France. She is suspected of killing fourteen people in a ten-year career of car bombs and machine-gun attacks and is also thought to have planned the assassination attempt against King Juan Carlos when he opened the Guggenheim Museum in Bilbao in 1997. As a member of the Eta commando unit operating in Madrid, she was one of a number of women who included Belen Gonzalea Penalva and Rosario Delgado Iriondo. A police officer has described her as 'a vixen whose wiles have kept her from being captured'.

Eta is efficient, it is rich, and it proactively seeks very young people to join its army – forging strong links with the radical youth movements and in particular Jarrai, which is also run by a woman, Anne Lizarralde.

Eta is technologically sophisticated, knowing as much about explosives as the authorities against which it is warring, and able, for instance, to detonate a bomb with a mobile phone, meaning that the guerrilla does not need to be near the scene of the explosion. These advantages did not come into play in July 2001 when 22-year-old Olaia Castresana accidentally blew herself up with a 4 lb bomb in an apartment block near Alicante. Police later found bombs and plans that indicated Eta were planning to target tourist areas – an obvious enough strategy since it causes the most disruption that it is possible to cause to a country whose economy relies on this industry.

Revolution, once hailed as a worthy cause, and often dignified by the pursuits of thinking women, has long lost its charisma and, nowadays, hardly manages to achieve even the glamour of nostalgia. Revolution no longer means a struggle for equality and freedom; it means terrorism.

Author Walter Laqueur attempted to describe the 'terrorist personality' in his book *The New Terrorism*.

'Investigations have shown that women terrorists are more fanatical and have a greater capacity for suffering. Their motivation is predominately emotional and can not be shaken through intellectual argument.'

He might also have mentioned that women are more subtle than men; more instinctual and thus better at hiding. They do not feel the need to macho it out with counterintelligence. They do not go to their 'regular' pub, get drunk and boast about their exploits (which has been the downfall of many a criminal, terrorist and otherwise). Feminine intuition senses danger and feminine cunning plans the best escape route. She is good at getting away with it.

Anthony Storr, in his book *On Human Aggression*, repeats the historian Gibbon's point that 'deplorable manifestations of aggression share identical roots with the valuable and essential parts of human endeavour.' That is, the instincts that produce anger are an essential asset to human survival. Intelligently harnessed they can produce change. In the arena of politics and oppression, where truth is entirely dependent on individual perspective, a female terrorist sees herself as a goodly warrior. Overreaching the traditional characteristics of female anger (manifest in the protection of children or the fight for a male) to achieve a higher cause, she exhibits a selfless courage that supersedes her gender. The paradox is, of course, in the nature of her battle, whose end result is a destruction that obliterates any honour implicit in her intentions.

SOURCES

Laqueur, Walter, *The New Terrorism: Fanaticism and the Arms of Mass Destruction*, Oxford University Press, New York, 1999

MacDonald, Eileen, *Shoot the Women First*, Fourth
    Estate, London, 1991
Storr, Anthony, *On Human Aggression*, Bantam Books,
    London, 1970
www.IrelandsOwn.com

8. SHE MADE ME DO IT

Team killers and deadly duos – but are the blokes always to blame?

The annals of crime do not support the archetype in which society still likes to believe – that is, woman as evil seductress and tempter to sin who, as described by Christian lore, is so evil she will contaminate any innocent man who has the misfortune to come upon her. Eve, as entity, remains alive as a primal character of the collective unconscious cultivated by fear and misogyny, but not actually apparent as a common, recognisable phenomenon, eternally reappearing in the patterns of biocriminology.

Nevertheless, there are Eves about the place, encouraging, supporting, subverting, hiding, killing – enjoying a symbiotic frenzy of savagery with their husbands and lovers – showing themselves as able to help him throw a body into a ditch as to cook him up a chicken pot pie.

The last twenty years of insupportable acts committed by duos tend to reveal the woman pleading as a supplicant. 'I killed because I was scared of him' goes the common cry. Evidence, and there always seems to be a wealth of it, often supports the conclusion that she was doing far more than loving, honouring and obeying.

Charlene Gallego received only sixteen years for aiding her brutish spouse Gerald in the murder of ten people. Gerald Gallego was a California-born career criminal who, delinquent by the age of six, married five times before settling for Charlene. She would helpfully procure women for him on the order, 'I want a girl, get up!'

Gerald, with his wife's encouragement, would then rape (at gunpoint) and kill the various unfortunates that she managed to lure into the Nevada desert. One, 21-year-old Linda Aguilar, was four months pregnant. Another, Virginia Mochel, having suffered his assault, actually begged him to kill her. Forensics showed that the lovely Charlene had bitten the breasts off more than one victim and had forced them to provide her with sexual satisfaction before her husband killed them. When one man interfered with an abduction, she punched him in the face.

The law finally caught up with them in 1980 when a witness noted their numberplate. Charlene copped a plea. She was released from a Nevada prison, at the age of forty, in 1997. Gallego, meanwhile, having escaped the death sentence, was, in 1999, declared to be mentally incompetent. A doctor counselled that he had suffered from brain damage caused by the head injuries sustained during an abusive childhood. Surprise, surprise: evil is mundane in its secular reality.

Paul Bernardo and Karla Homolka showed a similar pattern. They were known as the 'Barbie and Ken' murderers because they were both unusually good-looking in the bottle-blonde way that Americans revere. Based in Toronto, Canada, they had married in 1992 and remained a convincing, happy, yuppie couple until the day that Karla appeared at her parents' house with two black eyes and was persuaded to go to the police.

The cops told her that forensic evidence had come through which showed that Paul Bernardo was the 'Scarborough Rapist' who had terrorised the neighbourhood of Scarborough, near Toronto, in the 80s. Nineteen women had been raped at knifepoint.

Karla got herself a lawyer and used her battered face to serve her ends. It was only a matter of time before the police in Ontario, where she lived, would start to look more closely at the cases of the teenage girls whose bodies had been dumped in the neighbourhood.

Paul Bernardo, once a cute boy scout with angelic looks, had turned into a psychopath whose preferred recreation was anal rape. A scam merchant with a homicidal temper, he was only interested in sexually submissive women and, in 1987, that is what he got. He and Karla Homolka quickly became sexually obsessed with each other, sharing each other's tastes for advanced sado-masochism.

He would tie her up and beat her, but it wasn't enough. His imagination knew no limit, and nor did his compulsion to find stimulation that travelled far beyond the borders of SM foreplay. This was not dressing up in leather and larking about. This was murder.

The first victim, in 1990, was Karla's fourteen-year-old sister, Tammy, whom she drugged in order to allow her lover to rape the girl. Tammy, unfortunately, choked on her own vomit and died. Later, in a letter to her parents, Karla claimed, 'He (Paul) wanted me to get sleeping pills from work to drug her with. He threatened me physically and emotionally abused me when I refused. I don't expect you to ever forgive me, for I will never forgive myself.'

Then there was Jane, aged fifteen, who hero-worshipped Karla as, at 21, she was older and more sophisticated. Jane was most unfortunate in her choice of role model. Karla gave her to Paul as a Christmas present on 23 December 1990. They drugged her and videotaped the action as he forced himself into the comatose teenager's anus.

Fourteen-year-old Leslie Mahaffy had the misfortune to encounter Bernardo in the dark in 1991. He pulled a knife on her, took her home and filmed her as she lay naked and blindfolded. Then Karla took the camera and directed the actions as her husband anally raped the teenager.

Mahaffy's body was found in Lake Gibson, her braces a clue to her final identification. In 1992 Kristen French was filmed and tortured for two days before her body was dumped in a ditch. Karla's voice can be heard on the film. 'Suck him now, Kristen,' she says. 'Now use your hand. Yeah. Good girl.'

Bernardo strangled Kristen French while his wife watched. It took seven minutes. Then she went downstairs to blow-dry her hair. Karla Homolka, manipulative and intelligent, managed to command leniency and a relatively short prison sentence (twelve years) in return for telling the authorities everything she knew about the atrocities committed by her husband. He was to later say, 'I thought she was strong-willed and independent and a little weird.'

Her defence, in 1993, was that she was so frightened that she bent to his will, though the gruesome facts of the crimes rarely supported her – it merely supported an extraordinary level of savage amorality and bloodless narcissism combined with a genius for dissimulation. The fact of the matter was that she had colluded in murders two years before marrying the man who had supposedly bullied her into these conspiracies. She had smothered her sister with Halothane at her parents' house. An audio cassette recording of Tammy's end revealed her order to Bernardo to 'hurry up' to 'put a condom on' and, finally, to concede to performing cunnilingus on Tammy, who was menstruating at the time. All these 'festivities' were carefully documented on video and audio, for they were the product of the digital age, and this compulsion to voyeurism was to provide a hideous testimony against them in exactly the same way that it had against Ian Brady and Myra Hindley and the Wests.

Three weeks after Tammy's death the video camera again filmed the lovers. 'I loved it when you fucked my little sister,' says Karla. A 'little weird' went a long way.

Nevertheless, a psychologist making a report for her plea-bargain concluded that she 'knew what was happening but she felt totally helpless and unable to act in her own defence or in anyone else's defence. She was, in my opinion, paralysed with fear and in that state became obedient and self-serving.'

During her trial Mrs Bernardo was described as wearing false eyelashes, deep red lipstick, and heavily caked foundation that made her look like a 'matronly Lolita'. Nevertheless, as Patricia Pearson comments in her book *When She Was Bad*, reporters were 'literally unable to perceive Homolka as a sex offender'.

Pearson concludes that Homolka benefited from 'chivalry justice': 'Within our culture we are not taught to view well-mannered pretty young women as possible criminals. Certainly we are unable to see a woman who has been battered, if only once, by her husband as having been an equal in harming someone else ... A woman who has been hit, a good woman, good looking, white, middle class, cannot possibly be culpable in her own right.'

Paul Bernardo's trial in 1995 opened with the prosecution claiming that he had reduced his wife to a compliant victim through relentless physical and mental abuse, and had then exploited her. The opening speech was followed by the presentation of a video showing Karla masturbating herself. This, claimed the attorney, was evidence of Bernardo's control of his wife – she had been his sex slave, he argued, and would do anything to realise his sexual fantasies.

Karla then took the stand against her husband and described their marital years of untrammelled deviance, whereupon his defence lawyer attempted, with some success, to show that she was not the victim that she purported to be, but a vacuous bitch untroubled by remorse.

Paul Bernardo was sentenced to life in prison.

In March 2001 Karla Homolka was denied parole, which came as something of a relief to the parents of the teenage girls who had suffered so much. They doubtless agreed with the board report that described her acts as 'monstrous' and said that the public was in danger from a woman whose violent sexual impulses suffered no control.

Society never forgets women like Karla Homolka. Their crimes are so often committed as a part of the drama of love, inextricably bound up in a savage but intractable union, where there are passions with which it is possible to relate.

Who, rejected, has not wanted to harm a thoughtless lover?

Who has not loathed a rival?

Who has not played with sexual fantasy?

The human mind is not full of pure thoughts but, luckily for what we laughingly describe as society, the human person does not tend to act them out. You can read more about Karla Homolka in the final chapter.

Martha Beck remains a grand dame of classic crime, fascinating to observers if only because her obesity and ugliness led people to wonder how a woman so unaligned with the cultural expectations of beauty could become a seductress. And not only a seductress, but one who succeeded in persuading her lover, Raymond Fernandez, to commit serial murder.

Born Martha Seabrook in 1919, Beck's first affliction was to mature fast and gain excess weight. By the time she was twelve she had a woman's body and an abnormal sex drive, which was not helped by her brother who raped her when she was thirteen. Martha's mother's reaction to this incident was to beat her daughter and blame her for it.

Martha became a nurse, as crime's most dysfunctional women so often do, and, while working in an army hospital in California, took to having sex with any spare soldiers that were hanging about the place.

In 1944, pregnant, she married a truck driver named Alfred Beck, but divorced him soon afterwards. Working in a hospital in California she became involved in lonely hearts columns and, through these, met Raymond Fernandez.

Fernandez had once suffered a head injury, the classic wound of the serial killer – research has shown that damage to the frontal lobe can destroy impulse control. Fernandez, a conman and unstable, had an interest in voodoo and believed he was possessed of powers that gave him magical influence over women.

She was 26 with a treble chin; he had gold teeth and a toupee. He told her that he was a rich businessman and she fell in love with him. He allowed her to move in, but persuaded her to despatch her two children back to Florida.

His business involved seducing rich women. She suggested that they kill them. They killed more than twenty women in two years. Raymond's unpleasant modus operandi was to pick up women who advertised in the lonely hearts columns who, already vulnerable, fell prey to his attentions and often handed over their money to him.

In 1948 Mrs Janet Fay, a widow, gave Raymond $6,000 and moved to Long Island to live with him and Martha, who posed as his sister. Mrs Fay was clubbed to death and her body was buried in the cellar of a rented house in Queens, New York.

Mrs Delphine Dowling, who had also been writing letters to Fernandez, allowed him and Martha to move in with her and her two-year-old daughter Rainelle, in Michigan.

Fernandez proceeded to have sex with Mrs Dowling, to the fury of Martha, whose fury was dangerous, and, in this case, erupted into her overpowering her rival and forcing sleeping pills down her throat, aided by Fernandez. He then shot the woman in the head and, two days later, Martha drowned the screaming child in the bath.

Neighbours had reported that they had not seen mother and child for some time and the police arrived to find two bodies in the basement and an unremorseful couple.

Fernandez laughed as he admitted to seventeen murders while Beck boasted to police that she was the reason for them. Her man was so in love with her, he would do anything for her.

They were extradited to New York, where there was a death penalty, and the lovers enjoyed the fame of media frenzy. The mob wrestled with each other to get into the Bronx courtroom to see performances that rarely disappointed. On one occasion Martha threw her arms around Raymond, covering his grinning face with blotches of red lipstick, and shouting, 'I love him and always will!'

They were both executed in the electric chair in 1951, satisfying the appetites of their audience to the end by loud declarations of mutual love.

She wrote in one letter, 'My story is a love story. But only those tortured by love can know what I mean. I am not unfeeling, stupid or moronic, I am a woman who had a great love and will always have it. Imprisonment

SHE MADE ME DO IT

in the Death House has only strengthened my love for Raymond.'

Fernandez' last written words were, 'I want to shout it out. I love Martha. What do the public know about love?'

Sante Kimes had much in common with Martha Beck. She was fat – described by one court reporter as a 'shapeless blob' – she was manipulative, and she knew how to provide for the sensual needs of her men. Like Beck she was supposed to have suffered serious sexual abuse when she was very young and, like Beck, she also married a confidence trickster, managed him, over-powered him and led him to greater crimes than he might otherwise have committed.

Mrs Kimes was so good at persuading people to do as she wished that there were members of her husband's family who genuinely thought she practised black magic.

She was powerful and amoral. Domination and enslavement interlaced as a motif throughout her bizarre life. She was not personable. She was not attractive. Quite the opposite, in fact: she was cruel, and 'without her wig and make-up she was not a pretty sight'. Nevertheless people bowed to her will and could not break free from her. Her husband Kenneth could not and her son Kenny could not.

Kenny shared a bed with mom and he came to perform every crime that she suggested. But then Kenny had grown up in her shadow. There were many who said he never had a chance with a mother like Sante; a mother from hell. In May 2000 they were at the centre of a sensational court case in New York where they were accused of murdering Irene Silverman, an old lady who rented out the rooms of her upper-east-side house.

The body of Mrs Silverman was never found, confessions were never made, but the Kimes went down anyway and, on the way, their bizarre lifestyle came to light. They were quickly dubbed 'Mommie and Clyde'.

'She is indeed a scary woman,' one court reporter noted. 'Between rounds of evidence she picks out members of the press and public and fixes them with a cold sharp stare from her jet black eyes, deep-set beneath broad-brush black eyebrows.'

The jury heard much circumstantial evidence from various witnesses. Prosecutors said that Kenny Kimes, using the pseudonym Manny Guerin, plotted with his mother to steal Silverman's $5 million house.

They were arrested in Utah on the day that Mrs Silverman disappeared – 5 July 1998 – when they were accused of using a bad cheque to buy a Lincoln Town Car. A police search revealed two loaded guns, several wigs, $30,000 cash, and a 'date-rape' drug. There were also cassettes that had apparently been made by tapping Mrs Silverman's telephone conversations, and a forged deed purporting to transfer her property to the Kimeses.

The couple's chauffeur Jose Alvarez, meanwhile, testified that Sante and Kenny slept in the same bed, and the possiblities of their psychosexual union were evinced by their behaviour in court.

'Mother and son whispered to each other during the proceedings as if they were sweethearts,' wrote one reporter.

'I think my mother is a beautiful person,' Kenny told the American news programme *60 Minutes*. 'Spiritually and intellectually. And physically.'

Sante Kimes was the daughter of a prostitute and, consequently, grew up wild on the streets of Los Angeles until she was adopted by a childless couple from Nevada. Married twice before the age of 27, she finally ended up in LA where she alternated between prostitution and petty crime. Always able to exhibit the con-woman's mixture of amorality and nerve, she once walked into a car showroom, asked to test drive a Cadillac and never drove it back.

In 1971, when she was 36, she met 54-year-old Kenneth Kimes, a hustler who had conned his way to a fortune of ten million dollars. Sante, deploying the geisha skills that she had doubtless gleaned from her own mother and her own experience on the street, lured Kenneth with the kind of attention that men seem to like. She would stir his whiskey with her little finger; she had her perfume made to the scent of his favourite flower. That kind of thing. And he fell for it, as men do.

After four years together their son Kenny Jr was born into a household where, as author Adrian Havill has written in his book *The Mother, The Son, and the Socialite*, 'mother and father both loved to steal and con just for the thrill of it'.

Kenny Sr was 'operated as if he was a marionette' by his wife. He was drunk most of the time, while Sante's dishonesty ranged from dressing up as an old woman in order to con better prices while out shopping, to stealing fur coats, to burning down her own houses to claim the insurance money.

Most bizarre, though, was her practice of bringing impoverished girls from Mexico to work for her. She would incarcerate illegal immigrants in her house in California, pay them nothing and beat them. All of which was observed by her young son.

Finally the young women braved the threat of deportation and reported the goings on. Mr and Mrs Kimes were charged with 'conspiracy to violate slavery laws'. The girls told their stories and revealed their scars – one had been branded by a hot iron – and Sante was sentenced to five years in prison. Her husband got away with a $70,000 fine and agreed to enter rehab to be treated for advanced alcoholism.

Sante's cruelty knew few limits and she tended to pick victims characterised by defencelessness. One homeless man, employed to be the gardener, was driven back across town and handed an envelope with his 'wages', only to find that it was empty, and Sante gone.

An elderly aunt was kept in a locked room. When rescued by her family and placed in a nursing home it was found that part of her vagina had been sewn up with black thread.

Kenny was isolated from children his own age and taught by a series of tutors.

'Kenny didn't get enough exposure to other people and other families to know what was normal and what wasn't,' one acquaintance was to tell a newspaper.

'That kid didn't stand a chance,' said one of the scores of attorneys employed by the family.

When Sante went to prison on the slavery charge in 1985, Kenny went to school for five years. He lived with his father and went to McDonalds and nearly became 'normal'. Then, when he was fifteen, mommy came home. They had a physical fight and she won. From that point on he did not even try to get away. Then she started to murder people.

Elmer Holmgren was a lawyer who had, on her orders, burned their house in Hawaii to the ground. He got caught and started working against the Kimes, gathering evidence for the cops. In 1991 he went on holiday to Costa Rica with the Kimes family and never came back. His disappearance was to be followed, later, by the disappearance of Sayed Bilal Ahmed, a banker based in the Bahamas who had become suspicious of Sante's illegal pilfering of her late husband's bank accounts. In 1998 the bullet-riddled body of the 53-year-old businessman David Kazdin was found dead in a dumpster near Los Angeles airport. His name had been used on fraudulent documents by the Kimes and he was threatening to take them to the authorities.

Sante and Kenny Kimes were both sent to prison for over a hundred years for the murder of Irene Silverman despite the lack of any forensic evidence. Kenny screamed for his mother as he was hauled away.

'Sante Kimes is surely the most degenerate defendant who has ever appeared in this courtroom,' said the judge, Justice Rena Uviller. 'Her son, too, has become a remorseless predator.'

Some months after Kenny Jr was sent to prison, he attacked a female interviewer from Court TV with a Biro and held her hostage for four hours before being wrestled to the ground by prison officials.

Kent Walker, Sante's other son by her second husband Edward Walker, had, at times, tried to extricate his half-brother from their mother's clutches. But, at some point around Kenneth Sr's death of a heart attack in 1994, Kenny started to collude with all Sante's activities, and Kent realised that he had become 'borderline insane'.

Kent Walker wrote a book detailing their childhood years – a saga of cruelty and dishonesty summarised by the story of the afternoon that Sante took ten-year-old Kent shoplifting and, when caught, secretly punched him in the face in order to deflect the blame from herself to the store manager whom she then accused of the assault.

Screaming, she pointed to the blood running down the child's face. The police let her go and arrested the store manager. That was the thing about Sante: she always got caught. And it was when she got caught that she became really dangerous.

Sante Kimes was described, through the various legal proceedings and uncountable newspaper stories, variously as an 'incredible manipulator', 'a skilled actress and liar' and a woman with 'deep-seated psychological problems'.

Kent Walker wrote of her: 'I think she had a manic desire to control everything, and she had to create chaos in everyone's life to satisfy her addiction to attention.'

Sante Kimes' addiction to attention must have been well satisfied when it was announced that Mary Tyler Moore was to play her in a CBS television film. The actress, not an obvious choice to play a psycho, spent a day in Rikers Island prison researching the character of Sante. She discovered that the people there liked her, both the guards and the inmates – the younger women called her 'mom'. But, for every relationship, there was a price – Sante was always negotiating for more chits to spend in the commissary, more telephone time and so on.

'I was attracted to the story before the script was written,' Tyler Moore said in an interview to promote the film. 'I felt a kinship in some way. I don't know what it is.'

And Kenny? 'Their relationship is very complicated to say the least and I think there was a sexual attraction. I think it was a part of the manipulation that allowed her to function, having her son really in the palm of her hand.'

As Momma Kimes managed to hold her Kenny in a vicelike Freudian grip, so in Texas, Diane Zamora managed to propel her boyfriend David Graham to murder. Diane Zamora, at seventeen, on the face of it, was not a homicidal maniac, nor did she seem to be a siren with the power to lure men to the penitentiary.

She appeared to be a quiet student, from a Mexican-American family, reserved and religious, who wanted to work for NASA. She was a virgin when she met David Graham and, though most authorities would not hold this against her, or see it as an incipient sign of insanity, Diane Zamora's precious virginity was to play an important part in the fatal battering of Adrianne Jones.

Diane Zamora's goal was to train at a military academy and, to this end, at the age of fourteen, she enrolled in classes in the Civil Air Patrol based at Fort Worth, near her home town of Crowley-on-Gatlinburg in Texas. Here she met David Graham, a buzz-cut jock-type who wore combat fatigues, carried a gun, and wanted to join the air force.

Three years later they started dating and soon announced their engagement. Zamora surrendered her body. Their marriage would be in the year 2000, after they had graduated from their respective military academies.

Then David Graham made a mistake. He fell for the charms of Miss Adrianne Jones, a blonde cheerleader who seduced him in his car. It was a one-night stand, but Graham, feeling guilty, confessed to his fiancée, who immediately convulsed into the violent enactment symptomatic of a borderline personality.

Diane Zamora was more complex than she appeared; she had been disturbed by her father's infidelities and she had a history of cutting herself. She was far from stable. She herself, in a confession to the police, described the scene that followed her boyfriend's revelation.

'I remember reaching out for this big brass thing, this brass rod, and aiming for him and trying to hit him because I was so upset. He took it away from me and tried to calm me down because I was screaming so hysterically . . . I kept ramming my head into the floor trying to crack my skull, I just didn't want to live with what he had said to me.

'I screamed at him "Kill her! Kill her!" He was just so scared that he wasn't about to say no to me. I was still banging my head against the floor. All David wanted to do was make everything better. It seemed like him agreeing to do that was the only thing that calmed me down. David promised me he would do that and David never has broken a promise to me before.'

So, from 2 December to 4 December, David Graham and Diane Zamora planned the murder of Adrianne Jones. The idea was to break her neck and sink her body to the bottom of a local lake.

Graham rang the girl at home and asked her for a date. She snuck out of her house after the parental curfew and he picked her up. Diane hid in the back of the Mazda Protégé.

'I remember wanting to turn back,' Diane wrote in her confession. 'I was afraid to move so I just lay still in the trunk. David later told me he felt the same way, that he wanted to turn back and take her home, but he was afraid of what I would do or say if he turned back.'

David Graham's fear of his girlfriend was greater than his fear of shooting a person in the head. Diane screamed at him to 'just do it!' There was a fight, and Diane smashed Adrianne's head with a dumbbell that was on the floor of the car. The heavily bleeding teenager escaped and ran away. She collapsed on the side of the road whereupon David Graham finished her off with his gun.

Diane again: 'He went back to where she (Adrianne) was 'cause I told him to. He shot her twice in the head. He ran back and jumped into the car and drove off as quick as he could. I remember the first words out of his mouth were, "I love you baby, do you believe me now?" I said, "Yes, I believe you. I love you too." '

A farmer discovered Adrianne Jones' body in a field the next day.

Zamora and Graham separated and went to their respective military schools – David to the Air Force Academy in Colorado, Diane to Annapolis in Maryland.

The police investigated the murder of Adrianne Jones for nine months without finding any leads. Then Diane told two roommates that she and David had proved their love for each other by killing for one another and the friends reported her to the military authority. Following questioning by police, Zamora was suspended from her academy and sent home. A week later David Graham was arrested for the murder of Adrianne Jones after failing a lie detector test. Zamora was arrested two days later.

The couple were tried separately and attempted to blame each other. Zamora told the jury that she did not know Graham was going to kill Jones and that she never intended to harm the victim. She only wanted to confront Jones. She was, however, convicted, and received a mandatory life sentence. She will not be eligible for parole for forty years.

David Graham's trial started four months after his girlfriend's conviction and her written confession was used as testimony against him. He, like her, was convicted of capital murder and sentenced to life without the possibility of parole for forty years. He did not help himself by sending letters to Zamora, after his arrest, which were used as part of Zamora's defence and portrayed him as the driving force.

'Don't tell them anything,' he wrote. 'I told them you would not say anything against me, that you would take the death penalty for me. There's no way I'm going to jail while you walk free.'

David Graham's confession to the police did not differ, in essence, from the one made by his girlfriend. He told them about the sexual encounter with Adrianne which was 'meaningless' and 'immediately regretted'.

When he told Diane about Adrianne a month after the event, 'I thought the very life in her had been torn away. She was angry, she was violent and she was broken. For at least an hour she screamed sobs that I wouldn't have thought possible ... The only thing that could satisfy her womanly vengeance was the life of the one that had, for an instant, taken her place.'

Terrified that he was going to lose Diane, Graham agreed to her request to murder Adrianne Jones. 'I was stupid,' he wrote. 'But I was in love.'

After the murder he was consumed by guilt. 'I saw Adrianne's mother in the grocery stores. I read articles of how her family was coping in the paper. One thing, in particular, has haunted me. I read a quote from Linda Jones in which she said, "I hope that her killer is out there and he's just being eaten up with guilt." When I read that, I just wanted it to all go away.'

The crimes committed in the form of demented co-dependence are intense and mystifying, but they are sometimes explained by the psychologist's term *folie-à-deux*. This phrase has extended to encompass such terms as 'induced psychotic disorder (IPD), infectious insanity, psychic infection, contagious insanity, collective insanity, double insanity, influenced psychoses, mystic paranoia, induced psychosis, associational psychosis, epacti psychosis and dyadid psychosis.'

Despite its plethora of clinical descriptions, this symbiotic psychic state is rare and is seen as occurring where one person suffers from psychosis and induces delusions in the other or, sometimes, others.

Classified by the World Health Organization in 1992, the diagnostic definition notes that 'delusional beliefs are transmitted only in uncommon circumstances. Almost invariably, the people concerned have an unusually close relationship and are isolated from others by language, culture or geography. The individual in whom the delusions are induced is usually dependent on or subservient to the person with the genuine psychosis.'

Various clinicians have compiled papers researching this disorder, drawing conclusions from case histories that have, more often than not, been dysfunctional and delusional rather than dangerous and lawless. It takes a degree of abuse and amorality for shared psychoses to grow from neurotic or antisocial behaviour to the full force of savage criminality that makes grim headlines and turns the protagonists into the antiheroines of death row.

Case studies show that psychotic symptoms and delusional ideas are seldom transmitted from a psychotic individual to a healthy one merely upon prolonged exposure. The clinical conclusion is that the passive person involved in a *folie-à-deux* usually has a pre-psychotic personality (i.e. a marked personality disturbance with suspicious, histrionic, dependent or antisocial traits) and may well have developed a mental disorder even if she or he had not been in contact with a psychotic individual.

Most cases of *folie-à-deux* show a pattern of dominance and submission. In other words one will be in charge, and influence the other, who will be younger, more vulnerable, even dependent. The process of identifying with the ideas of the dominant person may be unconscious; while taking the ideas up will provide gain (in a defenceless person, such as a child, it could be a matter of actual survival).

According to one report by researcher Paul Nutteing:

Folie à deux *is an example of a pathological relationship in which the dominant party strives to maintain a link with reality while the other fulfils dependency needs. The recipient is not necessarily entirely a submissive partner since in most cases he or she becomes delusional after considerable resistance and this may impact on the primary sufficiently to modify her delusions.*

The secondary partner seeks to preserve the relationship with the dominant one by adopting her delusions because the threat of loss is greater than the fear of psychosis. All families share a common reality and family myths that help the family to maintain a stable cohesiveness in the midst of internal or external threats.

Delusions function as psychotic defenses. In folie à deux *the mutual acceptance of delusions enables the inducer to stay in contact with at least one other person despite the loss of contact with reality. The more dependent recipient is willing to accept delusions as the price of maintaining the connection.*

All of which might go some way to explain why Kenny Kimes thought his mother was a beautiful person, why Martha Beck inspired the passion of love in Raymond Fernandez and why David Graham would do anything for Diane Zamora.

The report continues by saying that delusional disorders are largely under-diagnosed because patients retain relatively high functioning in the community, actively denying disability and avoiding help from psychiatrists, who also avoid these patients because of their litigious and confrontational nature. These individuals drift between delusional and normal modes and confound all but the most experienced clinicians. Often passing as eccentrics until they cause harm or significant conflict in the family or community.

Other medical specialists, non-medical professionals and law enforcement officers are the likely first contacts. Inexperience and lack of skill in identifying and eliciting paranoid phenomena leads professionals to accept delusion-based reasons for patient's actions as rational if they are not immediately bizarre. Delusional patients often do not meet criteria for involuntary treatment, leaving professionals with few opportunities to remove children from potentially harmful situations. Guidelines for the involuntary commitment of adults are often in conflict with child protection legislation.

Paranoid parents tend to demand secrecy and loyalty, interrogating their children to confirm their beliefs. They do not challenge the beliefs because they fear the parent's anger and retaliation, which in turn awaken separation and abandonment fears. A similar situation exists for children who are the victims of parental incest, whose obligation to secrecy is necessary to preserve their abnormal relationship with the parent.

The risk of the second parent becoming delusional is significant. Other emotional responses in the second parent include anger, perplexity, protective feelings, help-seeking behaviour or withdrawal and uncertainty, whether the partner is ill or not.

If the psychotic parent acts on her delusions, children are endangered, especially if the other parent cannot protect the children. There is a major concern when the delusional parent is violent towards the other parent.

SOURCES

Havill, Adrian, *The Mother, The Son, and the Socialite*, St Martin's Press, New York, 1999

'Paul Bernardo and Karla Homolka' by Marilyn Bardsley
   (www.crimelibrary.com)
'Texas Cadet Murder Case' by Jan Bouchard-Kerr
   (www.crimelibrary.com)
'The Last Stop: Martha The Lonely Heart' by Mark Gado
   (www.crimelibrary.com)
'Gerald and Charlene Gallego' by Marlee Macleod
   (www.crimelibrary.com)
www.CourtTV.com
www.nutteing.no-frills.net

9. GUNS AND GIRLS

In America the female murderess prefers guns; in England an axe or a kitchen knife will do.

It was a sunny day in the Land of Opportunity, 1998. A Californian bank-teller looked up to see a woman dressed in a black-rimmed hat and pink sunglasses with black polka dots, and wearing a blue, long-sleeved shirt teamed with clashing green trousers. As anyone who has visited California will know, this choice of apparel is not unusual in itself. The state may have been taken over by multinational retail outlets, but there is still the odd vintage store about the place. No, the clothes were not the cause for alarm; the note was the cause for alarm. The note informed the teller that the woman was armed and that cash should be handed over forthwith. Ten thousand dollars in neat notes were duly submitted. The bank robber tucked the money into her black 'tote' bag and walked calmly to freedom. Later the police informed the press that this suspect was thought to have 'knocked over' at least seven Santa Clara County banks in the last six months.

The female bank robber is still a rare phenomenon, and she is not always a clever one. A woman named Erika G had a 'blonde moment' while doing over a bank in Germany. She entered the place wearing a Stan Laurel mask, successfully scooped up thousands of marks, but was so nervous that on her exit she forgot to remove the mask and was immediately tackled by passers-by on the pavement outside the bank. They held her down until the police arrived and presumably advised her not to make a career out of it.

A woman in New Jersey had more nerve, but about as many brain cells, when she hit a bank in Cranford.

'I'm back,' she said calmly. She had robbed the same branch a couple of days before. Described as having dirty blonde hair, a bad skin condition and a fast red car, she made off with about $10,000.

When the female bank robber arrives she is inevitably compared to the girls in the film *Set It Off*, though she is much more mundane. There are, in effect, very few ways you can actually rob a bank and there are few original thinkers; all they need is criminal audacity and a car. The robber hands over a demand note and intimates that she is holding a weapon, though that weapon is rarely seen.

The FBI are always keen to tell the public that armed robbery is not such a profitable business; the remuneration from a hit can be in the hundreds, which does not balance out the length of the jail sentence that these crimes carry.

It is fair, considering that Hollywood has inspired so many courageous cinematic criminals, that California should get more than the normal share of Bonnie and Clydes, or, more recently, Thelma and Louises. In 1999 a reward of $5,000 was offered for information leading to the arrest of a couple in their twenties who were thought to have robbed seventeen separate banks in the Bay Area of California and who were described as 'armed and dangerous'.

A year later, after a series of different incidents, Tammy Hall and her boyfriend Shaughnessy Williams were finally arrested after a robbery spree that was thought to have included some twenty banks along the west coast. They were caught after hitting a Bank of America in Calle Real.

Hall would appear at the window, hand over a note saying, 'This is a robbery. There's a bomb in this bag', and then tell the teller, 'No dye packs. It will trigger the bomb.'

One of the FBI agents investigating the crimes said at the time, 'Overall, it's unusual to see a female bank robber. But there's really no profile. We see people in all walks of life with different motivations. Obviously, they're all interested in the money.'

Over in Nebraska in 2001 a CCTV camera caught a picture of a blonde woman wearing a baseball cap down over her eyes to conceal her face as she walked up to rob a Maha bank. She waited in line for the teller, handed over a note, and demanded money with the calm finesse of a trust fund kid asking Daddy to sign a cheque.

In America, where the fact of women carrying firearms has become part of both the gun and feminist debates, their use in crime is unsurprisingly reflected in scenes of both domestic and other violence. They are not the only weapons used, of course; poison has long been a favourite of the female killer and arson is also prevalent in the annals of female crime. In 1998 a woman in San Francisco poured petrol over her boyfriend and set fire to him, and a Letitia Ford of Missouri received a ten-year sentence for igniting her house while her boyfriend and child were sleeping in it. There are also many cases of women using their cars to mow down their victims in the method of assault that could be described as motorcide, but is more commonly called vehicular homicide. But guns remain the favourite method of despatching a hated one.

Hope Grudowski, a nineteen-year-old living in Colorado Springs, was told to leave by her husband Bill. Instead she waited for him to return to their apartment and, when he entered the bedroom, shot him in the back. At first she claimed that Bill, an alleged pimp and drug dealer, had committed suicide without realising, apparently, that it is a very difficult for a person to shoot himself in the back unless he is made of India rubber.

Jesus, apparently, told Priscilla Jansma, also of Denver, that it was 'OK' to shoot her husband, while Rachel Davis, a bounty hunter working in Augusta, was sentenced to five years probation after firing at the car of a woman she was attempting to pick up for a missing court appearance.

The Mills family of Paoli, Indiana, were, according to their neighbours, 'really strange people'. Violent rows and gunshots resounded around the trailer park until the day that Mrs Mills shot Mr Mills in the face. She then caressed the blown off section of his jaw and proceeded to eat it.

Household scenarios are still the most common place for a female shooter; again and again it is the husband or boyfriend who dies; again and again the story is a tale of marital discord. We have yet to see many female spree killers or psychotic cheerleaders who break into the school playground and mow down the pupils.

Increasingly common is the old chestnut 'domestic violence' – a defence that very often rings true, but sometimes does not. It did not in the case of Cecilia Johnson from Colorado, who was sentenced to 35 years or shooting her husband. She argued that he had beaten her; prosecutors said that she was simply angry that he had threatened to leave her and that the fatal row was the result of an argument over money.

The backdrop to all this shooting and killing is complex and typically American. As women wielding automatic weapons have become part of both cinematic culture and the often more violent scenery of real life, the stateside cityscapes resound not only to the sound of gunfire but to the political debates surrounding the right to arms.

Statistics from the Bureau of Justice reveal that since the year 2000 violent crime has, in fact, been very much on the wane. While victimisations involving a firearm represent 8 per cent of the 6.3 million violent crimes committed (including rape and robbery etc.), in the year 2000 66 per cent of the 15,517 murders committed in the good old US of A were committed with firearms.

Documented trends reveal one fact that is most palatable to conservative America – the decline of violent crime is running parallel with greater expenditure on prisons and greater numbers of people incarcerated in them.

After 11 September 2001 firearms dealers reported increased sales in guns and the National Rifle Association noted a leap in the number of women who enrolled in programmes designed to teach them how to protect themselves with guns. This was unsurprising in view of the widespread paranoia that seeped through the country after the attack on its heart. The Nanny State was not protecting its children so the children had to defend themselves even more than usual. And they never needed much excuse to take up arms.

Legions of law-abiding ladies in America have collected up into organised movements of effective activists – not only as members of the anti-gun lobby (lots of moms who have lost kids in shooting incidents) but as members of the pro-gun brigade (lots of moms who acclaim their right to carry arms, to defend themselves, and to equally and effectively compete in male-orientated shooting competitions).

This second group gathers under the umbrella of the Second Amendment Sisters and the magazine *Women and Guns*. *Women and Guns*, which has featured the predictable picture of *Terminator 2*'s Linda Hamilton on its cover, was started in 1988 by gun enthusiast Sonny Jones.

She noted in her first editorial, 'Female gun owners are being cast as potential saviours of the pro-gun movement. Think carefully ladies. Our combined influence can work to reshape American society. What do we want to accomplish and where do we want to start?'

As the sales of *Women and Guns* increased, so the manufacturers started to gear themselves towards the female marketplace with products that were women-friendly. Little purses designed to hold handguns arrived along with neat pocketbooks fitted with neat compartments and feminine lines.

In 1989, Smith and Wesson launched the LadySmith, a 9 mm semi-automatic handgun which was seen by enthusiasts as a 'marker in the evolution, emancipation and revelation of women gunowners'.

Paxton Quigley, a cool blonde who knew her bolt-actions, weighed in with the best-selling and rational book *Armed and Female*. Conversely, despite the rise of 'power feminism', *Ms* magazine ran a cover in 1994 featuring a cover story on guns which said, 'When we took up the fight for women's rights, the right to keep and bear arms was not what we had in mind.'

Women and Guns, meanwhile, ran a cover of a chocolate cake surrounded by six handguns. This was followed by a 1997 wedding cover, featuring not a dippy model in Versace froth, but the bride who appeared at the Beretta fashion show walking through an 'honour guard' of crossed shotguns.

Recently, progressive thinkers and pro-porn feminists have begun to dare to reveal the truth about the charisma of the gun and the female attraction to it. Respected American underground writer Katharine Gates broke ground in her contribution to the radical book of essays *Inappropriate Behaviour*, in which she addressed and defended the proclivities of women who think that guns are sexy and go as far as to include them in their erotic life.

'Women aren't supposed to use weapons,' she wrote. 'Aren't supposed to be aggressively sexual, aren't supposed to possess that tooth-and-claw urge to life and death. They're not supposed to be independent and intelligent manipulators of technology. Whereas some cultures worship a powerful, sexually ravenous woman (think of the Hindu goddess Kali), it just won't fit into our American psyche. If a woman acts like that, she must want to be a man . . .'

Peggy Tarturo, the executive editor of *Women and Guns*, estimates that the number of women who own guns in America is between eleven and seventeen million.

In England, where gun culture does not exist, other than in a very small criminal underworld, the murderess must take advantage of any other lethal weapon that comes to hand – and it is often a tool that is even more effective than her tongue (that ever useful means of defence).

Tina Nash turned a T-shirt into a ligature and attempted to strangle her lover with it, an assault that propelled her to Bristol Crown Court in March 2001.

The GAY GIRL COP ROMP headlines noted that Sergeant Tina Nash, 41, had attacked her girlfriend, Inspector Sara Glen, 31, after Glen had made love to another female detective in the back of a van. Nash, who wanted to marry Glen, attempted to strangle her in their bed. She then took 32 paracetamol tablets. She was cleared of attempted murder but tried for assault.

Inspector Glen, Sara, was something of a love goddess in the Hampshire constabulary. It was said that many women were vying for her affections, one of whom was a lady barrister. Nash lost it when she realised that she could not hold on to her beloved and, forming a T-shirt into a ligature, tightened it around Glen's neck until she lost her breath and suffered serious bruising to the throat.

'It is not clear why Nash found Inspector Glen so spellbinding,' said the *Daily Telegraph*'s court reporter Richard Savill. 'Perhaps the appeal lay in her inability to give a commitment. It became apparent that the inspector, a vivacious blonde, was not ready to settle down and their relationship became increasingly turbulent.'

'You let yourself become completely besotted,' said the judge. 'It falls on me to sentence you for serious assault.'

Nash received a term of two and a half years, though her exemplary career as a police officer of nineteen years' standing was taken into account. She had been well respected by her colleagues, who were saddened by the fact that a relationship had been allowed to destroy her professional career.

Jane Andrews' choice of weapons was a cricket bat and a kitchen knife – both used to despatch her boyfriend Thomas Cressman in his Fulham house on 16 September 2000. The murder was violent; Cressman had been hit so hard on the forehead with the bat that his skull was fractured; the stabbing with the nine-inch blade was so savage that there was blood all over the walls and floor.

He was found face down in his boxer shorts, clutching the blade of the kitchen knife that he had succeeded in withdrawing from his chest before the life passed out of him. The door had been tied shut with the bloody cord of a bathrobe.

Forensic evidence later revealed that Ms Andrews had committed this incredible attack while she was completely naked. She had waited for Cressman to take out his contact lenses, so that he was rendered semi-blind and helpless and, as he went to sleep, she had killed him. His crime? He refused to marry her.

Men rejected Jane Andrews at their peril. Other boyfriends who had been driven away by her obsessiveness and jealousy had ended their relationships only to find themselves both physically attacked and stalked. There was the story of a poisoned box of chocolates that was generally thought to have been sent by her. One man said that she punched and kicked him and then stole his wristwatch and an oil painting.

Jane Andrews was a vicious woman. For some time there was little sign of her dangerous derangement, although observers were later to say that they had seen signs of it when she worked for several years as a dresser to the Duchess of York.

It is difficult to imagine that anyone would want to be seen as being like the Duchess of York, who, when Andrews worked for her in the mid-90s, was portrayed in the tabloid media as graceless, undignified, badly dressed and very silly. She was reviled by the British press whose campaign of embarrassment culminated in 1992 when they photographed her topless and in the throes of love-play with the equally ludicrous John Bryan – an American who was photographed sucking her toes beside a swimming pool in the South of France.

No one sensible would want to walk in the Duchess of York's shoes, but Jane Andrews was not sensible. She was very unstable and, the closer she became to 'Fergie', the more their professional relationship resembled a version of that performed by Jennifer Jason Leigh and Bridget Fonda in Barbet Shroeder's *Single White Female*. Indeed, if this story was used as a screenplay for a sequel it could accurately be called *Divorced Royal Redhead*.

The closer Ms Andrews was pulled into 'Fergie's' confidence, so her manner became more royal, her hair more orange, her clothes more similar to the air-hostess-like accoutrements favoured by her employer.

She was the daughter of a social worker from Grimsby; very ordinary, but somewhere along the line Jane Andrews became bizarre – something twisted her, and she turned from a meek royal lackey into a savage murderess. But not overnight.

Allan Starkie's *A Date With Death* is proud to expound the 'metamorphosis of the personality of an impression-able ambitous young woman corrupted by power, insatiable passions and privileges.'

Starkie, a businessman ran with the Fergie crowd for a brief period, during the mid-90s, when she was in love with his associate John Bryan. Bryan had taken it upon himself to advise the (willing) duchess on her finances; an involvement that served not only to see her at the lowest-ever ebb of public esteem, but also culminated in crippling overdrafts.

According to Starkie, Bryan wanted to commandeer the duchess's life and to marry her, in approximately that order.

Jane Andrews worked in this milieu as the duchess's dresser and then, absurdly, her household accountant, a position to which she was promoted by her employer and for which she had neither training nor aptitude. Still, as the keeper of the royal purse strings, she liked the tiny power it gave her over the other servants.

Allan Starkie, a diary writer who recorded every detail, informs his reader that Jane Andrews' manner was that of 'a shy and somewhat depressed vampire' and that she was an 'empty shapeless vessel eager to accept the liquid that was poured into it'.

She suffered from a passion for him, though it is a little difficult to see why. At first he spurned Bryan's instruction 'to fuck her and treat her like shit', as the woman was equipped with a fretwork of canine teeth 'that always gave me a fright'. Furthermore she was 'needy and obsessive', and Starkie sensed that she could be real trouble – a 'volcano of potential explosiveness'.

The affiliation nevertheless culminated in a night of intimacy which he describes with ungentlemanly relish as being similar to two penguins having sex and concludes with the comment that she was a woman who 'knew her way around men's clothing'.

Jane Andrews spent nine years working for the Duchess of York and would travel with her, packing her clothes, mending them, making sure her hideous outfits were inventoried and in good order and, on one occasion, blow-drying the royal armpits after the duchess's shirt became sweat-stained during a royal appointment.

Her inefficiency came to light in a spectacular way in December 1995 when she was responsible for the loss of a £250,000 diamond necklace that the Queen had given to the Duchess of York. It had been checked in to a normal baggage compartment where, in an unlocked case, it had been easily lifted.

The Duchess stood by her servant in this instance and the necklace was recovered. The two were to fall out two years later in circumstances that remained a mystery but were thought to be related to the Duchess's burgeoning relationship with the Italian count Gaddo della Gherardesca.

Jane Andrews, a neurotic snob, had little to fall back on when she was expelled from the hallowed employ of Fergie, and it was largely thanks to her employer's reference that she found herself a position in the portals of noted jeweller Theo Fennell – a man with a perma-tan whose skill it is to construct glittering baubles for various majesties.

Jane Andrews met Thomas Cressman in 1998 on a blind date. He was quite rich and had a house in Fulham; she slept with him on the first night. At first all went well, though her snobbery and boasting about her 'career' in the palace did not impress Cressman's father.

The relationship with Cressman deteriorated, particularly after Andrews hacked into his e-mail correspondence and found a series of flirty letters to a woman with whom he was patently intending to have an affair. She later printed them out and faxed them to Cressman's mother and various other acquaintances who could doubtless have done without them.

After she murdered Cressman, an inoffensive and kindly man who had done his best for her, Jane Andrews drove away and spent some days wondering if she should jump off Beachy Head. Certainly she was suicidal; certainly she was shocked. She sent nonsensical text messages to the Duchess of York and other friends. They exhorted her to turn herself in to the police. Finally, thanks to help from one of the friends, the police picked her up in Cornwall where she was asleep in her car. She was immediately charged with murder.

Her defence offered various mitigating circumstances. There was the agony of the loss of the palace job; the supposed history of sexual abuse as a child; a polycystic condition which gave her mood swings; the supposed violence of Thomas Cressman, who, Andrews insisted, had abused and raped her. She had only reached for the cricket bat in self-defence, she claimed.

The jury was treated to a description of the effects that this cricket bat had had on Cressman's face, which could not have filled them with affection for the defendant. The prosecution pointed out the lies that she had told in an attempt to save herself. Various women came forward and testified that Cressman was neither violent nor a rapist. The judge, Michael Hyam, agreed and dismissed her claims of rape. He described the stabbing as 'a classic case of murder as a result of betrayal'.

On 16 May 2001 she was found guilty of murder. 'Nothing can justify what you did,' said the judge. She was sentenced to life.

Janet Charlton's choice of weapon was a two-foot-long fireman's axe which she planted into the head of her lover, 41-year-old Yorkshire businessman Danny O'Brien. Mr O'Brien, having incurred twenty or so injuries to the head, back and neck, died on 23 May 2001, with the axe still embedded in his skull. He was handcuffed, blindfolded and had a rubber ball gag in his mouth. The victim had obviously knelt to receive these blows (thinking to receive the love attentions of an affectionate dominatrix?). Hanging from the axe still in his skull, draped as if on a Christmas tree, were 'a black and silver leopard-skin-effect suspender belt and a pair of white fishnet stockings'.

His mother, 72-year-old Elizabeth, was not surprised. She had never liked the look of that Janet. When her son asked his old mum what she made of his new girlfriend, his old mum said, 'She looks like a murderer or something, Myra Hindley.' But Danny just laughed.

'Danny,' she said after his death, 'was the most gentle, kind, caring, generous and thoughtful son.' So were the Krays, of course: nice to their mum, that is. The evidence pertaining to the character of Daniel O'Brien did not reflect quite such a rosy vision. The judge presiding over the six-week case in Leeds Crown Court described him as a 'flawed man with extremely depraved sexual proclivities'.

Janet Charlton, 36, had most of the characteristics required by the tabloid press to create a female demon.

She was a killer. She was blonde. And she loved sex. She told the court in May 2002 that she had had some sixty lovers, including the ten men she had had sex with in a sauna while Daniel O'Brien watched. A police officer who had spent some months investigating her observed that this was a very conservative figure. 'You can certainly quadruple that,' he suggested.

Janet Charlton was born in Oldham to an unassuming paint sprayer. She moved to Huddersfield when she was eighteen and went on to take a diploma in business studies. Working for a temp recruitment agency she met her first husband, Tony, and, in 1997, bore him a daughter, Amy.

After her divorce in 1998, Charlton spent her settlement on a pair of new breasts, then followed her instincts and slept with whom she liked. On a holiday in Spain she slept with three men in a week; in Australia she posed nude for 'lewd' photographs. One female friend told the London *Daily Mail*, 'She has always been the life and soul of the party. Even when she was married Janet was pretty wild and loved to be the centre of attention. But after she split from Tony she just went for it, going out drinking all the time and picking up men in clubs.'

One ex-boyfriend told the court that 'she has always slept around. When we met she turned to me in bed and said, "You do know that I'm going to have sex with other men, don't you?" I adored her but she just used me for sex. Her sexual appetite was fierce. She wanted threesomes, foursomes, group orgies ... you name it, Jan wanted it.'

Janet, then, showed all the signs of being a normal woman. In 1999 she decided to turn her pleasures into business and signed up with an Internet escort agency where she would earn £150 an hour for doing pretty much what she was doing anyway. She went about now as 'Natasha'.

'I realised it was not quite right,' she said. 'But I couldn't see any harm in it.' A friend, Jane McNamara, claimed that Charlton did not know what she was getting herself into. 'She was naive.'

Then along came Daniel O'Brien – rich, keen, with tastes that ran from A to bondage and back again. Not one to muck about when it came to the important things, Janet checked out his £300,000 house in Midgley, west Yorkshire and, within a week, she and her daughter Amy were living in it.

As they all settled into the businessman's swish red-brick home, surrounded by bluebell woods, O'Brien began to talk marriage and Ms Charlton started to keep a diary in which they both made notes. The book was found later by police.

In it, Mr O'Brien had written, 'When we first met, I think we scared ourselves to death. It was like looking into a mirror. We so quickly fell in love. I hope we always add to it with our great feelings, hopes and not so many fears. We love each other with a love which is honest and true.'

Charlton's entry read, 'When we met I didn't ever think I would be as happy as you made me. You make me feel like the most wanted woman in the world. Life without you in it would be so empty.

'I want to grow old with you and have so many special moments. We have found a love that is magical. I will love you forever. Let's make sure we both have a lot of life to live together.'

Denise Dugan, a cleaner who worked for the couple, testified in court and said, 'He was fastidious and could be difficult. She was good for him because he was too serious and she was fresh and bubbly.'

O'Brien's pre-marital demands were imaginative and extensive. His bedroom was described as being suitably stocked with everything from whips, harnesses and masks to a comprehensive porn library of 22 videos that encompassed gay sex and bestiality.

Starting with a request that Janet have sex with a stranger in a car while he watched, he proceeded to enjoy sessions with sex toys and various other equipment. Janet told the jury that she felt degraded; that she would have been happy with a 'normal' sex life, whatever that is. She said that Daniel became vindictive when he was not in control; she needed to keep him happy, then she would be given anything she wanted.

Daniel, however, had a lover – Lynn Golland – with whom he enjoyed orgies in clubs and, most notably, on a seventeen-foot waterbed in a Manchester swingers club named Xanadu – a club that, when visited by *Daily Mail* journalists, for the purpose of serious investigation, of course, was described as having the 'odour of decay'.

Lynn Golland, testifying, confirmed that O'Brien enjoyed SM sex and, on one occasion, had invited a man named 'The Master' to his house in order to watch him use nipple clamps on Ms Golland's person.

Their relationship had ended, though they occasionally met and on one occasion enjoyed sex outside in the garden at Chatsworth House, the stately home owned by the Duke and Duchess of Devonshire, which was not, presumably, what the Duke and Duchess had in mind when they opened their famously beautiful grounds to the public.

Janet Charlton's defence was that she, though a good-time girl, was not a pervert and began to become both oppressed by and resentful of her boyfriend's incessant demands. The crime was not murder, she said, it was manslaughter, committed in an act of self-defence. O' Brien had finally gone too far and threatened to kill her and drag her three-year-old daughter Amy into sex sessions.

The jury bought this and her charge was reduced from murder to manslaughter, which brought her the relatively light sentence of five years. The prosecution, however, described her as a 'callous killer and consummate actress', which was evinced, to a certain extent, by Ms Charlton's behaviour after the murder.

She lied to the police for six weeks after O'Brien's body was found, saying he had been murdered by a mystery assailant. Then she finally confessed of her own accord. She had claimed that she discovered the body after she returned to the Midgley home after an outing with her daughter. The truth was that she had found the axe in the dressing room off the master bedroom and had attacked her boyfriend with it, having blindfolded him and handcuffed him.

She told the police that she had believed her boyfriend's threat that he planned to kill her, that it was he who had brought the axe upstairs and, petrified, she had lured him into a bondage sex session then 'just hit him and hit him'. The prosecution's argument was that here was a sexually sophisticated promiscuous woman giving the 'performance of a life time'.

The story was not, in fact, of a woman terrified by her deviant lover, but of a woman enraged by rejection. Daniel O'Brien had told her that he had had sex with Lynn Golland the day before and that he planned to go back to her.

Janet Charlton showed little emotion until, after twenty hours, the jury delivered a unanimous guilty verdict and a five-year sentence was passed. Then she slumped forward, put her head on her hands, and wept out loud. One can only hope that she was thinking about her daughter.

Summing up, the judge, Norman Jones QC, recorder of Leeds, said:

The evidence in this case indicated that O'Brien was a controlling man and from what I have heard was often described as a 'control freak'. He could not tolerate you to have any degree of personal freedom and meticulously set about establishing that control in the relationship.

I am satisfied that he introduced you to some of these practices, although to keep him happy you were quite prepared to go along with them. Your own attitude to sex was relaxed, if not promiscuous, and you were more ready to indulge in these practices than others may have been.

To some extent you were attracted by his obvious trappings of wealth which you felt would have kept you in comfortable style if he married you.

He divorced you from your house, money and friends and tried to separate your daughter from her father. When you showed signs of resistance he would use sexual or other force to punish you. Eventually you decided there could be no more and you determined to leave him.

He took an axe upstairs and he threatened to kill you with it and sexually assault your daughter and kill her. He permitted himself to adopt a vulnerable position and you took an axe and attacked him.

You did not take the axe upstairs. It was only because he did so that you are here at all. Nevertheless, to take a man's life, even in those circumstances, is a grave offence.

You were imbued with a desire to kill or cause very serious bodily injury to Danny O'Brien.

The mystery of this case was the exact nature of the motivation. Police, judge, jury, press and public had to decide whether they believed the account given by Janet

Charlton. There were no drugs and drink involved in these scenarios. This mother was a sane and functional woman. The story of her bludgeoning the man she apparently loved into a bloody pulp threw up questions that were not answered by her, or by anybody.

Had she been genuinely repelled by his demands? It seems unlikely given her background and liberality, and they had not, after all, had the same effect on his other girlfriends. If every man who wanted to be whipped had an axe shoved into his head, there would be a lot of corpses about the place. Had he really threatened to have sex with her small daughter and triggered a lioness attack of protectiveness in a woman with no record of hysterical emotional response? Why did she not simply leave the house and go somewhere else? She had friends and a bank account.

Perhaps, as the prosecution believed, jealousy was the trigger for Ms Charlton's temporary lapse into animal savagery; perhaps she did truly love Danny O'Brien with all the passion that she described in her diary. Perhaps she, as the promiscuous person, had indulged in casual sex in order to camouflage her own fears of rejection and this was the first time that she had had to manage the feelings of pure hatred that are inevitably triggered by such an event. There are those who might think that to fuck about is to avoid getting fucked about; to reject first is to avoid rejection. But there was no evidence of any previous neurosis; this appeared to be a woman who simply enjoyed a lot of sex and went for it. Janet Charlton's explosion of murderous violence remains unexplained.

SOURCES
Quigley, Paxton, *Armed and Female*, St Martin's Press, New York, 1994

Berens, Jessica, Sharp, Kerri, *Inappropriate Behaviour –
    Prada Sucks! and Other Demented Descants*, Serpent's
    Tail, London, 2002
Starkie, Allan, *A Date with Death*, Mainstream
    Publishing, London and Edinburgh, 2001
the *Guardian*, 28 May 2002
www.goletavalleyvoice.com
www.sfgate.com
www.telegraph.com
www.womenshooter.com

10. BRIDES OF SATAN

Some women practise black magic. Some insist that they are vampires. Murders are committed in the Devil's cause.

Satan does not exist, but this salient fact has done little to prohibit his popularity. Satanism – cult, religion, a group of spotty teenagers, call it what you will – continues to attract enthusiastic acolytes from all over the world. Who to blame? Well, not Satan himself as he does not exist. Or does he? The evil committed in his name has succoured a tangible presence of demonic forces whose atrocities are Old Testament in their violence and fury. Christ on a bike, they shot a child in the eye out there in Tennessee. They stabbed a man in Germany. The Bible-bashers might be right! Lucifer is walking on this earth and we are destined for doom.

Books, records, Net communities, chat 'grottoes', the Goth boutique in London, the Marilyn Manson T-shirt in Los Angeles, the Urban Decay glittery black lipstick, the vampirella nightclub, tattoo parlours, the popular records of Venom, Slayer, King Diamond, and Korn – the Devil is so well marketed. Black magic is easier to buy than Hello Kitty.

The Dark Side, eternally attracting the imaginative teen-loner, is always reactive when added to hallucinogens or personality disorders or anger or angst or alienation or just good ol' desensitisation. There will always be somebody who thinks the Antichrist is a pop rebel antihero, some wild boy in leather to be worshipped and obeyed. It wasn't so long ago that the blues was condemned as the 'Devil's music', after all.

So the commerce of the death cult remains as immortal as the fantasist vampires in its midst. No youth cultural trend has ever killed Goth – not punk, not disco, not techno, not garage and certainly not Britpop. For every clone in Top Shop flares, there will always be a theatrical youth dressed up as the Count, a woman dressed up as his Bride, and a bookshelf full of Bram Stoker and the late Anton La Vey.

Anton's Church of Satan manifestoes, mainly served up in the pages of his Satanic Bible, still inspire leagues of urban ghouls. His words have been read in many of the places where ritualistic mayhem has come to call. Said he, 'Satanism is a blatantly selfish, brutal religion.'

His exhortation to embrace indulgence and vengeance combines with the black magic idea that it is possible for an individual to harness invisible forces in order to impose their will on the development of everyday circumstances. These provide mesmerising options to those who feel they have no power – the dork without a girlfriend, the girl being raped by her stepfather, the bored, the frustrated, the poor . . .

The Nine Satanic Sins seem designed to befriend those who pride themselves on being intelligent and of independent thought. Stupidity, for instance, is the cardinal sin of Satanism. As are pretentiousness, herd conformity and 'lack of aesthetics'.

Until recently members of the Church of Satan tended to number ten men to one woman. Blanche Barton addressed this with her essay, in *Blue Flame*, on Satanic Feminism.

The smartest, most passionate, most beautiful women I've met have been Satanists. It takes a special woman to be a Satanist. Wicca and feminism share a flaccid, lacklustre attitude and presentation. Satanic women like drama/adventure and know how to conjure it for themselves. Satanists have an innate complexity of mind

*that hungers for uncompromising examination and
speculation, not superficially comforting pap. We don't
need to be comforted; we prefer the invigorating, bracing
winds of truth and terror.*

*Many young, bottom-of-the-clock women who are
looking for gothic strength in a man can't find it in the
simpering she-males around them – so they manifest their
Demonics themselves, dressing in black leather, black
stockings and carrying a big black whip. A compleat
Satanic witch can best spend her time in constant,
intimate, spiritual and sexual contact with her strongest
Demonic archetype – Satan Himself.*

Step forward Manuela Ruda.

Siouxsie Sioux herself could not have looked more glam;
no John Carpenter Hollywood bloodsucker could have
paraded a more belligerent attitude. A dangerous
woman, Manuela, and not only because she was a
homicidal maniac. Or femmicidal womaniac as they may
say in post-fem circles. Manuela was dangerous because
she looked like the quintessential Goth queen. She
looked so good the newspapers ran her pictures big, big,
big.

So there she was in February 2002, photographed at
her court case, dolled up and a pin-up. The black
mohawk was teased to show the shaved head and
inverted crucifix tattoo; perfect white matte make-up;
long green nails; defiant, slanted, witchy green eyes.

Remorseless, rude, defiant, she stuck her tongue out
and rolled her eyes and made the sign of the Devil to
the cameras – forefinger and little finger pointing up. It
was an occult salute and it doubtless attracted like-
minded fans sympathetic to her dress sense if not her
dreadful cause.

She was straight out of a death metal gig, this one. You could see the bookshelves lined with Rice (Anne) and the record collection full of Rice (Boyd). Except Manuela was no freaky clubgoer; no mere modernist dressing up for a laugh. In Germany Manuela and her husband stabbed a man to death and then left his body to decompose in their flat.

Frank Hackerts was found with a scalpel protruding from his stomach and the sign of the Devil carved into his chest. 'These are sick people,' said their lawyer.

As an unnerved assembly gathered at the courthouse in the small town of Bochum in west Germany, Manuela's defence team asked that the windows be blacked out because their client preferred to live at night and sunlight hurt her eyes. The judge, unimpressed, allowed her to wear sunglasses while others were left to wonder if this request was a cool tactic to set up a defence plea of insanity.

Manuela was born in Germany in 1979. By 1993 she had dropped out of school and had made one suicide attempt. In 1996 she went to meet the Leopard Man of Skye, or Tom Leppard, an ex-soldier whose body is so covered in a leopard tattoo that he is mentioned in the *Guinness Book of Records*. Having marked himself thus to earn a living as a 'freak' he subsequently moved to the remote island to live as a recluse.

Leppard lives happily alone in a tiny dwelling without electricity. Interviewed by reporters after the Hackerts murder, the eccentric hermit remained baffled about the effect he was supposed to have had on the German girl who kept following him around.

'She seemed like an ordinary teenager,' he told the *Observer*. Ruda, however, wrote him letters which became more violent and, after her arrest, Leppard wrote to her wondering why she had shown no remorse for what she had done.

Manuela was not an ordinary teenager. There is more to a murderess than a smudge of purple lipstick and an acrylic nail. Somewhere along the road the fiction of the dark side blended into reality for Manuela, as it so often does for those who 'dabble'. If you believe in voodoo, then voodoo has the power it purports. It's a faith thing. Manuela believed in 'the forces' and she acted on them. She became the person in the horror movie; the evil spirits existed for her; she lost her grip on reality then entered a delusional state full of demons and death.

She told the jury that Satan had called her when she was fourteen and that she had subsequently embraced a vampiric lifestyle at 'bite parties' in London. 'We drank blood together from willing donors. I also slept in graves and allowed myself to be buried in a grave to test the feeling. I signed my soul to Satan . . .'

She took to sleeping in a coffin and she had two teeth pulled out and replaced with animal fangs. This unusual cosmetic choice did not increase her chances of attracting a nice young man, and a nice young man did not arrive. Daniel Ruda arrived and he shared her inclinations. They met after she answered the advertisement he had placed in a heavy metal magazine. It said, 'Pitch-black vampire seeks princess of darkness who hates everything and everyone.'

Daniel Ruda, a car parts salesman, told the court that following his necromance with Manuela he received a vision that told him that they must marry on 6 July 2001 and then make a human sacrifice exactly a year later which would be followed by their own suicides. The Devil had told him this. It was a direct command and had to be obeyed.

Their friend Frank Hackerts was chosen because he was funny and they saw him as a suitable court jester for Satan.

'We had to kill,' Daniel explained. 'We could not go to hell unless we did.'

'It was not murder,' Manuela added. 'We are not murderers. It was the execution of an order.' The couple lured their victim to their flat and then attacked him.

'Daniel struck him twice on the head with a hammer but he suddenly stood up again and walked towards the television,' said Manuela. 'Then my knife started to glow and I heard the command to stab him.'

They stabbed the pathetic Hackerts 66 times with a variety of weapons including a knife, a carpet cutter and a machete. As the maimed corpse lay on the floor they drank his blood and had sex in Manuela's coffin.

The Rudas then went on the run and, having failed to kill themselves, were arrested at a petrol station in west Germany. The defence led on the grounds that the couple were mentally unfit, and various analysts said that they were suffering from severe narcissistic personality disturbances and chronic inability to develop feelings of self-worth.

Mr and Mrs Ruda are currently serving fifteen and thirteen years respectively in secure psychiatric wards.

Manuela captured the public imagination as a shameless daughter of darkness for whom there seemed no rational explanation except for the presence of evil – she had the serial killer eyes, angry and dead. But the crimes committed by other brides of Satan reflect similar influences and similar levels of violence, all signified by the rise of demented witches influenced by belief in the powers of the Horned One.

In 2000 Silvina Vazquez, 21, and her sister Gabriela, 29, stabbed their father Juan Carlos a hundred times and then ate his face. The family, based in Buenos Aires, Argentina, were members of a cult called the Alchemy

Centre for Transmutation. The killing took place as part of a ritual designed to invoke the power of the Devil. And the Devil, it seems, came to call. When police arrived they found a sitting room full of liquids and lexicons and two hysterical women screaming that they had successfully invoked him.

Over in Mexico Sara Aldrete became a legend when she was arrested in a shoot-out in Mexico City that marked the bloody end to a bizarre saga of atrocities committed in the Devil's name.

Aldrete, from Matamoros in Mexico, was the daughter of an electrician and was, for some time, a model student and all-round good girl. Attending college in Texas, she held down two jobs while she studied physical education, intending to pass a certificate that would allow her to teach sport. She was six-foot tall, popular and ambitious.

All might have been well for Ms Aldrete had it not been for her choice of boyfriend – one Gilberto Sosa, a drug dealer connected to the local narco-barons, the Hernandez family.

In 1987 Aldrete met a handsome Cuban named Adolfo Constanzo when he cut her off in traffic and nearly caused an accident. He emerged from his shiny Mercedes to apologise and managed to charm her, an intention that was all part of his plan.

Adolfo Jesus de Constanzo was a very dangerous man and he had been watching Gilberto Sosa for some time. A drug dealer with multinational aspirations, he wanted an introduction to the Hernandez family so that he could augment his business.

Constanzo lured Aldrete to his bed and into his life, which was dominated by the Haitian voodoo cult known as *palo mayombe*. When he was six months old a priest had told his mother that he was destined to harness great power. Mrs Gonzalez, delighted and impressed, ensured that Adolfo received a full education in the black arts. She directed practitioners in San Juan and Haiti to teach him the ritual of *palo mayombe* before he received a formal magical apprenticeship with a Haitian priest.

Mrs Gonzalez was arrested thirty times for everything from shoplifting to child neglect. The houses she rented around Miami were stained with blood and cluttered with the remains of sacrificed animals. Adolfo, meanwhile, having decided that he was gay, divided his time between cruising gay bars and robbing graveyards. In 1981 he was arrested following an optimistic attempt to shoplift an electric chainsaw.

Constanzo, bisexual, savage, amoral, pledged his soul to Kadiempembe, the devil figure of *palo mayombe*. He was to spend the rest of his life worshipping evil.

In 1984 he moved to Mexico City and began to gather devotees who believed in his powers and who participated in the blood-sacrifices and ceremonies led by their revered black priest. Constanzo's reputation as a powerful magician, based on the belief that he had genuine psychic powers, attracted drug dealers who called on him for predictions and protection.

The criminal mind is not always the most intelligent – it tends to be blessed with cunning rather than common sense. The narco-traders believed Constanzo when he told them that his magic would make them both invisible to the police and bulletproof against the attacks of their enemies. They believed him, and they paid him. Thousands of dollars. But, as crime-writer Michael Newton observed, Constanzo's hold over the police was more peculiar. 'In or out of uniform they worshipped him as a minor god,' he notes.

Hocus pocus had gone mad.

Constanzo increased his coke connections so that his 'business' was bringing in thousands of dollars. He and his night-stalkers robbed graveyards to find bones for the bubbling cauldron of stew that provided the focus of his ceremonies. This mixture of boiling animal guts, known as *nganga*, was soon to be filled with human organs as Constanzo and his gang began to murder both his friends and his enemies and sacrifice them to his discarnate demon.

In April 1987 the mutilated remains of several members of the Calzada drug clan were fished out of the Zumpango River. Their ears had been removed, their genitals severed and, in two cases, the brains were missing.

Three months after this fiesta Sara Aldrete was lured to Constanzo's scene and introduced to the rituals of Haitian magic. Accepting the leader's preference for men, she became his priestess, La Madrina, or the 'godmother' of the coven.

As Constanzo had planned, Sara Aldrete introduced him to the Hernandez family which, fortunately for him, had been weakened by internecine fighting.

El Padrino, the 'godfather' of the family, agreed to pay Constanzo 50 per cent of the profits in return for the protection supplied by his magic.

Constanzo, Aldrete and various other deranged individuals then moved to a ranch outside Matamoros where, in the same way that such an arrangement had empowered the perverse proclivities of the Manson family, the protection of isolation and the intensity of sexual relationships combined with deviant belief systems and ignited the passion of murder.

Adolfo Constanzo told his followers that in order for the demons to work for their benefit the humans that died in the blood sacrifices must die screaming. This they did. The victims were tortured and sodomised and cut up. Then their hearts, brains and lungs were dropped into the *nganga*.

The bubbling brew in the cauldron seemed to emanate genuine forces of power. Following the sacrifice of one innocent victim at the ranch in order to magically procure the release of a member of the Hernandez family captured by rivals, the Hernandez hostages were released without ransom.

Constanzo's spells seemed to work; credulity and coincidence fuelled his reputation; his lethal magick mayhem now knew no limits.

Over the next two years, 1988–89, Constanzo and his cohorts killed one of their members (an ex-cop), tortured a smuggler to death, murdered two dealers and kidnapped and shot a member of the public before despatching a fourteen-year-old boy.

Keen to sell his stash of marijuana (800 kilos) under the aegis of magickal protection, Constanzo ordered his cronies to bring him a victim that would scream. The next morning they brought him Mark Kilroy. This was their big mistake. Kilroy was connected; he was white and he was a tourist. Suddenly the police cared. They began making arrests and they moved in on the ranch.

Constanzo and Sara Aldrete went on the run with two members of the gang. Aldrete enjoyed a brief moment of criminal fame as her picture appeared on the 'most wanted' section of crime programmes. One rumour circulated that she planned to kidnap and murder ten children to avenge the ten 'disciples' that had been jailed in Mexico.

The gang holed up in an apartment in Mexico City. Aldrete, fearing for her life, wrote a note and tossed it out of the window. It begged for help.

By a strange coincidence police arrived in the barrio looking for a missing child. Seeing them Constanzo fired with his machine gun and revealed his hiding place. Nearly two hundred cops surrounded the place and opened fire on the apartment block.

Constanzo persuaded another member to shoot him and his lover Martin Quintana Rodriguez.The bodies of the two men were found in a cupboard, blood-soaked and entangled. Three survivors, including Sara Aldrete, were arrested and jailed.

The brides of Satan can appear anywhere at any time. In Brisbane, Australia, a couple described as 'two sadistic lesbian teenagers' stalked and stabbed a tourist. Their victim, 59-year-old grandmother Dulcie Brook, was walking in Noosa National Park in 1998 when she was attacked by the two demented dykes who called them-selves 'Antichrist' and 'Angel of Sorrow'.

Sarah Bird stabbed Mrs Brook 22 times with a blunt knife and then proceeded to cut her throat. Her girlfriend, Aleaha Schipper, then hit the victim on the head and helped to throw her body over a cliff.

Prosecutor Peter Ridgeway told the court that Mrs Brook had only survived due to the fact that Bird's knife was blunt. The couple were caught eight days after the attack. Bird, gratified by her bloodbath, said, 'that's cool' when investigators informed her that Mrs Brook had been stabbed 22 times. She added that it had long been her dream to kill. 'I have no idea how it came to be an interest for me,' she said.

Ridgeway described the two girls as 'loners' bonded by an interest in Satanism which provided an insidious system of belief and distorted their reality with complicated lexicons and fantasy games in which they both took on roles as princesses of the underworld and engaged in sexual rituals.

Bird's journals revealed a rich fantasy life in which she (so patently powerless in reality) was an all-powerful killer – She Who Must Be Obeyed.

'I will be feared by everyone,' she wrote.

The American state of Kentucky produced two of the most notorious cases of covens gone wild. Photographs of Rod Ferrell, taken when he was arrested in 1996, show an ugly youth in an orange prison overall. Aged sixteen, with long Goth black hair, he looked older than his years, far from an adolescent – a man at least, and a plain one at that, with pulpy features from a life lived at night and on a diet of substances and Satan.

Nevertheless, with all the charisma of a Bela Lugosi bat, Ferrell managed to attract brides to his cabal. At the time of his arrest for murder, the white-trash warlock had three women in tow – Heather Wendorf, Charity Keesee and Dana Cooper – all of whom were willing to join in with his black magic and two of whom were proved to have colluded in the brutal bludgeoning of Wendorf's (unmarried) parents, Richard Wendorf and Naoma Queen.

There are many who think that all the true facts of this case have still not come to light.The case of the Kentucky vampires became distorted by hysteria and rumour to which people are prone and which seem to continually re-echo the witch-hunt resonance of the seventeenth century. Nevertheless these kids were not innocent. They were far from innocent.

They had first come to the attention of local officials when they were implicated in a break-in at a Kentucky animal shelter in which one puppy had been kicked to death and another had had its legs pulled off.

Rod Ferrell was to later claim that his mother, Sondra, was involved in black magic and that, at an early age, he witnessed human sacrifices. He also claimed that his grandfather raped him when he was five.

Sondra moved around, remarried and, briefly, abandoned her son. Her son, at this point, began to cut himself; in other words, he turned into a clear-cut psychiatric case. Almost textbook. Wounded boy, no facility to express pain, internalises pain, cuts himself, disappears into his imagination, comes up with a new character.

Rod Ferrell began to tell people that he was a 500-year-old vampire named Vesago. He also started to play a vampire role-playing game. It was probably easier than dealing with Sondra who was charged with soliciting one of his friends, a 14-year-old boy, to whom she wrote a letter insisting that she wanted to be his 'vampire bride'.

So Ferrell took drugs, dropped out, stayed out all night, and collected a damaged tribe of people whose imaginations were running along similar lines. One of these was Heather Wendorf, all purple hair and dog collar, who, it was reported, told Ferrell that her parents were hurting her and that she wished he would kill them.

Ferrell initiated rituals where his followers would cut their arms and then drink each other's blood. Enthused by the idea that he could open the Gates to Hell he stated that in order to do so he would have to kill a large number of people and consume their souls.

On the day that the Wendorfs were killed, Heather and Rod had performed a bloody drinking ritual in a cemetery in order to cross over to the 'dark side' and induct her as a vampire. She told investigators that Ferrell had discussed murdering her parents but she had told him not to harm them.

Nevertheless, on 25 November Rod Ferrell and Howard Anderson entered her family home through an unlocked door in the garage. Collecting a crowbar, they entered the house and pulled the telephone out. They then smashed the skull of Richard Wendorf who was asleep on the sofa.

At this point his partner Naoma arrived to find a blood-soaked teenager brandishing an iron bar. She threw coffee in his face, but Ferrell threw her to the floor and beat her to death.

He and Anderson then stole a credit card and the keys to a Ford Explorer and went to pick up the three girls – Heather Wendorf, Dana Cooper and Charity Keesee. The five headed towards New Orleans where they were picked up and arrested. Ferrell, Anderson, Dana Cooper and Heather Wendorf were charged with murder; Charity Keesee was accessory after the fact. Ferrell and Anderson were sent to prison for life; Dana Cooper received a prison sentence of seventeen years, Keesee went down for ten. Heather Wendorf walked.

Presiding Judge Jerry Lockett pointed the finger to the fifteen-year-old Heather, and clearly felt that she was not as innocent as she proclaimed. Since then the bride of Satan has had her share of defenders, not least the crime writer Aphrodite Jones, whose book about the case comes down on her side.

The same month, February 1998, that Rod Ferrell pleaded guilty to murder, a coven from the same state pleaded guilty to killing a couple and their six-year-old daughter. There were three women involved in the murder of the Lillelid family; three women and two youths aged twenty and fifteen. They all fingered the fifteen-year-old, Jason Bryant, as the shooter but it was generally agreed that the ringleader was nineteen-year-old Natasha Cornett.

Cornett was a classic Bride of Satan. She hailed from Betsy Layne, east Kentucky, where her mother, Madonna, inhabiting a trailer, described a litany of domestic dramas to reporter Jesse Fox Mayshark.

She claimed that, at the age of four, she had been molested by a pastor and, later, entered into a series of violent and abusive relationships. She was arrested after firing a gun at her first husband, an alcoholic. Her second husband was reported to have molested her eldest daugher, Velina. By the time Natasha was born in 1979, to a man with whom her mother was having a fleeting affair, Madonna Wallen was both unstable and violent. Abusive to Natasha (she once threw a Bible at her), she finally attempted to commit suicide. Natasha found her mother's comatose body and raised the alarm.

As a child, Cornett had a hole in the heart and an early memory was waking up to find her body scarred and itching. Later, when she was five, her mother worked in an army surplus store and dressed her up in camouflage outfits. The little girl discovered knives in this shop, then she started to cut herself, first on the ankles, then on her arms. She was scarred: first of all by surgeons; then by her mother; then by herself.

As a teenager she started to manifest the problems of a severely troubled young woman. She stopped eating and, having lost 30 lbs, was hospitalised, where she was diagnosed as anorexic and manic depressive. By the time she was thirteen the hair was purple, the jewellery was Celtic and the clothes were black. Ditching school, her hours were spent with Tarot cards, Ouija boards and the role playing-game 'Dungeons and Dragons'.

At the age of seventeen she married Steve Cornett. By then she had become involved in witchcraft – power for the powerless – and the wedding ceremony, held in a community centre near her mother's trailer park, was characterised by a black cake and black balloons. The bride wore a black gown and the bridesmaids were chained together with dog collars, like the cover of an Ozzy album, or something.

'We weren't like most of the kids around us,' her friend Brandon Reynolds told the *Kentucky Post*. 'We listened to different music. We had different ideas about the world. And we were all mad about the way things were.'

Steve Cornett, brought down by his wife's unstable behaviour, filed for divorce. Having stopped drinking because she wanted to get pregnant, she became hysterical and possessive. She often refused to let him leave the house, threatening to kill herself if he did. Suicidal ideation was a psychic norm for Cornett. She told one investigator that she had first tried to kill herself in her crib, at the age of four. Her mother had been shouting and screaming; she could not win her love; she felt herself giving up and tried to suffocate herself with a blanket.

After the split from her husband, Cornett, rejected and angry, wandered aimlessly in New Orleans. Sleeping rough, shooting smack, she began an inexorable stalk towards savage criminality.

By April 1997 she had gathered a coven around her. They would go to her mother's trailer and pierce themselves. She and Karen Howell, a dark beauty straight out of David Lynch, studied magic, cut each other's wrists and drank each other's blood. Howell claimed that she 'heard voices' and wrote a diary so violent that when it was found by her mother she was taken to see a psychiatrist. Howell, like Manuela Ruda, lived her life like a horror-movie script and once said, 'evil spirits have always been around me.'

The third 'bride', Crystal Sturgill, ended up in Natasha's trailer because she had nowhere to go. She had filed charges against her stepfather, claiming that he had repeatedly raped her. Her family took his side and threw her out. At first she and her friends had wanted to be accepted but, finding that this was not to be, they embraced the path of the outsider and followed it with enthusiasm.

'We dressed in black,' she was to say later. 'We did self-mutilation so that we would stand out. We were the freaks, the outcasts . . . We were trying to find answers. We had all been to Church but it didn't provide answers. We were interested in Wicca and books on spells. We were anarchists.'

The three youths, Jason Bryant, Edward Mullins and Joseph Risner, joined the girls in a car and drove from Kentucky to Tennessee, where they planned to embark on a *Natural-Born-Killers* style killing spree. Holing up in a room at the Colley Motel on Interstate 23 they held a seance and a ritual in which Natasha Cornett took up a blade and carved her initials into Jason Bryant's arm. You can imagine the six of them – all in black and pierced and chained and wild. A pack.

The Kentucky coven was carrying two stolen handguns and a wad of stolen cash. The plan was to steal a car, as Joe Risner's old Chevy was overheating. They stopped at a parking place outside Baileyton in Tennessee. Here they came across the Lillelid family who were driving their van from a religious meeting to their home. Ironically they had moved to Tennessee from Miami because they wanted to protect their children from the high crime rate there.

The Lillelid family, innocent and naive, were not intimidated by the gang of teenagers. But then, as Jehovah's Witnesses, they were perhaps protected by that sect's thick skin of faith. They were not, however, protected by anything else on that night.

Vidar and Delfina Lillelid asked the group if they believed in God, supremely ironic in the light of both the previous and subsequent circumstances. Natasha Cornett's few possessions included *The Book of Black Magic*, and her bedroom wall had been painted with an inverted cross. No, she told them, she did not believe in God, he had never come to her aid when she prayed to him as a child.

Instructing Sturgill and Mullins to follow in the car, Jo Risner climbed into the Lillelids' van, produced a gun and told them to drive away. Bryant, holding the second gun, also climbed in with Cornett and Howell. Terrified, the Lillelids said there would be no repercussions if they let them go as they would not recognise them; all teenagers looked the same to them.

Natasha Cornett testified that after the shooting Jason Bryant jumped into the passenger seat of Lillelid's van and tried to force a Marilyn Manson tape into the deck. She said that Risner instructed Vidar Lillelid to drive to a dirt track and then Bryant shot them with both guns. Bryant denied this and blamed the other two youths. The Lillelids died with their children in their arms. Six-year-old Tabitha died in hospital later.

Two hours later the maimed family was found by police sprawled in a ditch, lit by the headlight of the car that the teenagers had abandoned. The coven, having stolen the van, had run over the adults as they made their getaway – Risner apparently laughed as he felt the thud of the vehicle going over their bodies. There were muddy tyre tracks on their legs. Vidar Lillelid had been shot six times, his wife eight times. Their daughter had been shot through the head; their son, two-year-old Peter, had been shot in the back and through the eye. The little boy survived. Later he was fitted with an artificial eye, but the wound had paralysed him and he was unable to walk.

The coven was arrested trying to cross the Mexican border. Cornett told her first lawyer that she was the daughter of Satan. She had seventy razor slashes on her arm. The other two girls had collected trophies. Sturgill had the keys to the Lillelid home; Howell had the lock to Tabitha's Hello Kitty diary hanging on a chain.

An angry mob greeted the teenagers when they were transported from Arizona, where they had been arrested, to Greenville, Tennessee, where they were to be tried. As the kids waited on remand in Greene County Jail, their crime caused hysteria in the coalmining town of Pikeville, Kentucky, in the next-door state, from where they came.

The local carnival that month was heavily policed as the rumour spread that there were more vampire kids in town who were planning to run through the crowds slashing people with razor blades.

The defence for all six highlighted broken homes and violent families. Joe Risner had never met his father; Sturgill did not know who hers was. Jason Bryant had looked after himself after his mother had abandoned the family home leaving her children in the hands of her alcoholic husband. Karen Howell's father was a drunk; her mother had had a nervous breakdown. And so on. It all fell on the deaf ears of the judge Berkeley Bell, whose own son was the same age as Peter Lillelid. He saw the case as a conspiracy to kill made by all six and as an involvement in Satanism that had lost control. The case convinced him that there was such a thing as 'spiritual evil' and he sentenced all six individuals to a life in prison without parole.

Crystal Sturgill subsequently found God. Alone in jail, without a bed and facing a life sentence, she received a letter from a pastor who told her that the good Lord forgave everybody. Later he visited her in jail and converted her to Christianity. Interviewed by *Campus Life* magazine, she said, 'Everyone has done bad things, even Moses. I never knew Moses was a murderer. The people in the Bible weren't perfect either.'

SOURCES
Campus Life, June 2000
Cincinnati Post
the *Guardian*, 1 February 2002
Knoxville News, 22 February 1998
the *Observer*, 10 February 2002
'A Blackened Rainbow' by Jesse Fox Mayshark (www.weeklywire.com)
'All About Adolfo Jesus de Constanzo' by Michael Newton (www.crimelibrary.com)
WICA.org.uk
www.churchofsatan.com
www.CourtTV.com
www.kentuckypost.com
www.time.com

11. THE SUPERBITCHES

AILEEN WUORNOS

The 'science' of the serial killer was developed at the Behavioral Sciences Unit at the FBI headquarters in Quantico, Virginia, where a department of agents work to collate data that point to the uniform characteristics of this type of homicide. The method has given rise to the technique of psychological profiling, where a killer's 'clues' are thought to point to determinant characteristics about his age, place in society, level of insanity, deviance of sexuality and so on. Agent Robert Ressler defined this type of crime in 1978; since then the FBI's information and techniques have been used by police authorities all over the world and the methods have become part of the curriculum for those studying criminology at an academic level.

But as criminal insanity defies belief, so it often defies logical explanation, escaping through the data and statistics, evading the rules. There have been enough serial killers caught to cause the expectation that they will be youngish, white, poor and sexually disturbed. Most of them (but by no means all) will have had horrifying childhoods and some of them will have suffered serious injuries to the head at some point in their lives.

Some facts have become apparent since these strange killers have begun to appear with ever-increasing frequency. The most salient is that women do not tend to wander about, alone, murdering people, at random, for sexual reasons. This is not to say that they are not serial killers – it is merely to say that if they kill a lot of people it tends to be in a different way. And, unlike men, they do not tend to show off about it.

There have been relatively few serious studies, but one made by Eric Hickey in 1991 noted that women are 'quiet killers, every bit as lethal as male serial murderers, but we are seldom aware of one in our midst because of the low visibility of their killing'.

Hickey also stated that, in terms of psychopathology, women exhibited similar characteristics to their male counterparts in that they were 'insincere, amoral, impulsive, prone to exercise manipulative charisma and superficial charm, without conscience and with little insight, since they failed to learn from their mistakes.'

The ongoing statistic is that 72 per cent of female serial killers are American, but that they make up 8 per cent of the total number. In 2002 Hickey surveyed 62 women who were multiple murderesses to establish their motives and methods. He found that the primary motive was money, followed by drugs and a feeling of inadequacy then control, with sex at the bottom. The favourite method is poison (80 per cent), followed by shooting, bludgeoning and suffocation.

Michael and C Kelleher, in their 1998 book *Murder Most Rare*, outlined five types, coming up with the Black Widow (killer of family members), Angels of Death (nurses), Sexual Predator (sexual homicide), Revenge and Profit.

Aileen Wuornos was described as the 'first female serial killer', which was not to say that she was the first multiple murderess; she was not. Belle Gunness killed 49 people between l896 and 1908; Margie Velma Barfield managed to despatch seven husbands and her mother before being caught in 1978.

As Patricia Pearson has pointed out, at the time of Wuornos' arrest, 'only four years earlier ten female serial killers had been arrested across the United States, but the media went wild over Wuornos, as if she were a new species of serpent found in the sea'.

Most female killers kill where they live and/or work – and they kill for reasons that are darkly connected to their needs and to their femininity. They kill their children, they kill their husbands and, if they are nurses, they kill their patients. They kill people whom they know and who exist in their vicinity, dependents who often rely on them completely. It is no coincidence that mothers and nurses are the types that recur so frequently in the high-profile cases of homicide committed by women. While fantasy and pornography seem so often to be part of the male sex criminal's make-up, the minds of the women tend not to be so much fuelled by dreamy notions of sexual conquest and control as deluded by paranoia or motivated by hatred, revenge and money.

Wuornos killed in a manly way. Her cool executions were random and unrelated to her home as, to all intents and purposes, she did not have a home and, even if she had, she was not the type to be in it making a Victoria sponge.

Wuornos' actions were more predatory and thus more threatening, and it was this that imbued her with an aura which, in reality (like most killers), she did not have. Serial killers are like Hollywood celebrities in that way: the 'reality' of their reputation is not the product of an accurate assessment of their genuine presence, it is the result of a combination of media exposure and public perception – meet the real thing and you meet a monosyllabic paranoid neurotic. Aileen Wuornos was sad, dumpy, dull and angry, but she became a myth because she presented a genuine threat to men.

A strange respect surrounds her; she is so American in so many ways – her life a B-movie plot where the female dominatrix sets out to avenge herself for the punishments meted out by life and, in particular, by the men lurking therein. Here, the darkest anima of them all, wandering around the stateside highways, homeless, hopeless, penniless, promiscuous, but not defenceless. Aileen had her anger. And she used it. If he was a man it was simple – he deserved to die. She was a butch gone bananas. The simplicity was almost comical.

If she had been the heroine in a film she would be up there with Tura Satana, but she was not. She was a real-life white-trash maniac who escalated to billboard notoriety. Scarred (thanks to the fact that, as a child, she set fire to herself while playing with a lighter), uneducated, inarticulate, abused, Miss Aileen Wuornos was out of control.

Suspected of at least seven murders, she confessed to six, maintaining that the victims, whom she met while working as a hooker along the I–75 freeway in Florida, were despatched because they attacked her first.

Wuornos, like many of America's rootless sociopaths, wandered under the guise of many identities. Born Aileen Pittman in Rochester, Michigan, on 29 February 1956, she was the daughter of teenage parents who separated months before she was born. Her father served time in a mental hospital as a child-molester. Her mother Diane abandoned Aileen and her older brother Keith to the care of their grandparents. Lauri and Britta Wuornos legally adopted the children as their own.

Pregnant at the age of fourteen, Aileen had a son in 1971. Grandmother Britta, a heavy drinker, died in the same year. Her death was blamed on liver failure. Aileen and Keith became wards of the court, but they were neither protected nor contained. Aileen dropped out of school to work the streets full time, earning her way as a teenage hooker, drifting across the country as the spirit moved her.

The next twenty years were to see a range of delinquency that portended the the savage hatred that turned her to the final nihilism of the outlaw. In May 1974, using the alias Sandra Kretsch, she was jailed in Colorado for disorderly conduct, drunk driving and firing a .22-calibre pistol from a moving vehicle. She skipped town before the court case. In July 1976 she was arrested in Michigan after lobbing a cue ball at a bartender's head. In May 1981 she was arrested in Florida for the armed robbery of a convenience store. Sentenced to prison she was released thirteen months later. In 1984 she was arrested for trying to pass forged cheques at a bank in Florida. In 1985, under the alias Lori Grody, she was named as a suspect in the theft of a pistol and ammunition. In 1986 she was arrested in Miami under her own name, charged with stealing a car and resisting arrest. Police found a .38-calibre revolver and a box of ammunition.

Later that year Volusia County deputies detained 'Lori Grody' for questioning after a male companion accused her of pulling a gun on him and demanding $200. Then she met a lesbian named Tyria Moore in a Daytona gay bar. They became lovers and remained close for four years. In 1987 police in Daytona Beach detained Moore and her companion 'Susan Blahovec' (Wuornos) when they were suspected of hitting a man with a beer bottle.

A year later Wuornos, now sporting the eccentric moniker 'Cammie Marsh Green,' accused a Daytona Beach bus driver of assault and claimed that he pushed her off the bus following an argument. Tyria Moore was listed as a witness to the incident. On 23 July a Daytona Beach landlord accused Moore and Susan Blahovec of vandalising their apartment, ripping out carpets and painting the walls dark brown without his permission.

In November 1988 Susan Blahovec launched a six-day campaign of threatening calls against a Zephyr Hills supermarket, following an altercation over lottery tickets. Aileen Wuornos' anger was not internalised – that all too common female trait that propels victims to self-harm and mutilation and masochism. By 1989 her litany of previous convictions showed an alcohol-aggravated compulsion that was destined to escalate into a combination of paranoia and serious violence. She began to carry a loaded pistol in her handbag.

Working bars and truck stops, she thumbed rides and hitched up and down the freeway. If the man did not want to pay for sex, she stole as much as she could from him. And all the way she dreamed of revenge. It was one of the things she would reveal about herself when chatting to her girlfriend: her desire to avenge herself for the endless injustices that had consumed her life.

Richard Mallory, a 51-year-old electrician, disappeared in November 1989. His car was found abandoned along with his wallet, condoms and a bottle of vodka. His corpse was found a month later. He had been shot three times with a .22 pistol. Mallory had been divorced five times, was a heavy drinker and was often seen in local strip clubs.

After Wuornos had been tried for Mallory's murder an investigative reporter unearthed material that seemed to substantiate her claim that he had raped her. Mallory had served ten years for rape, a salient fact that was neither discovered by her defence counsel nor brought forward at her trial.

On 1 June 1990 the naked body of 43-year-old David Spears was found dumped in a wood north of Tampa. He had been shot six times with a .22. The third naked corpse was Charles Carskaddon, aged forty, a part-time rodeo worker from Missouri. He had vanished along the I–75 on the way to meet his fiancée.

Peter Siems, a 65-year-old merchant seaman turned missionary, left his Florida home to visit relatives in

Arkansas. He never arrived, and a missing-person report was filed with police.

Eugene Burress, aged fifty, left the Ocala sausage factory where he worked to make his normal delivery rounds on 30 July 1990. A missing-person report was filed when he did not return. His body was found by a family picnicking in the Ocala National Forest. The corpse was clothed and had been shot twice with a .22.

Fifty-six-year-old Dick Humphreys, a retired Alabama police chief, was reported missing by his wife when he failed to return home one evening. He was found the next day with seven bullet wounds and the pockets of his trousers turned inside out.

Walter Antonio, aged sixty, a truck driver, was found in some woods. Naked except for his socks, he had been shot four times.

The police caught up with Wuornos thanks, in part, to her habit of pawning the possessions that she had stolen from her victims. In January 1991 they grabbed her at the appropriately named Last Resort, a biker bar in Harbor Oaks, Florida. A day later Tyria Moore was traced to her sister's home in Pennsylvania, where she agreed to testify against her lover.

Wuornos confessed to six murders, all performed, she said, in the act of self-defence. 'I shot 'em 'cause to me it was like a self-defending thing,' she told police, 'I felt if I didn't shoot 'em and didn't kill 'em, first of all . . . if they had survived, my ass would be gettin' in trouble for attempted murder, so I'm up shit creek on that one anyway, and if I didn't kill 'em, you know, of course, I mean I had to kill 'em . . . or it's like retaliation, too. It's like, you bastards, you were going to hurt me.'

Within two weeks of her arrest, Aileen and her attorney had sold movie rights to her story. A bizarre sideshow to the pending murder trial began in late January 1991 with the appearance of Arlene Pralle as Aileen's new best friend.

A 44-year-old rancher's wife and born-again Christian, Pralle told Wuornos in her first letter to prison that Jesus had instructed her to write. Soon they were having daily telephone conversations at Pralle's expense and Pralle appeared on chatshows speaking in Wuornos' defence.

'We are like Jonathan and David in the Bible,' Pralle said. 'It's as though part of me is trapped in jail with her. We always know what the other is feeling and thinking. I just wish I was Houdini. I would get her out of there. If there was a way, I would do it, and we could go and be vagabonds forever.'

Pralle then legally adopted the famous murderess as her daughter.

Aileen's trial for the murder of Richard Mallory opened on 13 January 1992. Eleven days later she took the stand as the only defence witness, repeating her tale of violent rape and beating at Mallory's hands, insisting that she shot him dead in self-defence, using her pistol only after he threatened her life.

There was no hard evidence to support this claim and the jury rejected it. They convicted her of first-degree murder.

'I'm innocent!' she shouted when the verdict was announced. 'I was raped! I hope you get raped! Scumbags of America!'

The jury recommended death and, as of writing, she remains on Death Row.

ROSE WEST
When Rosemary West appeared in Winchester Crown Court in October 1995 it was to answer ten counts of

murder whose details were to promote her into a league of her own. Portrayed as a sexually insatiable, aggressively deviant, sadistic murderess, Rose West emerged from a house in Gloucester to be planted in a unique niche in the realm of modern female criminality.

Born in November 1953, Rose came from an appalling family that could only have served to desensitise and twist her. It would have been surprising, given her circumstances, if she had been a normal functioning human being; her abnormality, however, was a study of violent cruelty whose grotesque specifics were beyond the imagination. You simply could not have made Rose West up; as a character she defies belief.

Her father, Bill Letts, was a drunken sadist who regularly beat his children with his belt, or a lump of wood, or whatever came to hand; and if they weren't around he turned on his wife, Daisy. Daisy suffered a nervous breakdown for which she was treated with electric shock therapy, enduring one bout when she was pregnant with Rose, her fifth child.

Rose showed some signs of mental dysfunction from the beginning, often rocking herself from side to side. Later, as a plump child, she was also slow in class and became isolated when she was bullied. At home she slept in the same bed as her brother Graham with whom she was believed to be enjoying sexual relations.

When Rose was fifteen, her mother left her father and took Rose with her, but Rose went back to live with her father with whom she was sleeping. She achieved a job as a waitress and, in 1968, she met Frederick West.

West hailed from a family of farm labourers who came from Herefordshire. An unattractive leering youth prone to fantastical sexual boasting, he was, nevertheless, his mother's favourite, to the extent, it was said, that he was the one she chose to have sex with. By the early 60s West had sustained two serious injuries to the head, one as a result of a motorbike accident (after which he was in a coma for seven days) and one when a woman he was chasing pushed him off a fire escape, knocking him out cold for 24 hours.

After these accidents his behaviour, never beautiful, became ugly and erratic; there were witnesses who said that Fred West was a Jekyll and Hyde character prone to terrible attacks of savage temper, and you never knew when they were going to happen.

In 1962 he married eighteen-year-old 'Rena' Costello, a wild girl whose education had been received in an approved school and whose remuneration was accomplished through low-level street prostitution. Her hair was bleach blonde, she was a drunk and, at the time of her marriage to West, she was pregnant by an Asian bus driver. Baby Charmaine was the result of this liaison.

The Wests lived in Scotland and Fred drove an ice-cream van. Rena gave birth to their child Anne-Marie in 1964. When he killed a child by accident in the van, Fred left the job and moved south, back to his home of Much Marcle. He and Rena lived in a caravan while Fred worked in an abattoir. At one point Rena left him and returned to find that he was living with her best friend Anna McFall, who became pregnant and demanded that he divorce Rena and marry her. Fred West killed her and his unborn child instead. In July 1967 to be exact.

In 1968 Fred met Rose Letts at a bus stop. She was fifteen and accepted his offer of a lift. A year later she moved in with him and found herself looking after the two little girls, Charmaine and Anne-Marie. They were taken briefly into care when West went to prison for various petty crimes.

Rose then became pregnant herself and gave birth to Heather in 1970. Fred went into prison again. When he came out he killed Rena; it is still uncertain whether he or Rose actually killed nine-year-old Charmaine, who disappeared in 1971 and whose body was exhumed twenty-five years later. West was supposed to have been in prison at the time of the murder and the authorities believed that Rose killed her and he later buried the body.

Fred West moved the family out of the caravan park and into a flat in Gloucester and Rose became a prostitute. Fred would watch her activities through a peephole and encourage her to expand her repertoire to bondage and sex toys. Fred was very interested in pornography; his sexual imagination knew no limits and Rose was willing to try anything. At this point a baby-sitter claimed that they had drugged and raped her.

Fred and Rose got married in 1972 (despite the fact that he was not officially divorced from Rena, not that she was in a position to complain since her body was decomposing in a field) and Rose had another daughter, Mae.

They then moved into 25 Cromwell Street, Glouces-ter, the house that was to go down as one of the most famous landmarks in criminal history. The large house had a garden, attic and cellar, all of which were to come in useful to Fred.

The Wests took lodgers in the form of young male students with whom Rose (then nineteen) immediately slept. At first she entertained her clients in a room at the front of the house. Her husband, meanwhile, turned the cellar into a 'torture chamber' in which Anne-Marie, aged eight, was the first victim.

Fred West, having constructed a metal chastity belt which held a vibrator, inserted it into the little girl's vagina. When she screamed with pain Rose sat on her face while Fred West raped her. Rose told her it was for her own good, and that she would be beaten if she told anyone. Anne-Marie suffered some internal damage and could not attend school for several days.

The treatment of Anne-Marie, who testified against her mother at the trial, runs as a hideous motif throughout the story of the West household. She has said that she was beaten, raped, humiliated and forced to have oral sex with her stepmother. She was propelled into prostitution, having sex with her stepmother's clients while Fred looked on through a peephole.

In 1992 the Wests employed seventeen-year-old Caroline Owens as a baby-sitter. She repelled their original advances to no avail. So Fred West punched her senseless in the van. She claimed that she was bound and gagged, and taken to Cromwell Street where Rose kissed her and Fred beat her genitals with a leather belt. Rose then performed cunnilingus on her while Fred had sex with Rose. When Rose left the room, Fred raped the teenager.

Caroline Owens escaped, alerted the police, and Fred West was arrested. The couple got off with a fine. Another baby-sitter, Lynda Gough, mysteriously disappeared. When her mother came round asking after her, she was fobbed off by Rose, who answered the door wearing Gough's slippers.

The Wests lived in Cromwell Street for twenty years. West always had a day job and, at night, he would bang around the house, putting up extensions, digging in the cellar. Always something.

Lodgers, students and au pairs came and went. One, Juanita Mott, disappeared in 1975. Shirley Robinson moved in. A former prostitute, she became pregnant by Fred at the same time that Rose was pregnant by one of her West Indian clients. Rose bore Tara in 1977.

Robinson, meanwhile, was murdered and buried under the concrete slabs of the patio.

Delinquent teenage girls favoured Cromwell Street as a place to hang out, a mistake as it turned out, as one was to find out when she turned up to have a cup of tea and a chat and found herself being bundled into a room where Fred was with two young girls and where there was a whip and pictures of people having sex with animals. Rose raped the girl anally with a vibrator, followed by Fred, who also anally raped her. She was then bound with parcel tape, flung down on a bed, anally raped with an implement and then raped again by Fred.

In 1978 Rose gave birth to Louise, and then to Barry. Rosemary, born in 1982, and Lucyann, born in 1983, were both by West Indian fathers. Anne-Marie left the house when she was fifteen, suffering premonitions that if she stayed she would die.

Her place as a teenage object of desire was taken by sixteen-year-old Heather, who was constantly beaten and fondled by Fred. In 1987 he killed her and buried her. And that was to become a family joke. Heather under the patio. It was also, more than a decade later, to cause his downfall.

Rose had seven children to look after in a house that often acted as a brothel, set up with a bar and porn videos, many of which had been made by Fred and showed Rose having sex with various clients and, at times, with her husband.

All the evidence pointed to the fact that Fred and Rose loved each other, and would do anything for each other, in a bizarre version of marital accord which set new standards for the diversity of romantic emotions.

The obsessive sexuality that pervaded Cromwell Street was, perhaps, the thing that set this extraordinary duo apart. Sex was their drive and their motivation and their entire reason for living; every day was coloured by it. No boundaries were drawn, and if the children were involved then so be it. Rose never wore pants and sometimes Fred would push his finger into her, hold it in front of the children's faces and say, 'Smell that. That's your mother.'

One acquaintance, Mary Halliday, who knew the couple at this time and slept with Rose, said, 'She was absolutely insatiable. She used to say that no man or woman could ever satisfy her. I don't think she got much sexual pleasure from Fred – he wasn't very well endowed.'

In 1992 a policewoman named Hazel Savage appears in this narrative and it is certainly due to her suspicions and to her persistence that other adult lives were saved and the young West children escaped with some hope for a safe future.

Pursuing a complaint of rape by a teenage girl, Detective Constable Savage organised a search of Cromwell Street which resulted in the finding of evidence of pornography and child abuse. Fred West was charged with the rape and sodomy of a minor, and the younger children were taken into care. Rose was arrested on a charge of aiding.

The witnesses faltered and failed to press on with the case. The Wests returned home. The pornographic material was confiscated and Rose, terrified that she would lose her children, attempted to pursue a more sensible path by deflecting some of her husband's more unpleasant suggestions.

But DC Savage's 'hunch' would not leave her alone. She had heard Anne-Marie's stories of abuse and incest (the teenager was now living in another part of town with her boyfriend) and she heard that the other little girls would not speak because they were terrified of ending up 'under the patio like Heather'.

Where was Heather? DC Savage wondered. She was not at home, neither had she paid taxes or been to see a doctor. How could she subsist without a job? She had not claimed social security. Her records were blank.

On 24 February 1994 the police arrived at Cromwell Street and started digging up the garden. Rose insisted that Heather had gone away, 'to be a lesbian', but the next morning Fred confessed to killing Heather, cutting her up and burying her.

The police found Heather and, over the next couple of months, they found a lot of other people as well – twelve bodies in all. Most were found buried under the patio and in the cellar at Cromwell Street, but Charmaine was found at their former home in Gloucester, while Rena West and Anna McFall were found buried in fields.

Fred provided the police with fantastic confessions in which it was difficult to discern truth from fiction. At one point he told them they 'didn't know the half of it'. Then, on New Year's Day 1995, he hanged himself.

Rosemary West's trial opened before Mr Justice Mantell and hundreds of journalists. In November 1995 she was found guilty of ten murders and sentenced to life imprisonment. Her stance was that Fred had died and left her to take the rap; that she knew nothing of the killing of the seven girls who had been buried in her house, and that she had known nothing of the death of Heather until the police had told her that Fred had confessed to the girl's murder.

Rose West took to the stand, which was a mistake as opinion could never be and would never be on her side and she did not present a sympathetic spectacle.

'It's all very well for someone to say I did this or I did that,' she said, 'because I'm the one now in the spotlight.

Fred West is dead and I've got to take responsibility for what he's done.'

There are some people who agree with Mrs West's perception of her own circumstances and think that that is indeed what happened – that Mrs West was imprisoned for her dead husband's crimes. Brian Masters, a respected and thorough writer, devoted his book *She Must Have Known* to detailing the irregular aspects of this case and to outlining a haunting and convincing argument for the innocence of Rose West based on the fact that there was very little concrete evidence to underpin her actually being guilty of murder. There was no evidence at all to specifically link Mrs West with the murder of most of the women who had been buried in her house. She did not know them.

The questions that acted against her centred on how Fred West, alone and at night, managed to lure women into his car without an accomplice and, although there was no testimony to say that Rose West was in the car at the time of the murders, there was testimony that, in one incident, she had been in the car in order to lure a surviving girl to their house so that they could have sex with her.

Mrs West did not aid her own cause when she denied that she knew Shirley Robinson, a woman who was carrying her husband's baby. Her son Stephen explained this by saying that his mother had 'a memory like a sieve'. Fred, meanwhile, told police that he had killed Robinson and his unborn child because she was trying to usurp Rose's place. And he wasn't having that.

The atmosphere surrounding the case was irrevocably discoloured by the speculation cultivated by pressmen who offered potential witnesses thousands of pounds to tell their stories before the trial – stories that went into the tabloid newspapers and were thus invalidated by how they were procured and where they were published. They were nevertheless perceived as true by a public ready to believe in Mrs West's demonism.These factors did not help the defence, which was regularly faced with witnesses whose personal interest was to exaggerate their stories so they would be more valuable.

Brian Masters points out that it is perfectly possible that Mrs West might not have known what her husband was doing. Fred West's sexual relations with Anne-Marie were, by and large, conducted outside the house and Anne-Marie, like most abused children, was ordered not to tell.

The record of the taped interview shows that Mrs West seemed to be genuinely upset and surprised when the police told her that Fred West had confessed to the murder of her daughter Heather. Fred had told her that Heather had run away and Heather's unhappiness was known to Rose; she might well have believed him. She was an unintelligent dysfunctional woman whose emotional make-up was the product of a seriously abnormal life and would thus fail to manifest any normal characteristics of demonstrative grief or affection.

People came and went all the time from her house; people came and went without saying goodbye. Some of them, later tracked down by the police, were aware that Fred West was an unpleasant fantasist obsessed by sex, but they, like Mrs West, knew nothing of the morbid mayhem that had been going on for years in the house where they lived.

Fred West was always 'doing things around the house'. Some women might have wondered what it was that their husbands were doing, a very curious woman might have made it her business to find out, but Mrs West had several young children and might well have been preoccupied by their lives.

Fred, from the start of his interrogation by police, insisted that his wife knew nothing about his activities, that he had buried the bodies without her knowledge. He also made it clear that Mrs West was not in the house at the time of Heather's murder and, though she returned later, he was able to bury the girl without his wife's knowledge.

He is thought to have committed suicide not from conscience – as a psychopath he did not have one – but because he could not live with the fact that his wife now knew everything and would reject him as a result.

There can be little doubt that Mrs West was guilty of dreadful cruelty to her children. There can be little doubt that she allowed a terrible sexual deviance and violence to pervade the atmosphere in which they lived and thus to afflict their lives. But there is much doubt as to the specifics of her supposed collusion in all the murders committed by her husband.

BEVERLY ALLITT

The cases of female homicide tell many stories of demented nurses who have taken it upon themselves to despatch the very people who are in their care. They tend to get away with it because everyone in their vicinity cannot register the truth of the reality that is manifesting itself among the hospital beds.

A nurse is an archetype about whom it is impossible to believe the worst, but who, oddly, is also capable of doing the worst and, in the last twenty years, she has manifested this with sinister regularity.

In 1985 Bobbie Sue Terrell was arrested in Illinois, having worked in many nursing homes where the fact was missed that the 29-year-old had been diagnosed as schizophrenic and suffered from Münchausen syndrome by proxy, a psychological condition that was to become a common defence for women who killed in hospitals. Its purpose seems to be to gain attention and it is characterised by the enjoyment of taking patients (particularly children) to the edge of death in order to resuscitate them, apparently save them, and thus gain the accolades and affection generally allowed to heroines.

Terrell gave lethal insulin injections to twelve elderly patients in Florida and then, having mutilated herself, would appear in the police station saying that there was a serial killer on the loose. Her plea of insanity was successful.

Gwendolyn Graham and Catherine Wood, two deranged dykes working in a Michigan hospital in the late 80s, started off by experimenting with sexual asphyxia and proceeded to murder. Initiating a spree entitled 'The Murder Game,' the duo picked patients whose initials would spell 'murder'. Their early attempts to kill elderly women were stalled by the strength of the victims' retaliatory struggles.

Finally Graham smothered a woman suffering from Alzheimer's. She proceeded from one patient to another, killing each one, and becoming so aroused that the murders acted as foreplay and, having killed, she would have sex with her lover, Wood, as soon as possible afterwards.

Graham's passions were further inflamed by stealing items from victims – dentures, jewellery and so on. She also gained enjoyment in the morgue when her duties involved washing the body.

Graham and Wood then began boasting of their activities to other people, boasts that were inevitably dismissed as reckless fantasy. Graham and Wood split up. Graham went to work in another hospital while Wood confessed everything to her husband. He took a year to turn her in to the authorities. Wood turned evidence against her ex-girlfriend, saying that she had been particularly alarmed when Graham informed her that she wanted to throw one of the babies against a window.

Gwendolyn Graham was convicted of five counts of first-degree murder and sentenced to six life sentences with no parole.

In America in 1996 Kristen Gilbert, 33, working in a hospital in Massachusetts, was suspected of murder after killing four patients and causing three to nearly die of heart failure. When the bodies were exhumed, epinephrine was found in the tissues. Gilbert, meanwhile, was sent to prison for phoning a bomb threat to the hospital in an attempt to stall the investigation. She was eventually convicted of four counts of murder and two of attempted murder, for which she was sentenced to life in prison.

England produced its own sister of no mercy when Beverly Allitt, a prolific and compulsive serial killer, materialised in 1991. At 23, she was unstable – desperate for attention – and was said to suffer from Münchausen's syndrome, the aforementioned condition where an individual will constantly visit doctors with imaginary ailments and, in severe cases, will (successfully) demand unnecessary surgery. It is an obsessive, delusional state and can be very dangerous. The most famous sufferer was Wendy Scott, who, having undergone 42 operations, finally contracted a genuine illness, intestinal cancer, at which point no doctor would treat her and she died of it it.

People who knew Beverly Allitt well said she had been a cruel person since the age of thirteen and, after she was arrested, an ex-boyfriend described her bouts of violence. Nevertheless, she was given a position on the children's ward at the short-staffed Grantham and Kesteven General Hospital in Lincolnshire. In the space of 58 days she murdered five children and attacked nine others, leaving some of them permanently disabled.

At first she avoided all suspicion. Liam Taylor, seven weeks, died in his parents' arms after his heart stopped. Tim Hardwick, eleven, died of a heart attack. Toddler Cayley Desmond's heart stopped twice. Baby Paul Crampton was injected with lethal amounts of insulin. Bradley Gibson, five, stopped breathing but was revived. Allitt had injected him with potassium. Becky Phillips, at three months, died after she was given an overdose of insulin. Her sister Kate's heart stopped; she was resuscitated but the attack caused permanent brain damage. Becky died in Nurse Allitt's arms; her parents thought she had saved Kate's life. They saw her as a family friend and even asked her to be a godmother.

When it was found that an injection of insulin had killed Paul Crampton, the staff at the hospital assumed that it had been administered by a member of the public. Meanwhile more babies were attacked. Christopher King nearly died of respiratory failure; Patrick Elstone nearly died twice; the same thing happened to little Christopher Peasgood. Finally, the thirteenth victim, fifteen-month-old Clare Peck, died of what was originally thought to be asthma but was, in fact, a lethal dose of potassium.

Finally the police were called in and related 26 attacks to Nurse Allitt. Missing medical records were found in her room and she was arrested. Her defence detailed the effects of Münchausen's syndrome.

In the case of Münchausen's syndrome by proxy the individual causes a child to suffer in order to gain attention to herself, and there have been many cases of children being severely abused in order to show the requisite ailments. It is a classic symptom that if the child remains ill the carer will be calm but if the child shows signs of recovery the carer will become alarmed.

In May 1993 Beverly Allitt was found guilty of four counts of murder, eleven counts of attempted murder and eleven counts of causing grievous bodily harm. She was given thirteen life sentences, the harshest sentence ever given to a female defendant in Britain.

Six years later Kate Phillips, permanently brain-damaged by Nurse Allitt, and suffering both partial blindness and partial paralysis, was awarded £2 million by the Lincolnshire Health Authority.

MYRA HINDLEY

Myra Hindley's demonisation as a definitive icon of female criminality goes beyond the actuality of her crimes, which, though unforgivable, have been far superseded by the violence of other psychopaths, both male and female, many of whom have killed more people and some of whom have involved children in their excesses.

Other killers who admit that fame is their spur would do well to survey the disadvantages of exposure when it comes to long-term legislative procedure or judicial relief. Myra's profile has served her no advantage and is the reason why the public can still remember the dead children on Saddleworth Moor.

Ten-year-old Lesley Ann Downey was raped and murdered. Ian Brady recorded her pleas for mercy before she died and the tapes were found in a left luggage office by policemen who found the ticket down the hollow spine of a prayer book in Brady's house. It is that little girl's cry that continues to drown Myra's loud appeals for clemency. Myra's voice was on that tape.

Hindley, rather than her partner Ian Brady (a clever but psychotic sadist who has never shown any sign of remorse), has become the face of evil, recycled into contemporary culture as art (Marcus Harvey's portrait), song (The Smiths' 'Suffer Little Children') and theatre (the play *And All the Children Cried*).

Myra Hindley has been in prison since 1966. She was sentenced to life for the murder of twelve-year-old John Kilbride and ten-year-old Lesley Ann Downey and being an accessory to the killing of seventeen-year-old Edward Evans. In 1986, having denied it for over twenty years, Brady and Hindley finally confessed to the murders of Keith Bennett, twelve, and Pauline Reade, sixteen. All the bodies were buried on Saddleworth Moor with the exception of Edward Evans, who was killed when Ian Brady attacked him with an axe in front of a witness. That witness then informed the police and Brady was arrested.

In 2001 Hindley supplied three maps to forensic archaeologists searching for the body of Keith Bennett. She had twice returned in an effort to find it but with no success. The little boy's brother, Alan, has never given up hope of giving the child a formal burial.

Myra Hindley came from Gorton, Manchester. At the age of nineteen she went to work in a chemical company where she met Ian Brady, the fatherless son of a waitress. He was older and had grown up in the Gorbals slums of Glasgow. Evincing early signs of criminal insanity, Brady was fascinated by Nazism and enjoyed torturing animals. He had a criminal record by the age of sixteen and a term in Strangeways had succeeded in confirming his nihilism and aiding his commitment to giving full vent to the ideas fanned by his arrogance and personal derangement.

Myra's story was always that she was in love with Ian Brady and would have done anything for that sullen, aloof and strangely glamorous man. In Myra's telling it was Brady who led the disastrous dance as a *folie-à-deux* over which she had no power. Except Myra's voice was on that tape. And Myra helped to bury the bodies.

One policeman who had dealt with her for years (and had taken her confession to the murders of Reade and Bennett in 1986) has opined that Hindley was a perfectly normal girl before she met Brady. If she had not met him she might well, by now, be living as a normal married housewife.

This notion was undermined by Ian Brady, who has written various 'open' letters about Hindley, all of which condemned her argument that she was powerless in the face of his personality and his violent threats.

'Myra can kill in cold blood or rage,' he wrote, 'In that respect we were an inexorable force.' Another letter (to the Home Secretary Jack Straw) said that their relationship was not a *folie-à-deux* and that she was a willing partner when they 'experimented with the concept of total possibility'.

He noted that she continued to write to him for several years after they were imprisoned. 'In character she is essentially a chameleon, adopting whatever camouflage will suit and voicing whatever she believes the individual wishes to hear.'

As Ian Brady campaigns for his right to commit suicide, Myra is campaigning for her freedom. Her original sentence, set by the Home Office, was for thirty years, which ended in 1996. She has done her time, she thinks – three times the average life sentence.

Several Home Secretaries have disagreed with her and, in 2000, the British House of Lords ruled that she was uniquely evil and should remain in jail for life. This position is politically comfortable in that it reflects public opinion. Polls tend to show that the British man in the van is against the release of Hindley. In 1997

Marcus Harvey's portrait of her, presented at the Sensation exhibition at the London Royal Academy, was pelted with eggs.

Trends in progressive liberal thinking are beginning to support the human rights argument to free Ms Hindley, a position that has been argued by more than one judge.

In 1993 Lord Lane, the Lord Chief Justice, chaired a House of Lords committee which argued that murder ranges from mercy killing to serial killing and should not carry an inflexible mandatory life sentence that takes no account of a wide-ranging set of circumstances, apart from the basic one that some murderers are twenty and some forty. A life sentence is a very different punishment to every individual condemned to serve it, and those differences do not necessarily reflect the nature of the crime that that individual has committed.

In May 2002 this stance was strengthened by British Lord Chief Justice Lord Woolf. His advisory panel set out new sentencing guidelines whose intent was to grant more flexibility to the idea of a 'life' sentence.

The same month the European Court of Human Rights stripped the Home Secretary of his ability to interfere with the sentencing of a criminal by exercising a power over tariff. Up to this point the minister had the right to increase a person's term in prison after the judge had convicted him and determined his sentence. The Home Secretary was further relieved of his 'right' to keep murderers in jail once the parole board has recommended their release. It is seen as incompatible with the European Convention of Human Rights (drafted by British lawyers) that a politician should have the power to decide sentencing.

At the time of writing Hindley, at the age of sixty, was working on using the system to avail herself of freedom.

She has lodged an application with the European Court of Human Rights against her 'whole life' tariff, arguing that, in the light of current judgements, successive Home Secretaries have acted beyond their powers by ordering her to stay behind bars.

'Should she be released?' asked a *Guardian* leader on 29 May 2002. 'Of course she should ... The main reason she has not been is that her release has been in the hands of politicians who have not dared take on the tabloids. The body which ought to take this decision – the parole board, which assesses risk – has scrutinised her minutely, and recommended an open prison, a pre-step to release ...'

In February 2000 Hindley communicated with Duncan Staff for a BBC documentary. As he correctly pointed out, despite the number of books written about the Moors Murderers, no one has come close to explaining what turned a good Catholic girl from Manchester into a woman capable of the most appalling crime; a woman who, by the time she was 23, had helped to viciously cut down five very young, very defenceless people, all between July 1963 and October 1965.

Hindley has not been in a position to offer the public many enlightening reflections based on self-analysis, though, she has, of course, had three decades to ponder upon this complicated subject. One of the most revealing statements she made to Duncan Staff was when she told him that she was aware that 'there must be a callous streak in my nature, a cruel streak even. I still don't know what it was rooted in, or where it came from. Sometimes I've thought I'd drive myself insane trying to discover what.'

Staff, visiting her in prison, described a woman with immaculately manicured nails, walking on sticks and wearing a lilac trousersuit. She told him her childhood had been one of violence, characterised by a drunken father. She also confirmed her stance that it was Brady who indoctrinated her and influenced her, drawing her away from her Catholic faith, and then repeatedly raping, beating and sexually humiliating her. 'Then, one evening,' she told Staff, 'he told me he wanted to do a perfect murder and I was going to help him.'

She agreed to scout for victims in her van. In July 1963 Pauline Reade was picked up and killed on the moor. Hindley says that Brady killed and raped the teenage girl but Brady contends that Hindley had been involved in the actual killing and had sexually assaulted Pauline Reade.

One of his open letters said that Hindley 'insisted upon killing Lesley Ann Downey with her own hands, using a two foot length of silk cord, which she later used to enjoy toying with in public, in the secret knowledge of what it had been used for.'

Duncan Staff repeatedly attempted to make Hindley address this, the most horrifying part of her abnormal biography. Finally she left a message on his answering service: 'I'm having a great deal of difficulty with the Lesley Ann Downey thing. I think I'll just have to keep it brief. I just find it hard to believe that I could have been such a cruel, cruel bastard.'

ILSE KOCH and IRMA GRESE
The Third Reich bred a population of monsters but there were few women among them. Ilse Koch and Irma Grese were unique, not only as demons of Hitler's regime, but as monsters of a criminal cruelty that was megalomaniac, murdering, and sado-sexual.

Despite the waves of genocidal mayhem and ethnic cleansing that have swept over world history since the end of the Second World War, few female contenders have pushed themselves to the upper echelons of political power where they have been allowed full vent to practice their homicidal mania. Isle Koch and Irma Grese still stand out.

Irma Grese was in charge of the female prisoners (thirty thousand or so) at Auschwitz at a time when it was considered to be a Nazi duty to eradicate the Jewish race. Grese immersed herself in the final solution with fanatical efficiency. Rising at 7 a.m. to spend the day killing, she wore the full SS (male) uniform, complete with jack-boots and whip. She was accompanied by two Alsatian dogs which would pin a prisoner to the ground while Grese jumped on the stomach of the woman (or child) until they died.

Her killing was explosive and often spontaneous; she would whip a female prisoner to death for no reason; she once stood in front of a woman, smiled at her, and then shot her in the face. Tried as a war criminal, she displayed neither regret nor remorse. She was hanged on 14 December 1945.

The legend that the Nazis made lampshades out of human skin has the aura of dreadful urban legend, but the truth was that both Irma Grese and Ilse Koch had these objects in their homes.

Ilse Koch, who lived at Buchenwald with her husband Karl, commandant of the camp, once ordered two Jews to be murdered because she wanted the tattoos on their backs. Their skins were treated and brought to her. She had them made them into lampshades. Later, when more skins were brought to her, she made a pair of gloves. Later her interior decoration ideas stretched to a sideboard on which she placed a display of heads. They had been severed from the bodies of Jewish prisoners and carefully shrunk down to the size of grapefruit.

It is interesting that this woman, given the political right to unleash the full vent of lethal and sexual psychomania, turned into a killer with similar characteristics to the criminal personality of male serial killers operating outside the war. The unfathomable 50s serial murderer Ed Gein also kept the trophies of death around his house (and on his body) as decoration.

As a teenage girl Koch was a buxom blue-eyed blonde with a penchant for sexy storm troopers so she was very ready to assimilate the doctrines of the Nazi Youth Party. At the age of seventeen she was working in a book shop in Dresden (selling propaganda) when, one day in the 30s, Heinrich Himmler walked in with his aide Karl Koch and ordered him to mate with her. They were married later that year.

Karl Koch was not a beauty. In fact, he has been compared to a pig. But he was a leading light of the Nazi party and was given command of the Buchenwald concentration camp. He installed his wife in a villa nearby and, while she dutifully 'bred' two appropriately Aryan children, he indulged himself in sex orgies.

Ilse, also somewhat voracious in the bedroom department, slept with every SS officer available and started to treat the Buchenwald inmates as pawns in her sex games. She became known as the Bitch of Buchenwald. She cavorted semi-naked in front of the prisoners, and Jews were beaten to death if they glanced at her by mistake. She encouraged officers to shoot people randomly, firing at the prisoners as they darted back and forth across the yard, where they could be shot down as if in a fairground game. Massacres such as these were seen to arouse Ilse to a sexual frenzy. Killing, it seemed, was her form of foreplay.

She was tried as a war criminal and sentenced to life in prison. She appeared again, on trial in Germany, in

1950, to answer more charges of murder. Outside the window a crowd shrieked Kill Her! Kill Her!

Her dairymaid beauty had turned into blowsiness. She did not blame her husband for this, but she blamed him for everything else.

'I was merely a housewife,' she wept. 'I was busy raising my children.'

BRENDA SPENCER

Teenage spree killers massacring children in school yards seem to be common nowadays, so common that in 1999 FBI agents from the aforementioned behavioural science department in Virginia visited various schools in order to impart information about the identification of 'warning signs and risk factors'. The belief was that having identified the characteristics of adult psychopaths, the same kind of techniques could be applied to illuminate 'risk factors' and the genuinely dangerous pupil could be differentiated from the normal sullen horror-movie-loving 'loner' by a process of 'evaluations'.

But profiling, as more than one person has pointed out, is not an exact science. The 'risk' stigma would be a difficult tag to stick on any young person, particularly as, to the rebel, it would doubtless be worn as a medal of honour. Meanwhile the teen-psycho continues to run riot in the art departments, the science labs and the canteens.

From 1996 to 2002, worldwide, 34 schools have been affected by this phenomenon – kids going crazy with guns, mowing down teachers and other kids. There have been terrible incidents in England and in the Netherlands, but most of them have been in Germany and in America.

In 1998 Mitchell Johnson, thirteen, and Andrew Golden, eleven, killed four people at Westside Middle

School in Arkansas. A couple of months later Kip Kinkel, fifteen, killed two people at Thurston High School in Oregon. The most high-profile school massacre, if only because of the numbers involved, was at Columbine in 1999 when two students rampaged through the Colorado high school and killed fifteen people.

Since then there have been twenty other incidents – from a school in Michigan where a six-year-old boy armed with a .32 shot a little girl, to Erfurt, Germany, in April 2002 where nineteen-year-old Robert Steinhaeuser killed thirteen teachers, two students and one policeman in a rampage which also wounded ten others.

The tragedies tell of disgruntled youths – depressed, angry, suicidal, deranged – planning revenge, arming themselves with semi-automatics and behaving like something in a movie. But it was a girl who had the original idea; a girl who could be said to have set this trend. Brenda Spencer was the first. This is is not an accolade but it is a fact.

In 1979 Brenda Spencer, at the age of sixteen, fired at the very young pupils going into San Diego's Grover Cleveland Elementary School. She was armed with a .22 calibre rifle she had been given by her father for Christmas. She killed two people and injured nine children between the ages of six and twelve.

The Spencers lived so close to the school that Brenda just waited for the principal to open up and picked people out as they were walking in. Then bam! She set a precedent which demented adolescent shooters have been following ever since.

The principal died, as did a school caretaker who went to help him. Authorities then drove a dustbin cart across the school gates to prevent further bullets and, after hours of negotiation with police (and interviews with newspapermen), Spencer finally surrendered.

'It was a lot of fun seeing children shot,' she was reported to have said. These words were to come back and haunt her subsequent bids for freedom in the same way that Lesley Ann Downey's screams were to always haunt Myra Hindley's appeals for clemency.

When Brenda Spencer was asked why she did it she famously answered, 'I just started shooting, that's it. I just did it for the fun of it. I just don't like Mondays. I just did it because it's a way to cheer the day up. Nobody likes Mondays.'

All this seemed quite punk so (Sir) Bob Geldof wrote a song about it and the Boomtown Rats had a huge hit – 'I Don't Like Mondays.'

Brenda Spencer, meanwhile, went to number one in the crime parade, achieving worldwide notoriety, which is what she had wanted. A week earlier she had informed friends that she was going to do something 'big to get on TV'. Photographs of her showed a chic young girl with fringe and shades and attitude written all over her. She could have been a pop star, with that look, but she went berserk instead. Postal, as they say in America. She liked violent films. And she had spent her formative years shooting at birds out of her bedroom window. She pleaded guilty to first-degree murder and assault with a deadly weapon and was sentenced to 25 years.

Cam Miller, who was nine when Brenda Spencer shot him in the back, testified at her trial and was to later say that the look she gave him was 'enough to scare anyone to death'.

She has spent most of her life in a women's prison and has been turned down for parole several times. Her mental state inclines towards depressive and she has been treated for that illness. At the age of 38 she said that she felt better. 'I'm not scared all the time.'

In 1993 she claimed, for the first time, that she had been under the influence of drink and drugs (PCP) when she opened fire, though why she should think this is an excuse is anybody's guess. Anyway, that was her claim and it was accompanied by claims that the reason tests had showed negative was because her defence attorney and various policemen had conspired against her. She also claimed that she had been given mind-altering drugs for two years after her arrest which had left her incapacitated and unable to present a fair defence for herself.

'People who saw me say I was a zombie during that time,' she has said. 'I said what they told me to say, I did what they told me to do.'

She claimed that the PCP had made her hallucinate that commandos in paramilitary combat uniform were advancing towards her father's house and her shooting was a defence. She also claimed that some of the children who were wounded were wounded by the police, who were also shooting.

The board of 1993 turned her claim down having been reminded that Brenda Spencer had shown no remorse and that she had planned the spree for some days before carrying it out.

Five years later Spencer tried again and was (unanimously) turned down again at a hearing at which she said she felt responsible for the school shootings that had occurred since 1979. 'What if they got their idea from what I did?' she said in a statement. She told that board that she was a different person. 'I know saying I'm sorry doesn't make it all right,' she said.

This time she claimed that she came from a violent home and had been beaten and abused by her father, Wallace Spencer, who has never spoken publicly about this case and has refused all interviews. Her claims were not viewed with great seriousness as they had never been made before. One attorney pointed out that there were signs of a woman whose rehabilitation was not all it could have been. She had recently burned a paper clip and carved the words, 'courage' and 'pride' onto her chest. This, he observed, showed an inability to deal with stress and an inclination to act out anger.

Brenda Spencer's victims are divided in their opinions. Some say she should stay where she is.

'A cruel monster,' said Cam Miller.

'You never forget,' said the principal's widow Kathe Wragg in 1993. 'It did a lot to our family.'

Others are willing to allow that she was very young and that she might have served her time.

Jeff and Kevin Karpiak, who had been in the yard when Brenda Spencer started shooting, gave an interview in 2001 in which they said they remembered the murders as if they were yesterday. But they observed that time heals and that they remained optimistic because 'evil can be outdone by good'.

CAROL BUNDY

Carol Bundy looked like one of the many white-trash housewives who smooth their old Chevys around the freeways of the San Fernando valley, the hot suburb of Los Angeles where property prices are cheapest, where the porn industry is based and where the drive-through culture centres on mart and mall.

Born in 1942, she did not start out life as a superbitch. She slowly became one, moulded by a mixture of grotesque personal circumstances and a personality that was predisposed to the protection of delusion in the face of grim reality. Addicted to the worst kind of men – thieves, drunks and liars – Carol skidded from one relationship to another, always believing that she was the beneficiary of true and everlasting love, that the man she had chosen was a hero, that she was right to do anything for him. She was co-dependency gone crazy – a mad masochist who slowly and inexorably turned into a terrifying and callous killer.

'Women like us aren't as rare as we thought,' she once commented, on finding herself in a cell next to the girlfriend of Kenneth Bianchi, also known as the Hillside Strangler.

It is unsurprising, given Carol Bundy's lethal outings, to learn that her father, Charles, was a maniac. He ended up killing himself, but before he succeeded in that welcome event he managed to terrorise his family with his violent outbursts and once shot the family cat.

Bundy's mother was a violent woman who did not like her and who died early. Carol and her sister Vicky were forced to take her place in their father's bed. Carol then began to behave very strangely and, at the age of fifteen, she took to running through the streets naked. Sleeping with both men and women, she became compulsively promiscuous, as so many incest victims do.

In 1968 she graduated as a nurse in California and married Grant Bundy, also a nurse. They had two sons, but Bundy was violent and Carol, vulnerable because her eyesight was deteriorating, took her children to a shelter for battered women. Soon after this, going blind, feeling alone, she met Jack Murray, a married man with whom she fell in love. Surgery on her eye provided her with better sight, which was not the advantage she thought it would be. It allowed her, for a start, to study her own appearance, and that particular reflection was of a fat woman to whom Nature had shown no favours. On the other hand her new sight did not allow her to see Jack Murray in his true light, proving, once again, that love is blind.

She held out hope that Jack Murray would leave his wife Jeanette and marry her. But Murray was a man who was pleased to take money from Carol, offer her vain promises, and provide very little else. Finally Carol offered Jeanette $1,500 to leave Jack. The result of this was that Jack, who preferred Jeanette, ended his affair with Carol.

In 1978 she met Doug Clark in a bar. Clark was a murdering psychopath but he had the veneer of normality and even sophistication. He had been educated in Geneva and he had travelled around the world. But he had been expelled from school for theft and inappropriate sexual behaviour. He was then sent to a military academy where his obsession with sex increased – one of his pleasures was to tape the groans of girls with whom he was having sex and then play the soundtracks to his friends in order to make them jealous.

He joined the air force, left with an honourable discharge, a National Defense Service Medal and his benefits. He bought an upholstery business and married a woman named Beverly who did not mind the fact that he liked wife-swapping, *ménage à trois* and wearing her underwear. In 1976 they divorced amicably.

By the time he met Carol Bundy he knew how to play women, and particularly plain ones whose low self-esteem meant they were grateful for anything they could get.

He immediately seduced her and she immediately fell in love with him. The next morning he asked to move in with her and whether he could have a pair of her underpants, both of which she agreed to, though the latter were rejected on the grounds that they were too big for him.

Clark introduced Carol to the idea of sexual fantasy and encouraged her to share hers. They indulged each other with tales of sex slavery and began to experiment with Carol's liking for bondage. Clark enjoyed testing her apparently non-existent sexual limits and was soon talking about homicide, mixing up murder and sex with their foreplay chats and pushing her towards the idea of its extending their reality.

He plied her with ideas about necrophilia and all the other philias he could think of, watching her reactions. She, always wanting to please, would giggle as he presented his most deviant suggestions.

In April 1980 he appeared in her flat covered in blood; there was so much blood on him it was in his teeth. He told Carol he had been in a knife fight, defending himself against a man who attacked him.

Two months later Doug Clark killed Cindy and Gina Marano, who had run away from home. He picked them up on the Strip, in Los Angeles, in his Buick. He pulled into a car park and forced Cindy to perform oral sex. Then he shot both girls in the head and took their bodies to his garage where he laid them out on a mattress and had sex with them.

Confessing this to Carol served to enhance her love and loyalty. As far as she was concerned she was made 'special' by his confidence and the secrets strengthened their bond. Soon she was beginning to provide Clark with a 'kill bag' (containing knives, paper towels, liquid cleaner, plastic bags and rubber gloves) as some women provide their husbands with sandwiches for their packed lunches.

In June 1980 they went for their first joint kill and picked up a seventeen-year-old hooker from outside a supermarket in Hollywood. Carol was sitting in the back seat with a gun in her handbag. Doug shot the girl after she failed to give him an erection. She did not die immediately and lay bleeding on Carol's lap while she undressed her. They drove off the freeway and dumped the comatose body in some bushes.

Carol Bundy's personal hobbies broadened from SM to necrophilia but it was Exxie Wilson who promoted her from run-of-the-mill psycho to a world famous major league freak.

Doug Clark lured Exxie Wilson into his car and shot her in the back of the head. Then he dragged the corpse out of the car, stripped it, and cut the head off. Leaving the rest of Exxie in a pool of blood in a car park, he put her head in a plastic bag and took it to Carol Bundy's flat.

She found it sitting on the kitchen sink when she returned home and showed suitable admiration when Doug swung it around and told her that he had had taken it into the shower with him and shoved his penis in the open mouth.

They decided to keep it in the freezer for a couple of days until they decided the best way to dispose of it. Carol came up with the solution when she bought a wooden chest. They took the head out of the freezer and Carol made up the face, as a little girl makes up those Barbie heads one often sees in toyshops. They dumped the chest outside a 'Sizzler' in Studio City where it was found by a horrified passer-by.

After this, Carol Bundy began to fall to pieces and she (unsuccessfully) tried to kill herself.

Finding herself alive she attempted to mend relations with Jack Murray but he refused to have sex with her unless another woman was involved. Carol offered an eleven-year-old girl with whom she had formed a relationship thanks to the fact that Doug Clark was having sex with her. Jack Murray showed similar enthusiasm for child molestation and Carol allowed him to fondle the little girl.

Carol Bundy told Murray about the murders she had committed but then regretted it and decided that he would have to die. She lured him into the car with the promise that he could have sex with her and the eleven-year-old. She told him to lie on his stomach then she shot him twice in the head and stabbed him in the back, on the buttocks and in the anus.

Realising that his head was full of ballistic evidence, she cut it off and took it home with her in her car. Heads were something of a motif for Ms Bundy. Doug made her throw Jack's head in a bin. He was beginning to panic. Carol had killed a man known to both of them, and suspicion was bound to fall in their direction. He was right. Police, having been alerted by the stench of decomposition, found Murray's body in an abandoned van where it was black and covered with blisters.

Carol behaved how she thought people would expect her to, crying and screaming, then lapsing into what she hoped would appear to be a state of shock. She lost control and, having confessed to a nurse at the clinic where she worked, was arrested there and taken to a police station in Van Nuys. She admitted that she had killed Jack because he was 'an asshole who deserved to die'.

She also said that Doug did not force her to do anything against her will. The Sunset Strip Murders task force worked overtime to obtain all the evidence they would need to charge Doug and Carol with murder. Doug, inevitably, tried to pin everything on Carol. He was unsuccessful as there was a wealth of physical evidence (blood, bullet holes, vinyl gloves, you name it) to link him with the killings of several prostitutes and run-aways. Clark could not tell the police their names; they were just girls he had killed.

Awaiting trial Carol wrote to everyone she knew, justifying her position as a poor housewife who had been driven to the edge. She wrote to Doug, avowing her undying love for him, and even wrote a love letter to one of the detectives who had interrogated her.

It was more than two years before Doug's case came to trial – in October 1982. On 16 February 1983 the death penalty was handed down for six counts of murder. On 2 May 1983, the day that Carol Bundy was to go to trial, she withdrew her 'not guilty by reason of insanity' plea and pleaded guilty to two charges of first-degree murder. By doing so she escaped the gas chamber and was sentenced to two consecutive life terms.

In 1990 she handed over all of her legal and psychiatric files to Doug's lawyers to help him prove his innocence. When asked why she still wanted to help Doug, she would say that she still liked him although she could not say why.

KARLA HOMOLKA

There are some people who, if they found themselves married to a murdering rapist, would admit that they had made a mistake and run screaming to the constabulary. Not Karla Homolka. She might spawn the chivalric argument that women commit their worst crimes in tandem with men, but she also represents the more recent feminist contentions that women are as capable of extreme levels of sexual violence and cruelty. Karla Homolka was a sex criminal and, in this, she was unusual. She was also relatively beautiful, which sets her apart in a gallery of gore where supermodels are a little thin on the ground.

Homolka's personality showed no sign of psychosis before she met her husband Paul. Oddly, after she had been in prison for some years, experts speaking to a parole board said that she was a psychopath and had never shown any remorse.

In 2001 she was denied early release because the board assessing her described her as a person 'likely to commit an offence causing the death of, or serious harm to, another person'.

As a teenager Karla Homolka was blonde, perky and popular; a normal middle-class high school girl. After meeting Paul Bernardo she became a twisted hench-woman despite a loving background and all the privi-leges that her middle-class family were able to bestow on her.

Homolka's argument, from the beginning, was that she had been terrorised by her husband. She had been beaten into submission by him and had done as he bade her.

They both lived in Canada and were called the Ken and Barbie killers because that is what they looked like: waxen dolls manufactured on the conveyer belt of the American Dream factory.

She worked in a veterinary clinic; he was an account-ant. On 23 December 1990 they killed Karla's younger sister Tammy. Paul served up alcohol doped with sleeping pills; Karla pushed a cloth with halothane (a surgical sedative) over her face. Tammy was sick. Karla held her upside down in order to clear her throat. Tammy choked to death before Paul could take her virginity, which was the point of the project.

Paul Bernardo came from a suburb of Toronto, the son of Kenneth, who was inclined to sleep with his daughter, and Marilyn, depressed and obese and living in the basement of their house. Relations with her son were not improved when she informed him that Kenneth was not his real father.

By the time he had enrolled himself at college Paul Bernardo was a violent bully and a sadist whose preferred excitement was anal rape. His modus operandi was to creep around Toronto hauling girls off buses and then making them have oral and anal sex.

He met Karla Homolka in 1987. She enjoyed SM sex. And she started to find him women so that they could join in too. Fifteen-year-old Jane, given as a 'gift', was drugged, raped and filmed on video. Karla making love to Jane; Paul forcing himself into her rectum. Jane bleeding. Soon after this the Bernardos were married.

In 1991 Bernardo pulled a knife on Leslie Mahaffy and hauled the fourteen-year-old home to his wife. Together they made a home porno film – Karla caressing Leslie – Paul anally raping her; Leslie screaming. The teenager's dead body was cut up with a chainsaw and dumped in Lake Ontario.

Leslie Mahaffy was followed by Terri Anderson, fourteen, who was murdered, and Kristen French, forced into the car at knife point, hauled to the Bernardos' delightful suburban home and sexually assaulted.

'You look good covered in piss,' said Bernardo, urinating on her face.

They filmed these activities for two days and then killed her. Her body was found in a ditch.

In 1993 forensic evidence came to light that linked Bernardo with the rapes that had been committed around his neighbourhood of Scarborough. As the police planned to put him under surveillance, Karla lodged an abuse complaint against him. He had started to punch her in 1992. In January 1993 she left him.

Police wanted to know more about Mr Bernardo. Karla got herself a good lawyer. In February police searched their house and found an extensive library of pornography. Karla plea-bargained her way into a light sentence (twelve years) in return for shopping her husband.

She appeared at her trial, in June 1993, demure but over made-up. A shrink, speaking on her behalf, opined that she was paralysed by fear. Her husband was tried two years later for the murders.

The prosecution at his trial presented a case for Karla as compliant victim who was exploited to help in the rape of the young girls. The video tapes, shown to the jury, starring Karla as a posturing readers' wives-style porno starlet, were intended to show how she was little more than an actress performing to his direction; a zombie who would do anything.

Bernardo was convicted of all the charges but his defence managed to cast doubt, if such a thing were needed, on the reality of his wife's personality. She seemed compliant enough making love to young girls who were then murdered. She seemed keen enough to accept and give sexual direction, and her voice, like Myra Hindley's, was on the tape.

Homolka's presence as a demonic icon exists on the web where one individual designed a game that took bets as to when she would be killed.

In 2000 Joliette, a prison in Quebec, Canada, where Karla was incarcerated, reviewed her conduct with a view to addressing whether she should stay in prison for the entire term of her sentence, which officially ends in 2005.

Her image was not helped by stories revealing that she was enjoying an affair with a lesbian convict due to inherit $1 million and by the appearance of a series of photographs in a Montreal newspaper in which she was shown partying with Christina Sherry, convicted for her part in a rape and torture case, and Sherry's accomplice, Tracy Gonzales.

Sherry and Gonzalez had lured girls to a flat in Montreal in order to allow them to be tortured and raped by the sex criminal James Medley. Karla has made some nice new friends. Her mother will be pleased.

VALERIE SOLANAS

Valerie Jean Solanas was a savage individualist from New Jersey who gave new meaning to the term 'militant feminism' when she formed the Society for Cutting Up Men in 1967. Solanas was the only member of this strange club, although her manifesto is still distributed as a tract, taking its place in the history of feminism and pored over by culture studies elites and anyone who can appreciate an entertaining diatribe that begins with the following paragraph.

'Life in this society being, at best, an utter bore and no aspect of society being at all relevant to women, there remains to civic-minded, responsible, thrill-seeking females only to overthrow the government, eliminate the money system, institute complete automation and destroy the male sex.'

In 1968 she was imprisoned for shooting Andy Warhol in the stomach, an assault which served to put her on the map. She was granted immortality in 1996 when she was the subject of director Mary Harron's sympathetic film *I Shot Andy Warhol*.

It is easy to condemn Solanas' violence, but it is also easy to sympathise with a hatred for Warhol and the Factory and everything it stood for; easy also to be entertained by the extremism of her manifesto which describes the male sex as existing in a 'twilight zone halfway between humans and apes'.

The man, she said, 'is a half dead unresponsive lump ... at best an utter bore ... unfit even for stud service . . .'

These levels of vitriolic vehemence should not be taken as a serious contribution to the process of feminist thought so much as the outrageously cynical output of a woman who, in the end, was clever but irrational. Solanas was an interesting 'turn' rather than a discursive philosopher sustained by academic validity.

'SCUM is hypothetical,' she explained in one interview. 'No, hypothetical is the wrong word. It's just a literary device. There's no organization called SCUM . . . I thought of it as a state of mind. In other words, women who think a certain way are in SCUM. Men who think a certain way are in the men's auxiliary of SCUM.'

So who was Valerie Solanas? She was born in 1936 to Louis and Dorothy Bondo Solanas. Her mother was later to tell an interviewer that Solanas 'fancied herself as a writer, and I think she did have some talent. For years, she even lived with a man. She had a terrific sense of humor.'

Her father molested her and, by the age of fifteen, Solanas was pretty much out of the house and hustling, although she did manage to put herself through college, supporting herself by working in the psychology department's animal laboratory. After this she supported herself through prostitution and ended up in Greenwich Village which, in 1966, was boho-central.

Solanas attempted to persuade Andy Warhol to produce *Up Your Ass*, a play that she had written about a man-hating hustler and murderess. The same year she wrote the SCUM manifesto and sold it on the streets in Manhattan. Warhol, intrigued by her, once observed that she 'had a lot of ideas'.

Maurice Girodias, the legendary publisher of risqué authors such as Henry Miller, took her up and gave her an advance for a novel based on the SCUM manifesto.

Andy Warhol paid her twenty-five dollars to appear in his film *I, a Man*. She plays a tough lesbian who rejects the advances of a male stud. She also appeared in Warhol's 1967 film *Bikeboy*.

In 1968 Solanas approached an underground news-paper publisher saying 'I want to shoot Maurice Girodias.' He gave her $50, which was enough to buy an automatic pistol.

Girodias escaped assassination thanks to the fact that he was out of town for the weekend. Solanas diverted her mission to the Factory where Paul Morrissey found her hanging around. 'I'm waiting for Andy to get money,' she told him. Morrissey told her that Warhol wasn't coming in that day. 'That's all right. I'll wait,' she told him.

Warhol turned up at The Factory at 4.15, riding up in the lift with Solanas and commenting that she looked good that day, dressed as she was in a black turtleneck sweater and a raincoat, with her hair styled and her face made up.

Morrissey told her if she did not get out he would throw her out. Then Warhol went to answer the telephone and Morrissey went to the bathroom. As Warhol spoke on the phone, Solanas shot him. She missed twice. The third bullet went through his lungs, spleen, stomach and liver.

As Warhol fell down in a pool of his own blood, Solanas fired at Mario Amaya, an art critic and curator who had been waiting to meet Warhol. She then turned to Fred Hughes, Warhol's right-hand man, put her gun to his head and fired; the gun jammed. Then the lift door opened showing that it was empty. Hughes, with the cool finesse that was always his personal style, said, 'Oh, there's the elevator. Why don't you get on, Valerie?'

'Good idea,' she replied and made her exit.

Solanas turned herself in at a police station in Times Square. She handed over two guns and said that she had shot Andy Warhol because he 'had too much control of my life'.

Later, when journalists asked why she did it, she told them, 'Read my manifesto and it will tell you who I am.'

Brought before Judge David Getzoff at the Manhattan Criminal Court she said, 'It's not often that I shoot somebody. I didn't do it for nothing.'

The judge might have asked her why she was speaking like a character from a Warhol film but, in fact, he asked her if she could afford an attorney. She replied, 'No, I can't. I want to defend myself. I was right in what I did! I have nothing to regret!'

She was driven off to the Bellevue Hospital psychiatric ward for observation.

Appearing in the Supreme Court charged with felonious assault, Solanas was represented by radical feminist lawyer Florynce Kennedy who described her as 'one of the most important spokeswomen of the feminist movement'.

She was indicted on charges of attempted murder, assault, and illegal possession of a gun. Declared incompetent, she was sent to a mental hospital the same month that Girodias' Olympia Press published the SCUM Manifesto.

Valerie Solanas did not stop harassing Andy Warhol. She telephoned him and demanded that he pay $20,000 for her manuscripts. She wanted him to drop all criminal charges against her, put her in more of his movies and get her on the *Johnny Carson Show*. Solanas said if Warhol didn't do this, she 'could always do it again'.

In 1969 Valerie Solanas was sentenced to three years in prison for 'reckless assault with intent to harm'.

She was released in 1971 then arrested again for writing threatening letters and making alarming telephone calls to various people, including Andy Warhol. After that she was thought to be in and out of mental institutions, though her mother denied this.

In 1988, penniless and alone, Valerie Solanas had a drug habit and was still earning money from turning tricks. Other hookers saw her walking about, like a true Jean Genet character, elegant in a silver lamé dress. She died, at the age of 52, of emphysema and pneumonia in a welfare hotel in San Francisco.

SOURCES

Hickey, Eric, *Serial Murderers and Their Victims*, Wadsworth, California, 1991

Jones, Glyn Richard, *Women Who Kill*, Robinson, London, 2002

Masters, Brian, *She Must Have Known,* Doubleday, New York, 1996

Wilson, Colin, *A Plague of Murder*, Robinson, London, 1995

the *Guardian*

the *Observer*

Valerie Solanas biography compiled by Freddie Baer (www.bcn.net)

'Angels of Death' by Katherine Ramsland (www.crimelibrary.com)

'Addicted to Love: The Sunset Strip Murders' by Fiona Steel (www.crimelibrary.com)

Look out for other compelling, all-new
True Crime titles from Virgin Books

MY BLOODY VALENTINE – Couples Whose Sick Crimes Shocked the World
Edited by Patrick Blackden

Good-looking Canadian couple Paul Bernardo and Karla Homolka looked the epitome of young, wholesome success. No one could have guessed that they drugged, raped and murdered young women to satisfy Bernardo's deviant lusts. Nothing inspires more horror and fascination than couples possessed of a single impulse – to kill for thrills. Obsessed by and sucked into their own sick and private madness, their attraction is always fatal, their actions always desperate. The book covers a variety of notorious killer couples: from desperados Starkweather and Fugate, on whom the film *Natural Born Killers* was based, right through to Fred and Rose West, who committed unspeakable horrors in their semi-detached house in Gloucester, England. With contributions from a variety of leading true crime journalists, *My Bloody Valentine* covers both the world-famous cases and also lesser-known but equally horrifying crimes.

£7.99 ISBN: 0-7535-0647-5

DEATH CULTS – Murder, Mayhem and Mind Control
Edited by Jack Sargeant

Throughout history thousands of people have joined cults and even committed acts of atrocity in the belief they would attain power and everlasting life. From Charles Manson's 'family' of the late 1960s to the horrific Ten Commandments of God killings in Uganda in March 2000, deluded and brainwashed followers of cults and their charismatic megalomaniac leaders have been responsible for history's most shocking and bizarre killings. Jack Sargeant has compiled twelve essays featuring cults about whom very little has previously been written, such as the Russian castration sect and the bizarre Japanese Aum doomsday cult that leaked sarin gas into Tokyo's subways.

£7.99 ISBN: 0-7535-0644-0

DANGER DOWN UNDER – The Dark Side of the Australian Dream
Patrick Blackden

Australia is one of the most popular long-haul tourist destinations, but its image of a carefree, 'no worries' culture set in a landscape of stunning natural beauty tells only one side of the story. *Danger Down Under* lets you know what the tourist board won't – the dark side of the Australian dream. With a landscape that can be extremely hostile to those unfamiliar to its size and extremes, and an undying macho culture – not to mention the occasional psychotic who murders backpackers, or crazed gangs of bikers and cultists – there is much to be cautious of when venturing down under.

£7.99 ISBN 0-7535-0649-1

DIRTY CASH – Organised Crime in the Twenty First Century
David Southwell

There was once only one Mafia: now every country seems to have its own. Until fairly recently gangsters kept to their territories, but crime – like every other business -has been quick to take advantage of the new global economy. Business, it seems, is good, with over $150 billion laundered each year in Europe alone. As links are formed between the Mafia, the Triads, the Yardies, the Yakuza, the Russian Mafiya and the South American cartels, a tide of misery spreads throughout the world. The book looks in detail at the specific groups involved, the horrifying crimes they commit and the everyday lives of their members.

£7.99 ISBN: 0-7535-0702-1

TEENAGE RAMPAGE – The Worldwide Youth Crime Explosion
Antonio Mendoza

Columbine High School, Colorado, Spring 1999. 12 of its school-children and one teacher lie dead. Two boys have gone on a killing spree, venting their anger at their classmates before turning their guns on themselves. Cases such as Columbine are occurring with increasing regularity – and guns are not always involved. In Japan in 1998, a 13-year old schoolboy murdered his teacher in a frenzied knife attack. What is happening in society that young people are running amok, fuelled by hatred and nihilism, with little regard for their own lives and the lives of those around them? Expert crime writer Antonio Mendoza investigates this problem and comes up with some shocking findings that call for a global rethink on how we bring up – and punish – those responsible for the worldwide teenage crimewave.

ISBN: 0-7535-0715-3

January 2003

MONSTERS OF DEATH ROW – Dead Men and Women Walking
Christopher Berry-Dee and Tony Brown

From the cells of Death Row come the chilling, true-life accounts of the most heinous, cruel and depraved killers of modern times. At the time of writing, there are 3,702 inmates on Death Row across the USA, many of who have caused their victims to consciously suffer agonising physical pain and tortuous mental anguish before death. These are not normal human beings. They have carried out serial murder, mass-murder, spree killing, necrophilia and dismemberment of bodies – both dead and alive. In these pages are to be found fiends who have stabbed, hacked, set fire to and even filleted their victims. So meet the 'dead men and women walking' in the most terrifying true crime read ever.

£7.99 ISBN 0-7535-0722-6